Ivan Markovic

Semantic Business Process Modeling

Semantic Business Process Modeling

by
Ivan Markovic

Dissertation, Universität Karlsruhe (TH)
Fakultät für Wirtschaftswissenschaften,
Tag der mündlichen Prüfung: 03. August 2009
Referent: Prof. Dr. Rudi Studer
Korreferent: Prof. Dr. Dimitris Karagiannis

Impressum

Karlsruher Institut für Technologie (KIT)
KIT Scientific Publishing
Straße am Forum 2
D-76131 Karlsruhe
www.ksp.kit.edu

KIT – Universität des Landes Baden-Württemberg und nationales
Forschungszentrum in der Helmholtz-Gemeinschaft

KIT Scientific Publishing 2010
Print on Demand

ISBN 978-3-86644-557-4

Acknowledgements

Writing of this thesis was a journey, the success of which would not have been possible without the support and guidance of many persons. Here, I would like to thank all of them. In particular, I wish to thank:

Professor Dr. Rudi Studer, for being my *Doktorvater* and for giving me the opportunity to be a part of the Rudiverse.

Professor Dr. Dimitris Karagiannis, for being my second supervisor and providing inspiration through his work on metamodeling.

Nenad Stojanovic, for insightful discussions and constructive criticism. Christian Brelage, for raising my interest in business process modeling and a great sense of humor. Ingo Weber, for setting high standards and always raising the bar. Orestis Terzidis, for being the best manager I worked with.

All my co-authors and anonymous reviewers, for helping to sharpen the ideas presented here.

My students, for their dedication and energy.

Colleagues at SAP Research Karlsruhe and Brisbane, for allowing me to become a friend over the years.

My family and good friends, for always having faith in me and encouraging me to make this thesis happen.

Geli, for unconditional love and understanding.

Ivan Markovic

Abstract

Process orientation was introduced to achieve a holistic view on an enterprise, using business processes as the main instrument for organizing enterprise operations. In this context, business process modeling has become a popular technique for capturing business processes. Business process models enable a better understanding of business processes, identify their improvement options, facilitate communication between business analysts and IT experts and serve as a basis for the management and execution of processes in IT systems. As such, they are regarded as valuable design artifacts.

However, several important problems in business process modeling have emerged. First, business processes are often viewed in isolation, without explicit consideration of their broader organizational context - business strategy and goals, business directives, etc. Second, the popular tools used for process modeling provide little modeling guidance or reuse functionalities to the user. Third, conceptual process models may contain formal errors which often can not be analyzed on a semantic level. As a result, business process models are decoupled form strategic concerns, the modeling of processes is still highly complex, and the modeling errors are propagated further down the development lifecycle whereby their cost increases exponentially.

In order to address these problems, this thesis contributes a business process modeling framework based on semantic technologies. The framework consists of modeling languages, methods and tools, which aim at facilitating the design and improving the quality of business process models.

As framework foundations, we first define a process-oriented enterprise ontology framework in order to integrate all relevant aspects for describing business processes on a semantic level. Second, we propose a methodology which provides guidance for utilizing semantic technologies in business process modeling. Based on these foundations, we design modeling techniques (languages and methods) that allow for semantic modeling of business motivation, business policies and rules, and business processes. In order to instantiate these modeling techniques, we develop modeling tools for semantic modeling of business motivation (Maestro4BM), business policies and rules (Maestro4BPR) and business processes (Maestro4BPMN). Quality of the proposed modeling framework is evaluated based on the modeling content of SAP Solution Composer and several real-world business scenarios.

Contents

List of Figures

List of Tables

Part I

Foundations

Chapter 1

Introduction

This chapter starts with a discussion of the general motivation of the thesis in Section 1.1. Next, we present the research contributions in Section 1.2. In Section 1.3, we discuss our findings in the context of design science approaches to information systems research. Section 1.4 gives an overview of the most important publications where the results of the thesis have been published. Finally, Section 1.5 closes this chapter with an outlook on the thesis structure.

1.1 Motivation and Problem

In the 1990s, process orientation was introduced [Ham90] to achieve a holistic view of an enterprise, with business processes as the main instrument for organizing the operations of an enterprise [Wes07]. Process orientation means viewing an organization as a network or system of business processes. The innumerable benefits of investing in business process techniques were demonstrated in efficiency, productivity, cost reduction, quality, faster results, standardization, and, above all - in the encouragement of innovation, leading to competitive advantage and client satisfaction [GD08].

Process orientation considered IT as a key enabler and thus followed with the introduction of business process management (BPM) [Wes07] and business process management systems (BPMS) [Cha05] as means to support the knowledge workers in performing business processes. Ever since, the industrial reports have shown strong interest and rapid growth opportunity in the BPM-related software and services market segment. By the end of 2006, the BPM market reached nearly US$1.7 billion in total software revenue [HCDK07]. Gartner estimates that this market will have a compound annual growth rate of more than 24% from 2006 to 2011, reaching US$5.1 billion in total software revenue by 2011 [HCKP09]. Furthermore, a large number of academic books [JB96, zur04, vdAvH02, Wes07, SF06, Cha05] and conference series e.g. [vdAtHW03, DPW04, vdABCC05, DFS06, ADR07, DRS08] on this topic confirm the relevance of BPM as an academic discipline.

The design of a BPMS is based on explicit process models, which are conceptual models of an organization's business processes. Business process models enable a better understanding of business processes, identify their improvement options, facilitate communication between business analysts and IT experts and serve as a basis for the management and execution of business processes. These models are created by business people who understand and know how organizational processes work.

In order to create process models, business people need a modeling framework which would allow them to express their business needs. Such a modeling framework consists of a language, a method and a tool that matches their requirements[1]. While there exists a plethora of work on modeling frameworks for technical specification of BPMS e.g. [IBM09, SAP, Ora09], there are very few modeling frameworks that target the business users, see [DB07, SAP05a]. The dominant language used for technical specification is BPEL [AAA+07], whereas for business specification the EPCs [KNS92] and the increasingly popular BPMN [Obj09] are languages of choice. We have identified three major problems with existing modeling frameworks for business specification of BPMS, which we discuss in the following.

First, business processes are often viewed in isolation, without explicit consideration of their broader organizational context - business strategy and goals, business directives, etc. This leads to a misaligned organization, where the supporting information systems are decoupled from strategic concerns [Smi07]. Second, the popular tools used for process modeling (e.g. MS Visio, Excel, PowerPoint) are in fact merely drawing tools that do not provide any modeling guidance or reuse functionalities to the user. In turn, this results in process modeling still being a highly complex and time consuming activity [GL07]. Related to the second one is the third major issue - formal errors in business specifications. Namely, as the modeling frameworks for business users only support creating very informal specifications, they often contain errors [Men08]. It has been shown that the cost of errors increases exponentially over the development lifecycle: "it is more than 100 times costly to correct a defect post-implementation than it is to correct it during requirements analysis" [Boe81, Moo05].

Therefore, due to many possible interpretations, the business specifications as such can not be directly used as input for technical specifications, creating the so-called business/IT gap [SF06]. This fact is unfortunate, resulting in the consequence that implemented (running) systems often do not match business requirements [ER03, Dav98, Gro94, Gro95].

We argue that if business users are provided with a modeling framework which addresses the above listed problems, the quality of produced process models will increase and therefore better supporting information systems will be built [BR02, CK99, WW02, Moo05], i.e. systems which correspond to business needs. This would also "raise BPM to the business level where it belongs, from the IT level where it resides now" [HLD+05]. In other words, it would give the control over the business to the right people.

On the other hand, Semantic Web (SW) technologies have shown great potential for integrating the knowledge coming from various sources [FG94, UG04] and providing its formal machine representation by means of ontologies [Gru93, UG96]. In addition, SW technologies provide concepts and tools for automated analysis and inference on the represented knowledge [GHA07]. Therefore, the usage of ontologies and reasoning in business process modeling seems to be a natural fit for solving the problems we identified previously.

The objective of this thesis is to investigate precisely this point, i.e. how can semantic technologies be utilized to improve the modeling frameworks for the busi-

---

[1]We discuss the notion of a modeling framework in more detail in Chapter 2

ness specification of BPMS. In the following Section, we discuss the main contributions we make towards reaching this objective.

1.2   Research Contributions

In order to address the identified issues, the thesis contributes a business process modeling framework based on semantic technologies. In the following, we list the components comprising the framework and state our respective contributions therein:

Process-oriented enterprise ontology framework This ontology framework integrates all relevant aspects of business process model description - from strategic concerns such as business goals and performance indicators down to detailed process flow and resources. It allows for supporting different process perspectives and abstraction levels present in business process modeling (see Chapter 2). We present the ontology framework in Chapter 3.

Semantic business process modeling methodology We propose a methodology which significantly extends the existing process modeling methodologies with the aim to provide guidance in utilizing semantic technologies in the early phases of a BPM project. The methodology is presented in Chapter 3.

Modeling of business motivation We first present a rich formalization of the business motivation notions in the form of a Business Motivation Ontology. Further, we provide an approach to visual modeling of business motivation based on this formalization. Finally, different types of analyses are provided in order to be able to i) perform what-if and gap analysis, ii) check for conflicts as well as to iii) make queries on the business motivation models. This contribution is provided in Chapter 4.

Modeling and verification of policies and rules We first provide an approach to visual modeling of business policies and rules based on the Business Policies and Rules Ontology and a metamodel of the WSML-Flight language. Further, we design a context-based policy matchmaking mechanism in order to automate the procedure of finding applicable business policies for a particular process. Finally, we provide an anti-pattern based approach to policy-based business process verification. The contribution is presented in Chapter 5.

Modeling, annotation and querying of business processes We provide a means for capturing the behavioral aspect of process models through the Business Process Ontology. The ontology allows for integration of other process perspectives which is realized by means of semantic annotation of processes. Finally, an advanced query mechanism for business process artifacts is provided which is utilized for guided modeling and reuse of process artifacts. This contribution is presented in Chapter 6.

In the next section, we position our research methodology with respect to an established research framework within information systems research.

1.3   Research Methodology

This section starts with providing an overview of the information systems research framework [HMPR04] as defined by Hevner et al. in Section 1.3.1. We use the framework guidelines to talk about how research work in this thesis meets the information systems research standards in Section 1.3.2.

1.3.1   Information Systems Research Framework

Research in the information systems (IS) discipline has the aim to "further knowledge that aids in the productive application of information technology to human organizations and their management" [ISR02]. Such knowledge can be acquired using two distinct research paradigms: behavioral and design science [MS95]. The behavioral science paradigm "seeks to develop and justify theories (i.e., principles and laws) that explain or predict organizational and human phenomena surrounding the analysis, design, implementation, management, and use of information systems" [HMPR04]. It stems from natural science research methods. On the other hand, the design science paradigm is fundamentally a problem-solving one and stems mostly from engineering disciplines. The two paradigms have different research goals, where the goal of behavioral science being *truth* and that of design science being *utility* [HMPR04]. Since this thesis follows the design science research paradigm, it is the main focus of our discussion in the following.

In Fig. 1.1, the conceptual framework for conducting, evaluating and presenting IS research using design science and behavioral science paradigms is presented. As shown in Fig. 1.1, the IS research is conducted in an environment that involves people, organizations, and technology in order to enhance the knowledge base of foundations and methodologies in this area. The environment defines the problem space and the context from which the business needs emerge (cf. Fig. 1.1). It is then the task of a researcher to align her activities to the identified business needs in order to assure research *relevance*.

The knowledge base consists of foundations and methodologies which offer solutions to problems that are already well understood (cf. Fig. 1.1). Building of artifacts can rely on foundations such as theories, frameworks, instruments, constructs, models, methods, and instantiations that have resulted from prior research. Methodologies on the other hand provide guidance for the evaluation phase. The researcher applies existing foundations and methodologies to a given problem in order to establish *rigor* (cf. Fig. 1.1). Naturally, the overall goal is to address the business need and to contribute to the knowledge base for future application. This is often used as a criterion to distinguish routine design and design research [HMPR04]. While routine design tackles business needs by applying existing knowledge, design research establishes either innovative solutions to unsolved problems or more efficient or effective solutions to solved problems. Accordingly, design research contributes to the knowledge base while routine design does not.

Design science is technology-oriented and strives to create artifacts that serve human purposes [MS95]. The artifacts are created through two design processes: *build* and *evaluate* (cf. Fig. 1.1). The produced artifacts may be categorized into four types, namely *constructs* (vocabulary and symbols), *models* (abstractions and representations), *methods* (algorithms and practices) and *instantiations* (implemented and

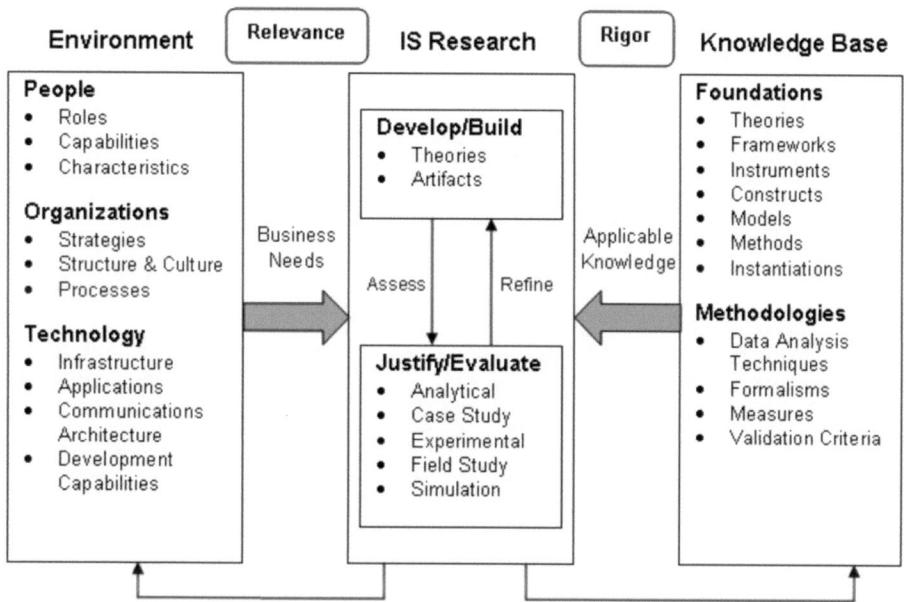

Figure 1.1: Information Systems Research Framework as defined in [HMPR04]

prototype systems). Through the build process the artifacts are created. Consequently, the evaluate process is performed to provide feedback and a better understanding of the problem so that the quality of the produced artifacts and the build process itself can be improved [HMPR04] (cf. Fig. 1.1). Central to design science is the iteration of this build-and-evaluate cycle for a number of times before the final artifact is created [MMG02].

As pointed out in [Sim96], the main characteristic of problems in design science is *wickedness*. This means that there is no definitive formulation of the problem due to unstable requirements, ill-defined environmental context, complex interactions, inherent change, and of psychological and social factors being involved [HMPR04]. This is also why the solution cannot be assessed by truth, but rather by utility of produced artifacts.

1.3.2 Adherence to the Framework Guidelines

In the context of their framework, the authors in [HMPR04] define a set of seven guidelines for design science in information systems research. In the following, we use these guidelines to discuss how this thesis meets information systems research standards.

Guideline 1: Design an Artifact Design science research must produce purposeful artifacts addressing business needs within an organizational setting [HMPR04]. In this thesis, we provide the process-oriented enterprise ontology, as well as business motivation, business policy and rule, and business process ontologies as constructs that can be used to describe and formalize various aspects of business process models. Furthermore, we define methods to provide semantic modeling and analysis functionalities for business motivation models, perform policy-based process verification and advanced querying on process models. Finally, we present prototypical implementations of these methods (i.e. instantiations) in form of the SAP Research Maestro semantic modeling framework in order to demonstrate feasibility.

Guideline 2: Problem Relevance Design science research must develop technology-based solutions for important and relevant business problems [HMPR04]. The general business need of this research stems from a growing popularity and wide-spread application of business process modeling and management in practice. The concepts and findings presented in this thesis contribute to several aspects of design improvement and verification in business process modeling.

Guideline 3: Design Evaluation The utility of an artifact in a given problem situation must be clearly demonstrated using evaluation methods [HMPR04]. We have evaluated the utility of the produced artifacts from different aspects. First, the representational completeness of the provided constructs is evaluated against the business knowledge contained in the SAP Solution Composer [SAP05a]. The constructs are also compared and contrasted with other existing efforts. Further, we test the performance and scalability of the methods using large sets of real data. Additional case studies are provided to demonstrate the feasibility and applicability of our approach and its instantiations.

Guideline 4: Research Contribution The design research has to provide a novel, significant, and general contribution to the knowledge base [HMPR04]. Our contributions have already been presented in Section 1.2.

Guideline 5: Research Rigor A researcher has to effectively make use of the knowledge base in construction and evaluation of artifacts [HMPR04]. In this thesis, we took advantage of prior research in business process modeling languages, knowledge representation, ontologies and reasoning, requirements engineering, strategy management, and business rules.

Guideline 6: Design as a Search Process Problem solving in design science requires utilizing suitable means to reach desired ends while respecting laws imposed by the environment [HMPR04]. The constructs in this thesis were designed iteratively based on thorough analysis of existing approaches and business knowledge contained in process models. At first, a minimal corpus of representational entities was created and then evaluated against the case studies requirements and numerous process models. The set of entities was increased and refined until the satisficing solution [Sim96] has been reached.

Guideline 7: Communication of Research Design science research has to be presented to both the academic community and to practitioners who might be interested in the findings [HMPR04]. The work on this thesis has led to the publication of two journal articles, twelve conference papers, seven workshop papers, and nine technical reports and popular publications. This implies that most of the concepts of this thesis are already publicly available as part of the information systems knowledge base.

Putting this thesis in the context of the framework guidelines underlines that it suffices research standards in this discipline and that it enhances its knowledge base in several directions.

1.4 Publications

In this section, we list the most relevant publications where the results of this thesis have been published.

In the following two papers, the foundations of our semantic business process modeling framework are presented. The first paper presents the process-oriented enterprise ontology framework and the second paper discusses a methodology for semantic business process modeling. These papers have been used in the writing of Chapter 3.

- Ivan Markovic, Florian Hasibether, Sukesh Jain, Nenad Stojanovic. Process-oriented Semantic Business Modeling. Proceedings of the 9th International Conference on Business Informatics (Wirtschaftsinformatik), Vol. 1, pages 683–694, 2009.

- David de Francisco, Ivan Markovic, Javier Martinez, Henar Munoz, Noelia Perez. Methodological Extensions for Semantic Business Process Modeling. Proceedings of the 10th International Conference on Enterprise Information Systems (ICEIS), Vol. 2, pages 410–415, 2008.

The following two conference papers discuss the Business Motivation Ontology and its relation to business process modeling. The concepts from these papers have been used in Chapter 4.

- Carlos Pedrinaci, Ivan Markovic, Florian Hasibether, John Domingue. Strategy-driven Business Process Analysis. Proceedings of the 12th International Conference on Business Information Systems (BIS), pages 169–180, 2009.

- Ivan Markovic, Marek Kowalkiewicz. Linking Business Goals to Process Models in Semantic Business Process Modeling. Proceedings of the 12th IEEE International Conference on Enterprise Computing (EDOC), pages 332–338, 2008.

In the following journal article, we present our approach to modeling and verification of business policies and rules on business process models. We start by explaining the method for visual modeling of policies and rules, continue with introducing context-based policy matching and finally present the policy-based verification of process models. This article is used as a basis for Chapter 5.

- Ivan Markovic, Sukesh Jain, Mahmoud El-Gayyar and Armin B. Cremers. Modeling and Enforcement of Business Policies and Rules in Semantic Business Process Modeling. Communications of Systemics and Informatics World Network (CoSIWN) Journal, 2009.

Finally, the following two conference papers discuss the Business Process Ontology and the semantic annotation and querying method for business processes. The concepts described in these papers have been used in writing Chapter 6.

- Ivan Markovic. Advanced Querying and Reasoning on Business Process Models. Proceedings of the 11th International Conference on Business Information Systems (BIS), pages 189–200, 2008.

- Ivan Markovic, Alessandro Costa Pereira, Nenad Stojanovic. A Framework for Querying in Business Process Modeling. In Proceedings of the Multikonferenz Wirtschaftsinformatik (MKWI), 2008.

Apart from listed publications, the research work described in this thesis has been published in other journal, conference, workshop and popular publications. A full list of publications is provided in Appendix A.

1.5   Structure of the Thesis

The structure of this thesis is represented as a business process model in Fig. 1.2. The thesis is organized into three parts: providing an overview of basic concepts and technologies used in this work, presenting the semantic business process modeling framework and discussing the evaluation results with concluding remarks. Each part is represented as a rounded rectangle that includes its chapters (see Fig. 1.2), whereas directed arcs indicate dependencies between chapters and suggest the recommended order of reading.

Part I: Foundations proceeds with Chapter 2 which provides the basic concepts of business process management, and discusses the basic technologies which constitute the semantic technologies stack. In the last section, a new research field created by merging the previous two, semantic business process management, is introduced. We position our work in the context of each introduced area.

Part II: Semantic Business Process Modeling Framework discusses the research contributions of this thesis. First, in Chapter 3, we provide the modeling framework foundations in the form of the *process-oriented enterprise ontology framework* and *semantic business process modeling lifecycle*. We continue in Chapter 4 with presenting a semantic modeling framework (see Section 2.2) for business motivation. Chapter 5 provides a semantic modeling framework for another strategic aspect - business directives (policies and rules). We include a policy-based business process verification method for detecting formal errors in process model specifications. Chapter 6 focuses on improving the modeling of business processes through better reuse and modeling guidance. Again, a semantic modeling framework is provided for this purpose. Chapter 4 can be read independently from Chapters 5 and 6, as shown in Fig 1.2.

Part III: Finale evaluates the proposed semantic business process modeling framework from various aspects in Chapter 7. Finally, Chapter 8 concludes the thesis and gives an outlook on future research.

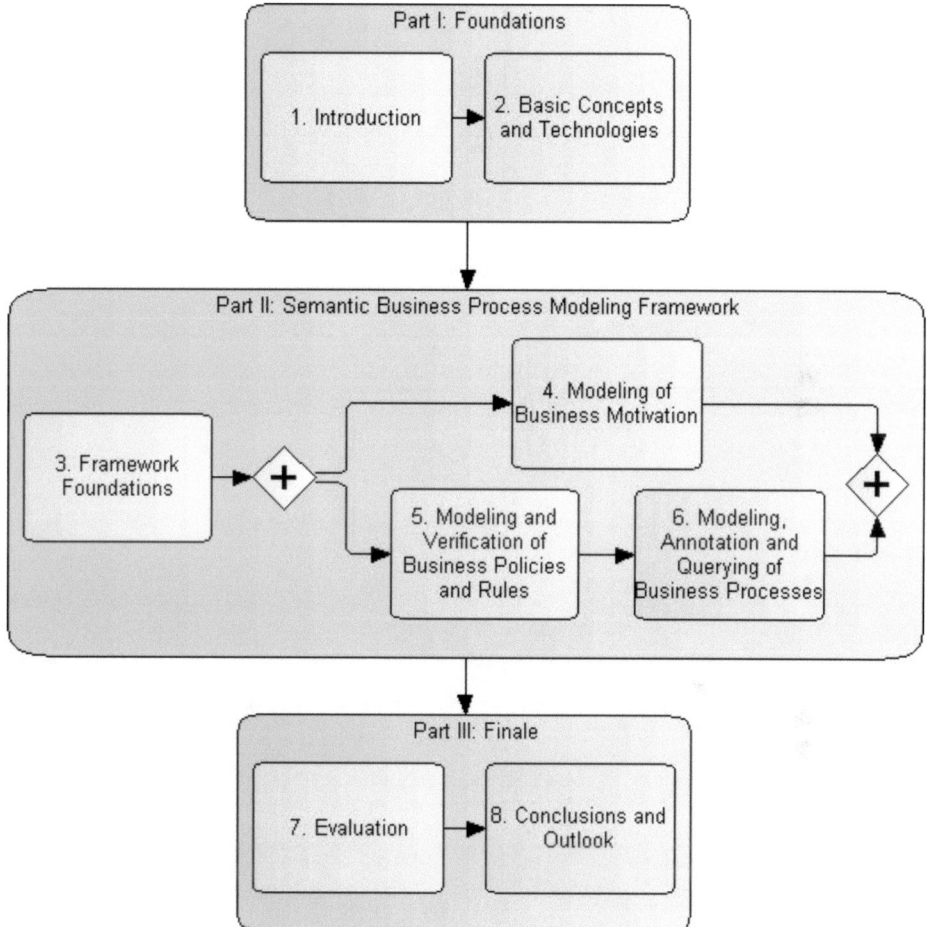

Figure 1.2: Structure of the thesis and recommended reading process

Chapter 2

Basic Concepts and Technologies

This chapter provides the background knowledge necessary to follow the rest of the thesis. First, we explain the most important concepts behind Business Process Management in general, and Business Process Modeling in particular. Second, we discuss semantic technologies in the form of ontologies and reasoning which are used extensively throughout our work. Lastly, we introduce a new research field yielded through the application of semantic technologies in BPM - Semantic Business Process Management.

2.1 Business Process Management

Business Process Management (BPM) is a discipline which aims at leveraging IT to implement and improve business processes. BPM makes processes more efficient through automation and enabling employees to better collaborate and manage deadlines. This includes the identification of bottlenecks and the planning of resources.

In order to talk about the management of business processes, we first need to define the term *business process* more accurately. Many definitions can be found in BPM literature. For instance, Hammer and Champy in [HC93] define a business process as a collection of activities that take one or more kinds of input and create an output that is of customer value. Finding this abstract definition too liberal, Davenport in [Dav93] defines a business process as "a set of logically related tasks performed to achieve a defined business outcome for a particular customer or market." For this thesis, the following definition of a business process is adopted:

> "A business process is a coordinated and standardized flow of activities performed by people or machines, which can traverse functional, departmental or organizational boundaries to achieve a business objective that creates value for internal or external customers" (Chang, 2005).

as it points out that the aspects of planning, ordering and value creation are central to the term process.

Business Process Management may be a new name, but the ideas behind BPM are quite old. The concept of BPM as we know it today has been referred to as the "third wave of process management" [SF06]. The first wave of process management has its roots in Taylor's theories on scientific management [Tay11], where the business process was implicit in the work practices and processes were standardized, but not automated. The second wave of process management (business process reengineering) began in the 1990s and business processes were automated using enterprise resource planning (ERP) and other standard systems. This was the first time that the information systems (IS) were seen as key enabler for effective processes [HC93]. In the third wave (process orientation), the business process is made the central focus and building block of automation and business.

Since BPM brings together business administration and computer science communities, the concept itself is perceived as dual. The computer science community is interested in information technology as the main driving force behind BPM, whereas the business administration community views BPM as a management discipline. As a consequence, there is no commonly accepted definition of BPM. In the following, we give the most prominent definitions from both perspectives. Weske [Wes07] provides the following definition of BPM:

> "Business process management includes concepts, methods, and techniques to support the design, administration, configuration, enactment, and analysis of business processes."

On the other hand, according to Gartner, BPM is defined as "a set of management disciplines that accelerate effective business process improvement by blending incremental and transformative methods. BPM's management practices provide for governance of a business process environment toward the goal of improving agility and operational performance. BPM is a structured approach that employs methods, policies, metrics, management practices and software tools to manage and continuously optimize an organization's activities and processes" [CH08].

BPM relies on a set of enabling technologies which are usually commonly referred to as Business Process Management System (BPMS), a term originally coined by Karagiannis in [Kar95]. We adopt the following definition of BPMS in our work:

> "A business process management system is a generic software system that is driven by explicit process representations to coordinate the enactment of business processes" [Wes07].

where the explicit process representations are provided by means of process models.

Business process management can be understood as a set of management activities concerning business processes. In order to categorize and discuss different management activities involved in BPM, we provide a BPM lifecycle overview in Fig. 2.1[1]. Broadly speaking, the lifecycle comprises the management activities of *analysis, design, implementation, enactment, monitoring* and *evaluation* of business processes (cf. Fig. 2.1). We now briefly discuss each of the lifecycle activities.

Analysis The lifecycle starts with the analysis activity (cf. Fig. 2.1). The analysis is based on the process context (environment), which spans from strategic

---

[1]It is worth noting that many authors tried to define different variations of the BPM lifecycle (cf. [zur04, vdAvH02, Wes07]). Here we mainly follow the lifecycle proposed by [zur04], with minor changes by [Men07], for two reasons: i) it does not only include activities but also artifacts and ii) it consolidates the lifecycle models presented in [GS95, NPC03].

concerns (business goals, directives, etc.) to organizational structure. The output of this phase is a set of requirements for business process design, which include process objectives, key performance indicators, process owners, etc.

Design Based on the set of requirements from the previous activity, this activity is concerned with capturing either an existing (as-is) or desired (to-be) state of a process. Based on information originating from various sources, an abstract representation in a graphical notation is used to cover knowledge about business processes at hand [Wes07]. This includes defining process activities, specifying their order and constraints, assigning process roles and resources, etc. The output of this phase is a conceptual process model which integrates these different design perspectives.

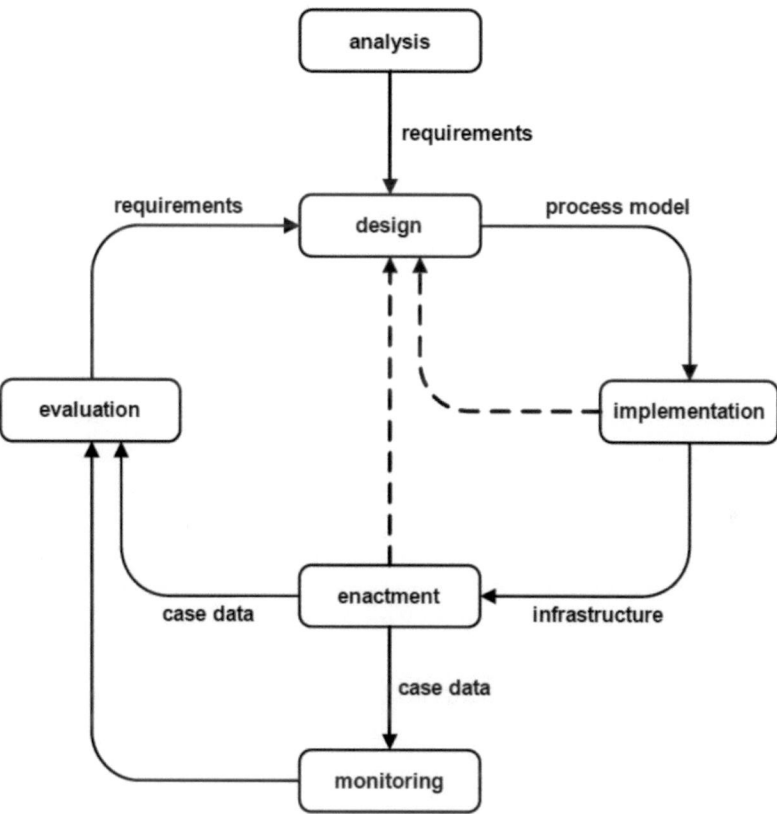

Figure 2.1: Business Process Management lifecycle as proposed in [Men07]

Implementation This activity uses the conceptual process model as input. Implementation means the selection and configuration of IT artifacts which implement process activities, according to process control- and data-flow. During implementation, it may be discovered that the process can not be implemented as depicted by the process model. This provides a feedback loop to the design activity in order to perform required modifications (see Fig. 2.1).

Enactment Process enactment is the phase where the business process management system is actually used. The BPMS infrastructure supports the execution of individual cases (process instances). During execution, different case data is recorded such as execution time, process branching decisions, resource access, etc. This data is used as input for the following two management activities.

Monitoring This activity is performed continuously for each case based on the assigned process metrics, such as maximum delay time. If a metrics threshold is reached, appropriate program logic is triggered in order to deal with the situation. This activity is essential in assuring the correctness of individual process executions.

Evaluation The evaluation activity is concerned with the aggregated view on individual process executions. Here, the process execution data is compared to the original design requirements of the process. The goal is to assess further potential process improvements and thus identify new requirements for process design. These new requirements are taken as input for the process redesign in the next iteration of the lifecycle (see Fig. 2.1).

The lifecycle activities are overlapping (picking up work of the last activity again is possible), as well as iterative (the whole cycle is repeated to achieve process improvement). Our work focuses on the first two described activities, namely *analysis* and *design*. In particular, this thesis aims to provide a framework based on semantic technologies which improves current practices regarding these two activities.

Within the lifecycle, business processes exist on different abstraction levels. Weske [Wes07] identifies five process abstraction levels in business process management (cf. Fig. 2.2). At the top level, the business *strategy* is defined, which often articulates the competitive advantage and sets the overall direction for a company. The strategy is broken down into business *goals*, which specify desired outcomes contributing to the realization of the overall strategy (see connecting arrows in Fig. 2.2).

Once the goals are specified, *organizational business processes* are defined to organize the work from a high-level perspective in order to meet the goals. For the previous three levels, usually only informal or semi-formal specification techniques are used such as plain text or forms-based approach [Wes07]. At the fourth level, for each organizational business process, a set of *conceptual business processes*[2] is defined. In conceptual business processes, detailed process activities are specified along with responsible roles, utilized resources, etc. The specification is done using *conceptual business process models*. In order to implement and execute such process specifications, additional implementation-relevant information must be added to the models. Such processes which contain the execution-level details are called *implemented business processes* (see level five in Fig. 2.2).

In this thesis, we target the first four levels of business processes from Fig. 2.2. Together, these levels form what we call the *business specification* of a business process management system. The business specification abstracts from implementation-level concerns. Careful reader may notice different specification techniques commonly used for these levels, i.e. plain text for strategy and goals,

---

[2]Weske [Wes07] calls them operational business processes, however in other business process modeling literature they are often referred to as conceptual business processes

Figure 2.2: Levels of business processes, adopted from [Wes07]

forms-based approach for organizational processes and conceptual process models for conceptual processes. In reality, this results in a mix of different modeling artifacts created on different levels which are difficult to integrate. Clearly, a unified modeling paradigm would improve the integration issues. Also, since the specifications are semi-formal at best, there is no possibility to perform any kind of verification of such specifications. This leads to the fact that the modeling errors introduced at one level are propagated all the way down the abstraction chain and the cost of errors increases exponentially [Boe81, Moo05]. Our aim is therefore to provide a modeling framework for these four levels which i) nicely integrates the modeling artifacts produced on each level by providing a unified modeling paradigm and ii) enables the verification of specifications created on each of the levels, thus improving the quality of business specifications.

As mentioned before, BPMS are driven by explicit process models. The authors in [DvdAtH05] identify some of the advantages of using process models in business process management systems: i) They serve as a means of communication between managers, business analysts and IT personnel; ii) process-aware systems are driven by models rather than code, thus only models need to be changed to support evolving or emerging business processes; iii) explicit representation of processes allows their automated execution; iv) management is better supported at the (re)design and control (monitoring) level by explicit process models. In addition, the market research reports that about 90% of companies participating in a survey conducted or considered business process modeling [Pal07]. We discuss the basic concepts of business process modeling in greater detail in the next section.

2.2   Business Process Modeling

Business process modeling comprises two activities in the lifecycle shown in Fig. 2.1: *analysis* and *design*. We adopt the following definition of business process modeling and business process model by Mendling:

> "Business process modeling is the human activity of creating a business process model. Business process modeling involves an abstraction from the real-world business process, because it serves a certain modeling purpose. Therefore, only those aspects relevant to the modeling purpose are included in the process model" [Men07].

> "A business process model is the result of mapping a business process. This business process can be either a real-world business process as perceived by a modeler, or a business process conceptualized by a modeler" [Men07].

In order to model business processes, a user requires a *modeling framework*, which consists of one or more modeling techniques and modeling tools as depicted in Fig. 2.3. A *modeling technique* is an operational approach for the creation of conceptual models [Men07] and it subsumes a *modeling language* together with its corresponding *modeling method*. It is an essential building block of a modeling framework.

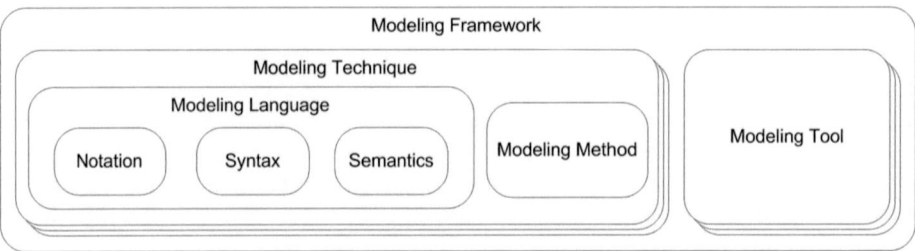

Figure 2.3: Concepts of a business process modeling framework, adapted from [Men07]

The modeling language consists of three elements: *notation, syntax* and *semantics*. The notation specifies the visual elements which can be used for the visualization of a model [KK02]. Multiple notations may exist for the same modeling language. The syntax provides a set of constructs along with the rules which specify how the constructs are allowed to be combined [WW95]. It is sometimes referred to as the modeling grammar [WW95, WW02]. The semantics provides meaning for the constructs defined in the syntax (see Fig. 2.3). It can be provided through different means, in our case it is provided using *ontologies* (see Section 2.3.1). Expressive power and usability of a modeling technique are mainly determined by the modeling language.

The modeling method specifies how a modeling language can be used [WW02]. If the modeling method is correctly applied, the output is a model which adheres to a particular modeling language. Finally, a *modeling tool* (see Fig. 2.3) is of critical importance for the practical application of a modeling technique [Men07]. It usually supports the specification of models, model administration and multi-user collaboration [Ros03a].

However, as argued in Section 1.1, current process modeling tools do not allow for incorporating strategic concerns in process models, offer too little modeling guidance to the users and lack analysis functionalities of models on a semantic level. In order to cope with these issues, while adopting the presented definition of a modeling framework, in Part II of this thesis we provide a business process modeling framework based on semantic technologies. The framework includes several modeling tools which enables the process modelers to create process models of improved quality in an easier manner.

2.2.1 Perspectives on Business Processes

In order to describe a business process, several forms of process concepts need to be integrated in a business process model. The authors in [CKO92] provide a popular categorization of concepts that a process model should capture. They argue that information in a business process model should provide answers to the following questions: what is going to be done, who is going to do it, when and where it will be done, how and why it will be done, and who is dependent on its being done [CKO92]. These questions helped to group the commonly used process concepts into four perspectives: functional, behavioral, organizational, and informational process perspective.

An example of a widely accepted method to capture different process perspectives is the so called ARIS House of Business Engineering [Sch99]. ARIS distinguishes between four perspectives: Organization (*who*), Data (*what*), Function (*how*), Product/Service (*output*), centrally connected by a process flow (*in what sequence*) [SKN92, DB07]. Recent research on process perspectives [Wes07] also reinforces the ideas outlined in [SKN92, CKO92], where function, data, and organization modeling are seen as the core ingredients of a business process model.

In section 3.2.2 we argue that this viewpoint lacks some important insights. The process-oriented view of an organization requires the process models to capture broader knowledge than considered in the aforementioned works. For example, too little attention is payed to strategic aspects of processes, such as business goals, KPIs, business directives, etc.

We now provide an overview of existing process modeling languages and briefly discuss their deficiencies.

2.2.2 Business Process Modeling Languages

Process modeling languages can be classified into three main categories: informal, semi-formal, and formal languages [Lin08]. Informal languages are natural languages, which are used on the first two levels of business processes in Fig. 2.2. Semi-formal languages are graphical languages which introduce a set of notations with semantics defined in the underlying metamodels. Formal languages have rigid and precise semantics defined in formal logics or mathematics. The work in [Lin08] compares most widely used process modeling languages such as Petri nets [Pet62], BPMN [Obj09], EPC [SKN92], which we introduce in the following.

Petri nets were introduced in the 1960s as a formal, graphical language for modeling distributed systems [Pet62]. Due to their well defined mathematical properties, they are widely used in workflow management and software design in practice. Petri nets are also still popular in the BPM research community (cf. [vdA04, Des05]), where various extensions regarding complementary process modeling perspectives have been proposed.

Event-driven process chains (EPC) [SKN92] were created in the 1990s as part of the ARIS framework. In its basic form, the EPC concepts bear close similarities to Petri nets, as they support modeling of processes as a chain of events, triggering a function which in turn again results in events. There are various extensions of the basic EPC concepts, which provide support for modeling the organizational and informational process perspectives. EPC is a graphical modeling language which is targeted to be easily understood and used by the business people. Although the language achieved its wide adoption during the 1990s, it can be noted that in the recent years, both in research and practice, the EPC language is gaining increasingly less interest and attention.

The Business Process Modeling Notation (BPMN) [Obj09] is a new standard for modeling business processes. BPMN belongs to the category of semi-formal modeling languages, intended to support business process management for both business and technical users. BPMN roots stem from the activity diagrams in UML [Obj07] and it is gaining increasing adoption in industry and academia. At the time of this writing, BPMN 2.0 version of the standard is being finalized. This new version includes extensions to the notation (e.g. for expressing collaboration between process participants), metamodel specification, and interchange format.

If we observe the historical development of the above mentioned modeling languages, it can be noted that over time they got richer in expressiveness (scope). In the case of EPC, if we compare the notation in [DB07] with the initial version in [SKN92], we notice that the trend of notation extensions aims to support a broader business context. For example, the extended EPC described in [STA05] and [DB07] allows for modeling of business objectives, key performance indicators, risks, and internal controls in the context of business processes. However, the proposed extensions i) remain underspecified with respect to their semantics, ii) are not well integrated to the basic EPC metamodel, and iii) have weak links to other extensions. In the case of BPMN, on the one hand it has been extended to allow for modeling of B2B collaboration, whereas on the other hand a formal semantics has been proposed for the behavioral process perspective [Obj09].

Extensions on the business process notation level in general fall short of seeing processes in the overall business context. For example, one of the major issues in BPM identified by the authors in [BIS+07] is the "broken link between BPM efforts and organizational strategy" [BIS+07]. We argue that in order to establish this link, the conceptual business process models need to be enriched with information regarding the strategic aspects coming from the higher levels of Fig. 2.2. Such information includes business goals, key performance indicators and business directives (policies and rules). In addition, formal modeling languages for these strategic notions need to be provided as they are currently specified in plain text or semi-formally using forms. Including as much of the semantics in the language itself would enable elegant model-driven verification mechanisms, rather than writing program scripts for even the simple checks as in the case of ARIS [DB07].

Further overviews of different process modeling languages can be found in [DvdAtH05, Wes07]. In the next section, we focus on the second aspect important for our work which will turn instrumental in providing semantics for our modeling languages.

2.3 Semantic Technologies

In this section, we present basic technologies for providing semantics to the represented knowledge and its automated processing. We start by introducing *ontologies*, computational artifacts that are used for formalizing the knowledge of a particular domain using different ontology languages based on different knowledge representation formalisms. We continue with explaining the automated machine processing of the formalized knowledge by means of *reasoners*. Finally, we discuss the syntax, semantics and reasoning tasks for the ontology language chosen for our purposes, WSML-Flight.

2.3.1 Ontologies

The notion of ontologies as computational artifacts[3] stems from the field of applied artificial intelligence (AI) [Gru93]. In this context, ontologies are conceptual models that formally represent the relevant entities and relations in a domain of interest [UG04]. A number of fields in computer science make use of ontologies: knowledge management, database design, software engineering, knowledge representation, information retrieval and extraction [Mcg03].

In order to define the term *ontology* more precisely, we adopt a fairly commonly accepted definition of ontologies in the computer science community, originally coined by Gruber [Gru93] and extended by Studer et al. in [SBF98]: "An ontology is a formal, explicit specification of a shared conceptualization." This definition contains four important characteristics of ontologies which deserve some further clarification. i) *conceptuality*: "A body of formally represented knowledge is based on a conceptualization: the objects, concepts, and other entities that are assumed to exist in some area of interest and the relationships among them. A conceptualization is an abstract, simplified view of the world that we wish to represent for some purpose" [GN87]. The way an ontology represents the knowledge of a domain is conceptual, using symbols that represent concepts and their relations. In addition, an ontology describes a conceptualization in general terms, trying to capture as many situations as possible [SGA07]. ii) *formality*: In order to make sure that the concepts and relations in an ontology are interpreted according to their intended conceptualization, a formal representation of these symbols is necessary. Knowledge representation languages are used to provide formal underpinnings for the concepts and relations contained in an ontology. iii) *explicitness*: Refers to the accessibility of domain knowledge to machines. All knowledge that is not stated explicitly in an ontology is not part of the machine-processable conceptualization. iv) *being shared*: It

---

[3]In philosophy, Ontology (uppercase initial) is a branch of metaphysics which investigates the nature of existence (reality). It seeks to answer fundamental questions such as "what is being?", or "what are the features common to all beings?" [Gua98]. Here, we focus on the perception of ontologies prevalent in computer science, i.e. ontologies as engineering, machine-readable artifacts [Gru93].

has been shown that for practical usage of ontologies, without a shared ontological commitment, the benefit of having an ontology is limited [GOS09]. Thus, ontology design is associated with a process of reaching consensus among the people in a community [SGA07].

One of the important factors determining the degree to which an ontology specifies a conceptualization is the axiomatization [GOS09]. A richer axiomatization allows for more precision of an ontology, i.e. better alignment with the intended model of a domain. However, rich axiomatization comes with a price, an insight which we will illustrate using Fig. 2.4. On the one side, there are rather informal approaches that may support definitions of terms only, without specifying the meaning of the term (see Fig. 2.4, left). At the other end of the scale are formal approaches that allow specifying rigorous and precise formal theories (see Fig. 2.4, right). When looking at the scale from left to right in Fig. 2.4, the level of formality increases, but so do the requirements for supporting machine interpretation of the ontologies. At this point one speaks of a trade-off between expressiveness and efficiency when choosing the appropriate level of formality for a specific application [GOS09].

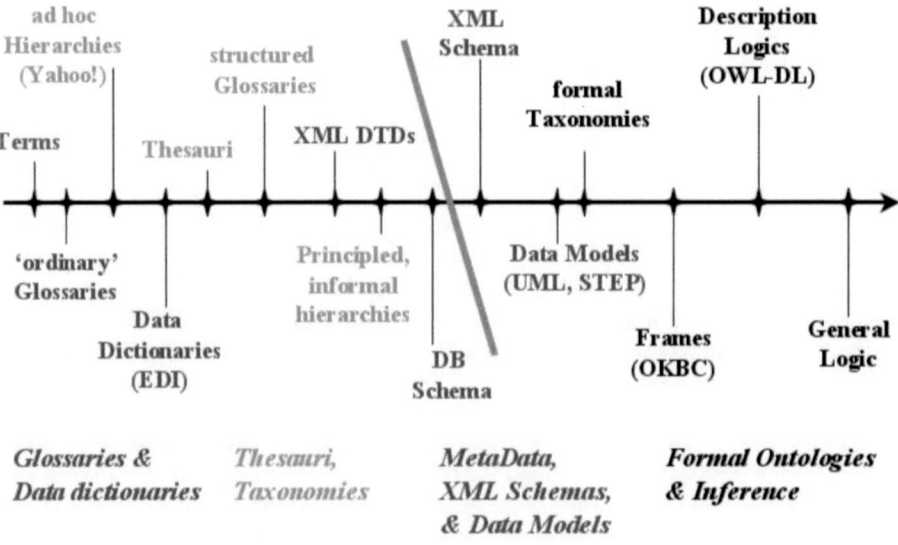

Figure 2.4: Kinds of ontologies, adopted from [UG04]

The development of ontologies was given a push with the coming of the Semantic Web [BLHL01]. Semantic Web visionaries claimed that ontologies have great potential to provide semantically richer representation of Web pages and their relations on the Web, thus better enabling people and computers to work in cooperation [GDDS06]. The vision of Semantic Web requires annotation of data with domain-specific metadata. Staab et al. [SSSS01] identify a two step process for achieving the annotation. The first step is concerned with all activities necessary for the creation of an ontology and outputs a set of terminology to be used in the second step, where the vocabulary created earlier is used to annotate information artifacts with metadata. The idea of semantic annotation of artifacts will prove instrumental within our approach in the domain of BPM, as will be shown in Section 2.4.

Depending on the intended application, different ontology languages with different degrees of expressiveness may be required. In the next section, we provide a brief overview of available ontology languages.

2.3.2 Ontology Languages

The authors in [BLHL01] stressed the importance of selecting an appropriate ontology language for the needs of a specific application scenario. Depending on the use case, there is a known trade-off between expressiveness[4] and decidability[5] when choosing the ontology language. Logical formalism underlying the chosen language must be powerful enough in terms of its expressiveness, but must also be decidable for its practical application. We use Fig. 2.5 to give an overview of the most important ontology languages and discuss their formal underpinnings.

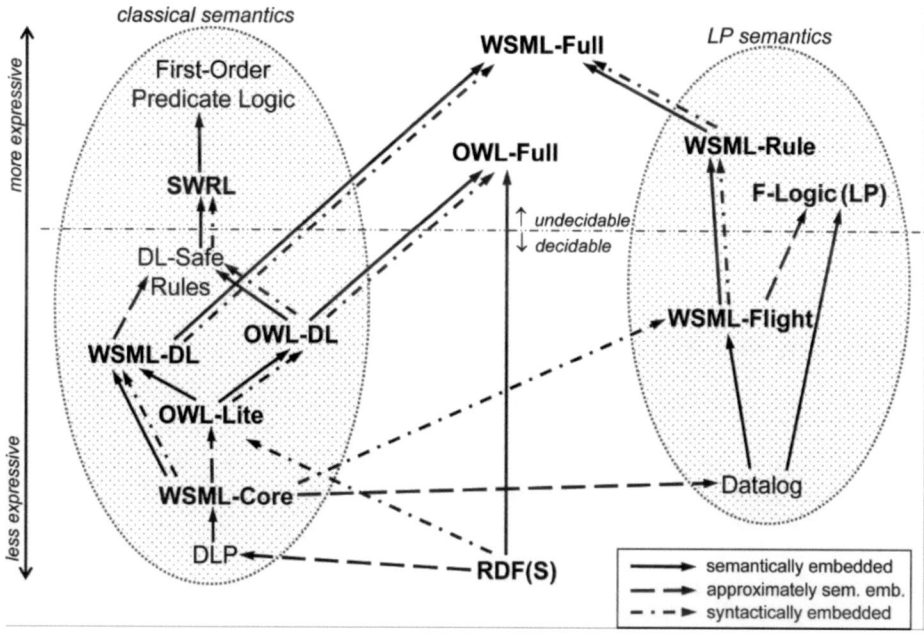

Figure 2.5: An overview of ontology languages. Source: [GHA07]

The ontology languages in Fig. 2.5 are presented hierarchically, where the connecting arrow type indicates the level of embedment between languages. For instance, a solid arrow denotes a complete semantic containedness, meaning that anything that can be expressed in the source language can also be expressed in the target language [GHA07]. A dashed arrow is used to denote a weaker embedment, where

---

[4]In this context, a language is more expressive if it allows for representing more complex knowledge and supports more complex reasoning algorithms over that knowledge

[5]A reasoning algorithm is decidable if it terminates with a correct answer in finite time [GHA07]

not all features of the source language completely fit the target language. A dash-doted arrow symbolizes that the source language syntax is a subset of the target language syntax, but their semantic interpretations may differ (see Fig. 2.5). The languages depicted near the bottom of the figure are the least expressive and decidable, whereas languages placed at the top are the most expressive but undecidable.

There is another important distinction depicted in Fig. 2.5. On the left side it shows a family of ontology languages based on Description Logics (DL) knowledge representation formalisms [BCM+03]. These languages are based on the open world assumption, which asserts that if a particular piece of knowledge cannot be deduced from existing knowledge – then nothing can be concluded about it [GHA07]. The best application example for the open world assumption is the World Wide Web. A widely used ontology language in this family is OWL [Wor04], which is also adopted by the W3C[6] as the ontology language for the Web. On the right side of Fig. 2.5 is a family of ontology languages based on the Logic Programming (LP) knowledge representation formalism [Llo87]. These languages follow the closed world assumption, which is based on the notion that *what cannot be proven is wrong* [GHA07]. The best application examples for the closed world assumption are all database and enterprise applications, including BPM. One of the most widely used ontology language in this family is WSML [dBLPF06].

Since our application scenarios require highly performant instance retrieval mechanism (e.g. querying the process artifacts space), we have opted for the LP formalism paradigm. WSML-Flight [dBFK+08] proves to be decidable (see Fig. 2.5), and having a scalable reasoner implementation [BF08] makes it the most appropriate ontology language for our purposes. We describe it in more detail in Section 2.3.4.

2.3.3   Reasoning

Within the semantic technology community, the term "reasoning" is frequently ambiguously referred to [dBFK+08]. We will use Fig. 2.6 to explain the basic concepts related to reasoning. In previous section, we discussed the importance of choosing an ontology language (see Fig. 2.6, left) for a given application scenario. Different ontology languages support different forms of reasoning.

In knowledge-based systems, two levels of knowledge are usually distinguished: schematic knowledge that applies to any situation in a domain, and situational (factual) knowledge that describes a specific situation (see Fig. 2.6, center). Ontologies can represent both levels of domain knowledge, and they are formulated in terms of an ontology language. Depending on which type of reasoning tasks are more important for the target application (see Fig. 2.6, bottom), the ontology language (knowledge representation formalism) can be chosen. For example, description logics-based ontology languages are best suitable for reasoning on schematic knowledge through subsumption-based reasoning, whereas logic programming-based ontology languages are efficient in data intensive querying or reasoning on situational knowledge and identification of constraint violations [FLP+06].

The reasoning component (see Fig. 2.6, right) serves as an interpreter of the formally represented domain knowledge to a target application (see Fig. 2.6, bottom). It provides the underlying machinery and infrastructure support by implementing

---

[6]http://www.w3.org/

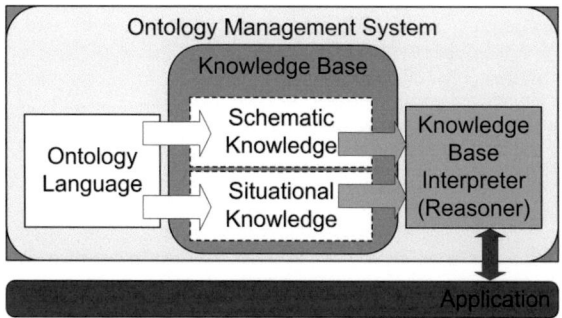

Figure 2.6: A schematic view of knowledge-based systems, adapted from [dBFK$^+$08]

the necessary algorithms required for specific reasoning tasks [FLP$^+$06]. We shortly describe the reasoning tasks for our language of choice, WSML-Flight, in the next section.

2.3.4 WSML-Flight Language and Reasoning

Web Service Modeling Language (WSML) [dBFK$^+$08, dBLPF06] denotes in fact a family of formal languages for the Web Service Modeling Ontology (WSMO)[7], the latter proposing a conceptual model for the description of ontologies, semantic Web services, goals and mediators [FLP$^+$06]. Since WSML defines a syntax and semantics for the WSMO conceptual model, it can be used for describing ontologies. WSML provides five language variants supporting both DL and LP logic-based knowledge representation paradigms, which are used to provide a formal meaning to ontology descriptions in WSML (see Fig. 2.5).

The WSML syntax has two main parts: the *conceptual* syntax and the *logical expression* syntax [GHA07]. The conceptual syntax allows for conceptual modeling of a domain in terms of concepts, instances and relations. It is based on the structure of the WSMO conceptual model and it is independent from the logical formalism used [dBFK$^+$08]. The logical expression syntax allows for formulating logical formulas (axioms) and thus depends on the expressiveness of the logical formalism underlying the language variant.

The WSML-Flight language is based on a logic programming variant of F-logic [KLW95]. More specifically, logical expressions are in the form of Datalog rules [Dah97], extended with inequality and locally stratified negation[8] in the body of a rule.

We now describe the most important parts of the language syntax in more detail. Listing 2.1 shows a WSML ontology which will be used as an illustrative example.

ontology Research
importsOntology { _"http://xmlns.com/foaf/0.1/" }

---

[7]http://www.wsmo.org/

[8]Locally stratified negation means that the definition of a particular predicate does not negatively depend on itself [dBFK$^+$08]

```
// The schema–level part
concept Researcher subConceptOf foaf#Person
        hasName ofType (1 1) wsml#string

concept Student subConceptOf foaf#Person
concept Project

relation leadsProject(impliesType Researcher, impliesType Project)

relation supervises(impliesType Researcher, impliesType Student, impliesType Project)
relation supportsProject(ofType Student, ofType Project)

// The assertional part
instance SUPER memberOf Project
instance Mario memberOf Student
instance Christian memberOf Researcher
        hasName hasValue "Christian"

relationInstance supportsProject(Mario, SUPER)
relationInstance leadsProject(Christian, SUPER)

// The logical expressions part
axiom supervisesDefinition
    definedBy
    supervises(?r,?s,?p) :– ?r memberOf Researcher and ?s memberOf Student and ?p
        memberOf Project and supportsProject(?s,?p) and leadsProject(?r,?p).

axiom leadsProjectConstraint
    definedBy
    !– leadsProject(?s,?p) and ?p memberOf Project and ?s memberOf Student.
```

Listing 2.1: An example WSML-Flight ontology

A WSML-Flight ontology is created by specifying the name using the keyword *ontology* in Listing 2.1. Using the *importsOntology* keyword one can import and extend elements defined in other ontologies. Keywords *concept* and *relation* are used to define concepts and relations in the ontology, whereas *subConceptOf* is used for specialization of a concept. WSML offers the possibility for range restriction to ensure that attribute values are of a certain type by using the keyword *ofType* when defining an attribute (see e.g. `hasName` attribute definition in Listing 2.1)). Keyword *impliesType* allows concluding or inferring that an assigned value is of the type specified in the attribute definition. Cardinality constraint can also be defined for attributes. In addition, there are pre-defined data types such as *string, integer, decimal,* etc. Example of an n-ary relation is the definition of relation `supervises` in Listing 2.1. Relations between concepts can alternatively be modeled as attributes defined in each concept participating in a relation.

Specific entities of a concept are defined using keywords *instance* and *memberOf*. Values to attributes are assigned using the *hasValue* keyword. Relations between instances are defined using the *relationInstance* keyword and specifying the instances as parameters for the relation.

The logical expression part allows for defining two types of logical formulas, namely inference rule and constraint. Inference rule allows inferring new knowledge based on existing facts in the knowledge base. For example, the rule defining the semantics of the `supervises` relation in Listing 2.1 infers that a researcher is supervising a student if the student supports a project led by the researcher. Inference rule syntax is similar to a Datalog rule [Dah97] with head and body of the rule being connected by the symbol ":-". A rule *body* defines a set of conditions. A rule *head* represents the conclusion (new knowledge) inferred on condition (body) being true. Variables are defined by using the symbol "?" preceding the variable name. Constraints are modeled using the symbol "!-" followed by the set of conditions (body). A constraint is violated when its condition or body is true and the target ontology becomes inconsistent. In the example ontology, a constraint is defined to ensure that students are not allowed to lead a project (see axiom `leadsProjectConstraint` in Listing 2.1).

WSML-Flight also allows for querying of ontologies. A *query* consists of a body alone, without the head. For example, the query `supervises(?x, ?y, ?z)` on the example ontology (see Listing 2.1) would return `Christian`, `Mario` and `SUPER` for the variables `?x`, `?y` and `?z`, respectively. For further details on WSML-Flight syntax, we refer the reader to [dBFK+08, dBLPF06].

The reasoning tasks that can be performed with WSML-Flight are realized by Datalog queries [Dah97] and include: *consistency check, entailment* and *retrieval* [dBFK+08]. The consistency check of a WSML-Flight ontology is performed by querying for the empty clause. If the result set is empty, this means that the empty clause could not be derived and the queried ontology is satisfiable, otherwise it is not [dBFK+08]. This reasoning task is used in Chapter 5 of this thesis. The reasoning task of entailment by a WSML-Flight ontology is performed by using queries that contain no variables. If the resulting set is non-empty, then the fact is entailed by the queried ontology, otherwise it is not [dBFK+08]. Entailment is used in Chapter 4 of this thesis. The retrieval is performed in a similar way to entailment, the difference being that the posed query contains free variables. The result set then contains all instances for which the query expression is entailed by the queried ontology [dBFK+08]. Retrieval reasoning task is used in Chapters 4, 5 and 6 of this thesis.

2.4   Semantic Business Process Management

In this section we will draw a connection between both fields mentioned before, namely Business Process Management and semantic technologies. The research field of Semantic Business Process Management (SBPM) was born from a need to increase the level of automation within the BPM lifecycle. In the SBPM vision paper [HLD+05], the authors propose to combine the technologies developed in the Semantic Web services (SWS) community [SGA07] with BPM community efforts in order to create one consolidated technology called SBPM. The remainder of this section clarifies the aims and the approach of SBPM.

The collection of everything that matches the definition of a process from Section 2.1 in an enterprise can be referred to as the enterprise process space. Different roles are involved in BPM efforts, as illustrated in Fig. 2.7, but we can broadly identify two perspectives on BPM: i) the business perspective on enterprise operations and ii) the actual execution of the operations by a number of IT systems, resources, and human labor. We adopt the view of Hepp and Roman [HR07] who see BPM as an approach for managing the execution of IT-supported business operations from a managerial view rather than from a technical perspective.

Business Experts' Perspective: Processes

IT Implementation Perspective

Figure 2.7: The critical IT/process divide. Source: [HLD+05]

The main idea in SBPM is to semantically represent the two perspectives (business and IT) using ontology languages and to employ machine reasoning for the automated or semi-automated translation tasks between the two perspectives. In this way, it is possible to overcome the problem of disconnectedness of management and execution levels through SBPM. At present however, businesses lack a machine readable representation of their process space. Hepp et al. [HLD+05] analysis is that therefore "the business process space inside the organization as a whole is not accessible on a semantic level". Not having this is a major obstacle towards achieving higher level of automation in BPM. The authors also claim that the current research results in the area of Semantic Web and Semantic Web services (ontology languages, repositories, reasoners and query languages) should be applied to the BPM space in order to achieve the vision of SBPM. Hence, the core idea of the SBPM approach is to i) represent and semantically describe each existing atomic and composite process in an organization as a Semantic Web service, ii) express business expert needs as WSMO goals, iii) use an existing SWS execution environment to mediate between business goals and available processes.

Hepp et al. [HLD+05] formulate two general usage scenarios for SBPM: i) querying the process space, and ii) manipulating the process space. For instance, in the first scenario, a query could give an answer to the natural language question, "In which processes is resource x used?", thereby exploiting both, the process space as well as further enterprise knowledge, i.e. resource structure. The second scenario subsumes the following tasks: creating a new business process, modify an existing process or abandon an outdated process. This scenario requires querying functionality plus the possibility to actually invoke Web services and execute processes. The work presented in this thesis loosely relates to the scenario i) in Chapter 6, where we present an approach for querying of business processes.

SBPM has received growing attention through workshops and conference tracks organized on this topic, e.g. cf. [HHK+07, BHK+08]. Although SBPM also aims at formalizing the knowledge within the BPM domain, in our opinion it is too strongly driven by the SWS community which tries to apply the existing mechanisms of automated discovery, composition, mediation [SGA07] of SWSs in the BPM domain.

Our perception is that the problems in the domain (in this case BPM) need to be thoroughly understood before rushing with off-the-shelf solutions. Only in this way can semantic technologies fundamentally improve BPM. The lack of this insight results in our work being considered "out of scope" for the SBPM approach.

2.5 Summary

This chapter introduced the basic concepts and technologies important for the realization of the semantic business process modeling framework. We have first discussed and clarified the broad concept of business process management in general and business process modeling as its subdiscipline in particular. In this context, we have positioned our work within the BPM lifecycle and identified some of the important problems with respect to specification of business processes at different levels of abstraction. We have also discussed the issue of the lack of formality of process modeling languages and its implications. The second part of the chapter describes the important concepts behind the term semantic technologies. We discuss ontologies as means of formal knowledge representation and reasoning as a mechanism for deriving new facts from the knowledge base. WSML-Flight as a kind of an ontology language is discussed in more detail as it is used extensively in this thesis. Finally, we introduce a new research field created by bringing together the ideas from the BPM and Semantic Web communities, the Semantic BPM and position our work in this context. In the next part we describe the main contribution of this thesis, the semantic business process modeling framework, making use of the concepts introduced here.

Part II

Semantic Business Process Modeling Framework

Chapter 3

Framework Foundations

3.1 Introduction

In order to provide a semantic business process modeling framework as defined in Section 2.2, there are some foundational aspects that need to be investigated first. They include the scope of modeling languages which need to be provided, the underlying techniques on which the modeling methods can be based on, and the guidelines for the usage of such a modeling framework.

In order to provide a unified modeling framework (as argued in Section 2.2), we first needed to better understand the knowledge used in creating conceptual process models, the roles involved in modeling, and the modeling abstraction levels. In this context, we further need to define a structure and building blocks required for the formal representation of such knowledge so that the process models can be analyzed on a semantic level. In addition, we need to describe how such formal representations can be used and the kinds of added value this provides in comparison to standard business process modeling methodologies.

Given the above discussion, this chapter is structured as follows. We investigate the categorization of knowledge captured in process models as well as process modeling perspectives and abstraction levels in Section 3.2. Based on this, in Section 3.3, we present a process-oriented enterprise ontology framework which allows for the formal representation of relevant process knowledge. Finally, Section 3.4 introduces the methodological guidelines for the application of ontologies and reasoning in modeling of conceptual business processes. We compare our efforts to the related works in the field where appropriate.

3.2 Understanding Conceptual Process Models

In our quest for a better understanding of a conceptual business process model, we follow [Mor98] where the authors claim that the subject of thinking becomes gradually clearer when it is observed from different aspects. Therefore, we start with the analysis of a large repository of process models in order to discover what process knowledge is usually captured in models. Next, we take a step further in organizing this knowledge into six process perspectives. Finally, based on the types of modeling artifacts in the repository, we define modeling abstraction levels and discuss them in the context of the process knowledge used in modeling.

3.2.1 Process Knowledge in Models

In order to better understand and categorize the business knowledge used in describing business process models, we have analyzed a rich business process repository (BPR)[1] provided by SAP. This repository contains over 1500 real life business process models which capture best practices and is a result of more than 35 years of experience in the design and customization of processes for customers from 25 different industries. The BPR repository design is based on a set of XML[2] schemas which were analyzed and consolidated for our purpose.

Categorization of the knowledge captured in process models from the BPR repository can be summarized using Fig. 3.1. In the following, we discuss each of the resulting knowledge categories in more detail.

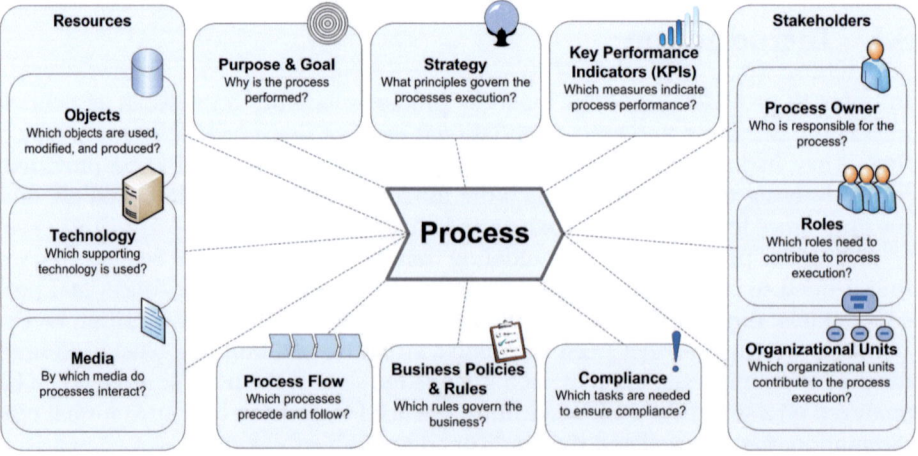

Figure 3.1: Process knowledge in models

The *process flow* could be seen as the core of a process representation and means the business logical sequence of activities and their dependencies from end to end. As processes essentially are transformations that manipulate *objects* (e.g. create, change or delete) it is relevant for the process to capture information on these and the states they take on during transformation. From a systems perspective, objects might form the source for system data. *Technology* can be seen as an enabler for certain steps in the process in terms of persistency and efficiency. Also, in tight connection to the questions on objects and data is the *media* used in a process. This is especially interesting since a medium often forms a process differentiation characteristic. A process could be quite different depending on the medium used, e.g. providing the customer of a telecommunication service with either an electronic or paper bill. We refer to the collection of objects, technology and media as *resources* (see Fig. 3.1, left).

A similar grouping under the label of *stakeholders* could be done for *organizational units*, *roles* and *process owners* (see Fig. 3.1, right). Given the end-to-end process perspective described in Section 2.1, it is important to stress that processes run across

---

[1]https://implementationcontent.sap.com/bpr
[2]http://www.w3.org/XML/

one or more organizational units within a functional or divisional hierarchy. We define a role as a task and responsibility bundle which is clearly distinguished from the person that is performing the role. It can be played by different persons and one person can play several roles. Talking about roles and processes allows to easily talk about the tasks that should belong together or should be separated from a process perspective before mapping them to the organizational structure. The process owner as an accountable manager for the process end-to-end execution can be seen as a special role in the context of processes.

Compliance is of high importance to today's businesses. The compliance regulations especially impact processes in the form of specific tasks in processes that are required in order to fulfill regulatory requirements. Thus, in process design it is important to capture and explicitly mark these tasks. The process *goal* is the ultimate reason for the process existence and the purpose it serves. When formulating a process goal, it is useful to already think about quantifiable results. The way to do this is to define appropriate *key performance indicators* along the dimensions such as time, cost or quality that measure the process and then determine corresponding values. A goal makes explicit where to go, whereas a *strategy* shapes the way in reaching a goal i.e. it channels efforts towards a goal.

Business policies and *business rules* exist to control, guide and shape strategies. They define what can be done and what must not be done. For example, a decision rule for a specific business situation states which alternative should be chosen according to predefined decision criteria. A prioritization rule applies e.g. when reserving resources. Business policies differ from business rules in that they are less formally-structured [OMG08a]. Business rules are in practice not necessarily stated explicitly, but likely incorporated into the process design [MK08].

The information associated to processes described in this section could be thought of as the answers to the questions illustrated in Fig. 3.1. In order to adequately organize the business knowledge from Fig. 3.1, we follow the approaches in [CKO92, Wes07], where the authors define process perspectives in order to reduce the complexity of process design (see Section 2.2.1).

3.2.2 Process Perspectives

Based on the result presented in Fig. 3.1, we define six key perspectives to organize business process model knowledge. We visualize them in Fig. 3.2, motivated by the "orthographic projection" paradigm used in mechanical and civil engineering to create detailed drawings of physical objects. The main idea is to enable the process modeler to easily manage and navigate the various perspectives of process design. In the following, we shortly describe each of them.

Functional perspective provides a functional breakdown of activities that an enterprise performs. Starting from high-level business functions (value chain), the coarse-grained functions are broken down into finer-grained functional units by means of functional decomposition. Functional decomposition has proven to be an important concept for capturing and managing complexity [Wes07].

Motivational perspective is inspired by the recent OMG specification, the Business Motivation Model (BMM) [OMG08a]. The notion of motivation is important for business processes because an enterprise should be able to say why it executes a particular process and how does it fit into the overall strategy. This perspective is divided in two segments: intentional and directional.

The intentional segment captures the enterprise aspirations - what it wishes to achieve, i.e. goals and the metrics used to measure the success in achieving goals - key performance indicators. The directional segment describes what the enterprise will employ to achieve its goals, i.e. strategies, business policies and rules (see Fig. 3.2).

Organizational perspective represents by whom (roles and organizational units) activities are performed. We depict it in Fig. 3.2 by a grouping under the label of stakeholders, encompassing organizational units, roles and process owners.

Resource perspective describes applications and resources that should be spent when carrying out certain process activities (e.g. objects, IT systems, or media needed in order to accomplish the activity) or that may be results of certain activities (see Fig. 3.2).

Compliance perspective represents compliance requirements within process models. The source of these requirements may be external (laws and regulations) or internal company policies and guidelines. In either case, this is a process aspect which can and should be modeled separately.

Behavioral perspective captures process control flow. It represents the logical ordering of process activities and their causal interrelationships. This perspective could be seen as the core of a process representation and acts as a connection point [Wes07] for the other perspectives (see Fig. 3.2).

We can think of the business process model knowledge depicted in Fig. 3.1 as being present on each business process level introduced in Section 2.1 in smaller or greater detail. In the next section we will investigate the mapping of this knowledge to individual process abstraction levels.

3.2.3   Abstraction Levels in Process Modeling

The analysis of process models from the SAP business process repository has shown that the abstraction levels in Fig. 2.2 are not investigated in sufficient detail. Based on this analysis, we now illustrate the types of artifacts usually created on each abstraction level and discuss how different modeling abstraction levels relate to the process knowledge in Fig. 3.1.

The modeling artifacts from the BPR created on different process modeling abstraction levels can be visualized using a pyramid-like structure, as shown in Fig. 3.3. *Business motivation* forms the top most layer of the pyramid. It models the various driving forces (i.e. goals, strategies, metrics, etc.) of the enterprise and the relationships between them (cf. top left of Fig. 3.3). The business motivation model is then structured along the industry-specific *value chain*. The value chain is composed of a sequence of value-creating functional areas - so called value chain elements. The top right of Fig. 3.3 shows the telecommunication industry value chain with its value chain elements. *Business scenario group* is a collection of business scenarios with the same business goals. A business scenario group can span across several functional areas (cf. center of Fig. 3.3) and sometimes even integrated with consumers and suppliers delimitating a value chain. *Business scenario* is a set of logically related business processes performed to achieve defined and measurable business objectives. Each business scenario is associated with a set of metrics (key

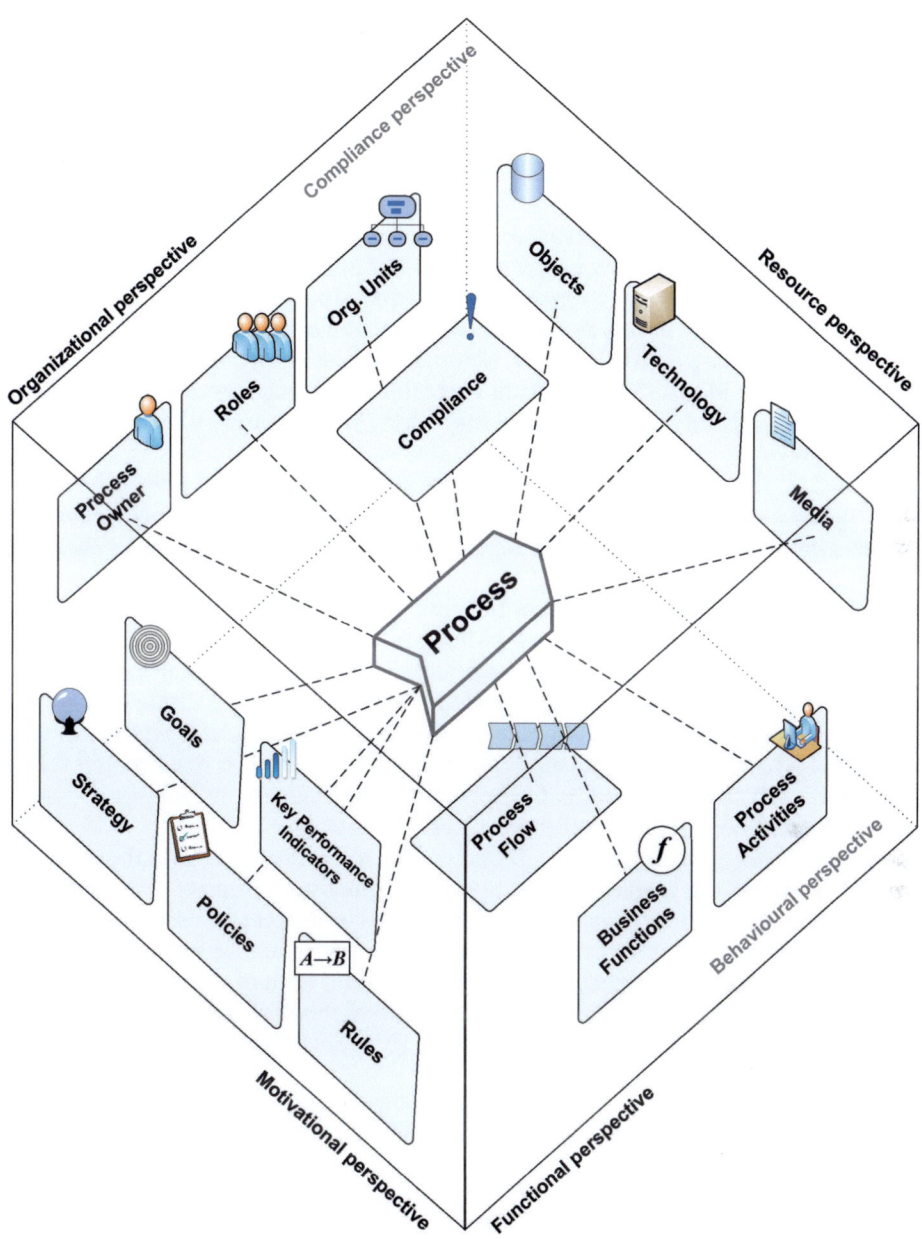

Figure 3.2: Process perspectives

performance indicators) which serve as efficiency benchmarks. Example KPIs are shown for the Lead and Opportunity Management scenario in the center right of Fig. 3.3.

Business process is a set of operations within a business scenario. All business processes follow a well defined flow in order to achieve the business objectives of its scenario. *Business process activity* represents an operation of a business process that performs a defined function. The bottom right part of Fig. 3.3 shows the process activities of the Lead Processing process. All business process activities are connected in a business logical flow in order to fulfill the purpose of the business process.

Business Process Frameworks[3], which are becoming popular in companies, also contain similar types of modeling artifacts. They provide a common language, set of high level processes and its associated metrics which one can use as a template to quickly and easily define new processes or evaluate and improve existing processes based on the provided metrics. Some of the best known examples are Supply Chain Council's SCOR (Supply Chain Operation Reference model)[4], TeleManagement Forum's eTOM framework[5] and the Value Chain Group's VRM (Value Reference Model)[6].

Based on the aforementioned types of modeling artifacts, we revisit the definition of process modeling abstraction levels and seek to establish their relation to process knowledge in Fig. 3.1. We define three modeling abstraction levels as follows:

Executive (strategic) level. Here the enterprise goals and the general strategic direction are set. Key performance indicators are determined for measuring the progress in achieving goals. Business policies are defined in order to govern the enterprise courses of action. Typical artifacts on this level may include goal specifications, strategy documents and policy guidelines (cf. Fig. 3.4, left). Artifacts on this level of abstraction provide the motivation ("why") for the processes within the organization, which are defined on further levels. The modeling techniques are rather informal or ad-hoc (plain text, flip chart techniques or mind maps).

Line of business manager level. Based on the artifacts produced at the executive level, line of business managers need to provide quick and intuitive overview of the business processes of an organization. The aim is to depict processes from a high-level perspective with a focus on understanding key points of the process. These high-level processes are called business scenarios and each of them represents a set of logically related processes performed to achieve defined and measurable business goals. Models such as Value Added Chain Diagrams [Por85] and SAP Business Scenarios[7] are used for this purpose.

Business analyst level. Unlike the other two perspectives, the business analyst faces a variety of purposes in modeling. This includes business process documentation, process improvement, system requirements specification, etc. Process models created at this level detail each of the business scenarios specified and serve as a

---

[3]http://www.bptrends.com/publicationfiles/spotlight_052008.pdf

[4]http://www.supply-chain.org/cs/root/scor_tools_resources/scor_model/scor_model

[5]http://www.tmforum.org/BusinessProcessFramework/1647/home.html

[6]http://www.value-chain.org/en/cms/1960/

[7]SAP Business Scenarios are delivered with the SAP Solution Composer, a modeling tool provided by SAP. http://www.sap.com/solutions/businessmaps/composer/index.epx

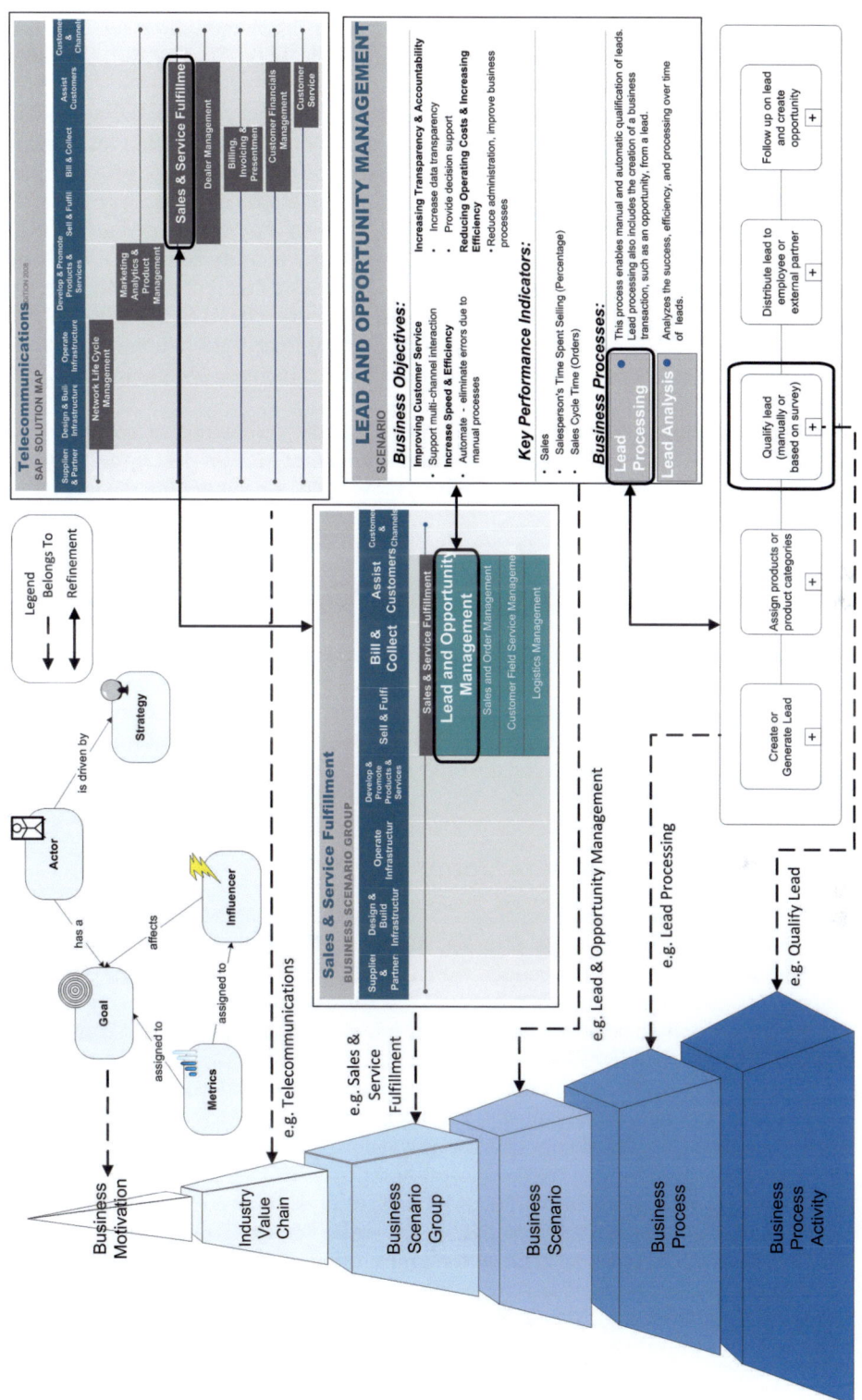

Figure 3.3: Processes at different levels of abstraction

starting point for the underlying information system implementation (cf. Fig. 3.4, right). There are numerous modeling techniques (EPC [KNS92], BPMN[8], UML Activity Diagrams [Obj07]) used in this space.

We can think of the process knowledge depicted in Fig. 3.1 as being present on each level of abstraction in smaller or greater detail. Parts of this knowledge tend to grow stronger as we move down the abstraction levels, e.g. process flow. Of course, high level knowledge such as strategic goals and core strategy plans do not vanish as we reach a level of higher detail. Rather, they get refined and superimposed by a more concrete view. Strategic goals grow to measurable and timed operational goals, strategic directions to detailed plans, etc. For example, the executive abstraction level strongly encompasses concepts related to the motivational perspective (goals, strategy, KPIs, etc.), while it is not interested in detailed process flow, information systems supporting the process or business objects (cf. Fig. 3.4, left).

In order to enable semantic analysis, querying and verification of business process models, there is a need for a comprehensive formal process description capturing all relevant process knowledge. In the next section, we show how we fulfill this need.

3.3 Process-oriented Enterprise Ontology Framework

Based on the insights gained in the previous section, we design a *process-oriented ontology framework* based on semantic technologies to provide means for the formal description of all relevant process perspectives identified in Fig. 3.2 and supporting all abstraction levels in process modeling from Fig. 3.4. In the following we briefly describe the ontologies constituting the process-oriented enterprise ontology framework.

3.3.1 Business Motivation Ontology (BMO)

The BMO acts as an umbrella ontology to capture the concepts from the uppermost level in the hierarchy given by Fig. 3.5. Based on the discussion in Section 3.2.2, there are two fundamental questions which are captured separately in the ontology, namely: *"what* to reach" and *"how* to reach it". First, what is needed to achieve what the business wants to achieve? And second, why does each element of a company's business plan exist? [OMG08a].

In order to provide means for modeling business motivation, the BMO distinguishes four top level concepts: *end, means, metric* and *influencer*. The notion of an *end* groups the aspirational concepts such as vision, goal and objective. BMO allows for hierarchical modeling of these concepts and provides a set of attributes and relations between them to enable different types of analysis on such specifications. On the other hand, *means* are a notion *dual* to the ends. Means group a set of concepts which are set up in order to achieve the ends: mission, strategy and tactics. Mirrored to the hierarchy of ends, a corresponding hierarchy of means can be modeled using BMO, establishing the means-end relationship. Following [OMG08a], we see

---

[8]http://www.bpmn.org

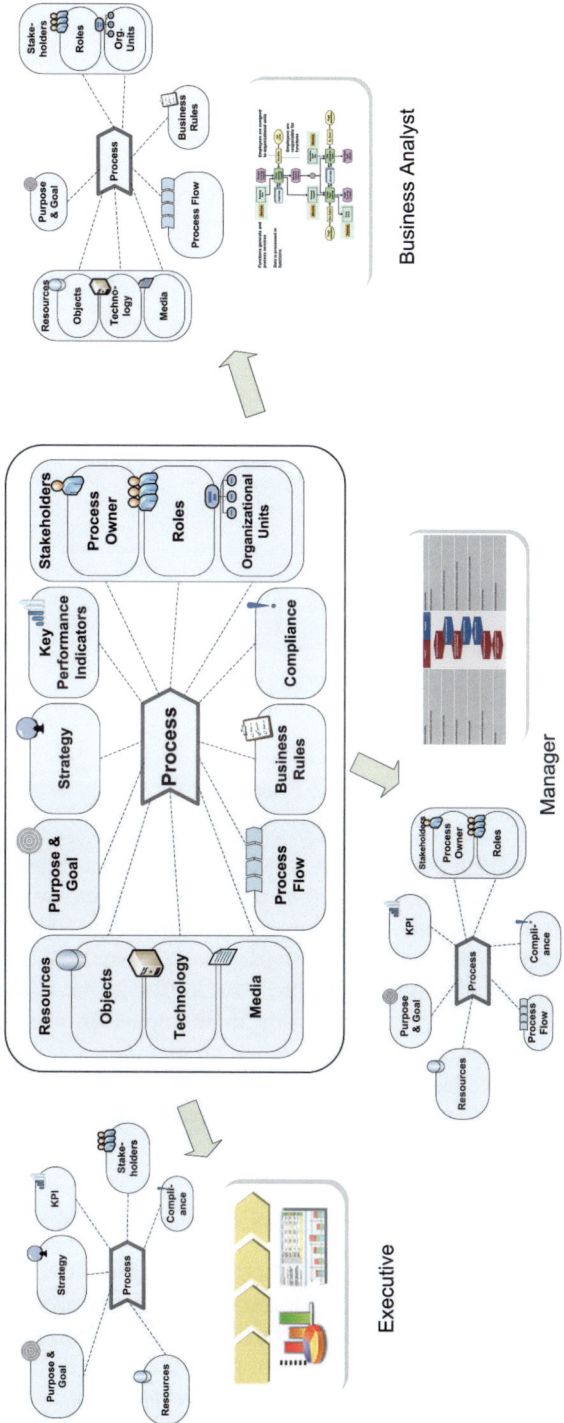

Figure 3.4: Modeling abstraction levels and the mapping to process knowledge

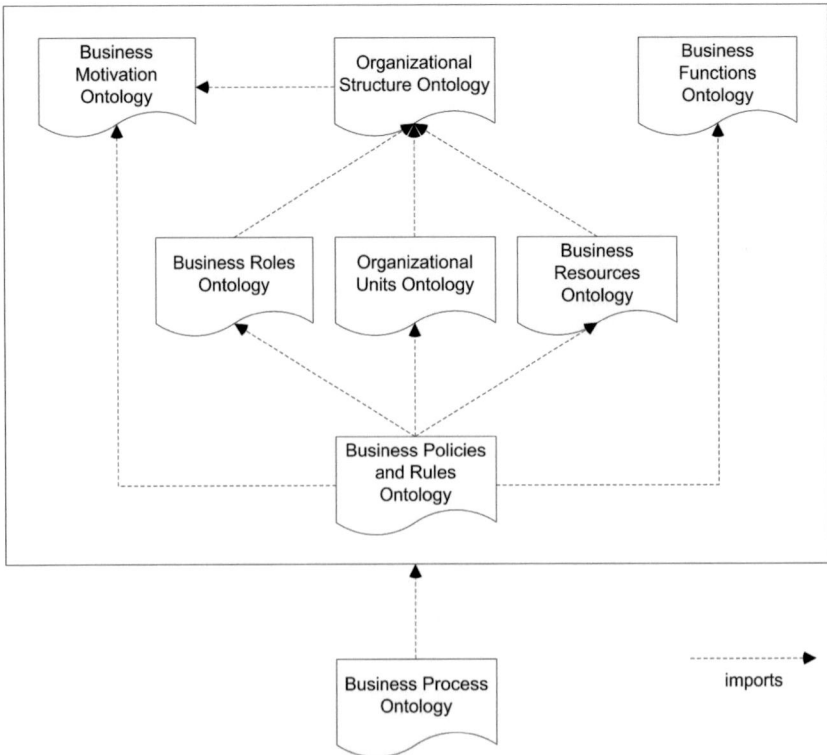

Figure 3.5: Process-oriented Enterprise Ontology Framework

an *influencer* as something that can cause changes that affect an enterprise in the employment of its means or achievement of its ends. Influencers may be internal or external. In order to judge how an enterprise should react to the change caused by influencers, a *qualitative assessment* is needed. The basis for assessments are metrics. *Metrics* can be assigned to ends (in order to monitor the achievement of ends) and to influencers (with the purpose of evaluating their impact on the organization). The BMO provides means for metric definition which includes determining appropriate metrics for a particular end or influencer, as well as defining their target values and desired tendencies (leading or lagging). We discuss the BMO in further detail in Chapter 4.

3.3.2 Business Policies and Rules Ontology (BPRO)

BPRO (cf. Fig. 3.5) allows for modeling constraints/guidelines that govern the behavior of processes. It is designed in a generic way to support the modeling of constraints coming from a variety of internal and external (compliance) regulations. Therefore, it corresponds to the compliance perspective in Fig. 3.2. There are two top level concepts in BPRO: *business policy* and *business rule*. Regarding modeling of business policies, BPRO allows for specifying the dependency and composition relations between policies, assigning contextual information and a set of implementing rules. The assignment of contextual information is done through the annotation of a business policy with other imported framework ontologies (cf. Fig. 3.5). The annotations have the purpose to characterize the application situation of a particular policy as precisely as possible. For instance, the annotations can specify on which resource a policy should be applied, in which functional area and for what type of a user role. Since business policies are less formally structured than business rules [OMG08a], the rules provide means for formalizing the meaning of a particular constraint using elements defined in other framework ontologies. A set of coherent business rules is then assigned for the implementation of a particular business policy. When modeling business rules using BPRO, it is also possible to specify dependencies between rules as well as assign the logical expression modeling the meaning of a constraint, in form of an ontology axiom. Further details on BPRO design are provided in Chapter 5. Since its first version reported here, it has been further developed and refined, which is documented in [KSMP08, EKSMP08].

3.3.3 Business Process Ontology (BPO)

For describing the behavioural (dynamic) perspective (cf. Fig. 3.2) of a process we use a process algebra, the π–calculus [MPW89]. We follow the argumentation in [Puh06b] to select the π–calculus as theory for describing the dynamic nature of modern business process management systems. A crucial benefit of using π–calculus are the facilities provided by the bisimulation theory [San96], which have been used in process verification [Puh06a], simulation [BP06] and process substitution [AS06]. The dynamic perspective of a process model stands for process control-flow, and we model it using the ontologized π–calculus, denoted by Business Process Ontology (BPO) in Figure 3.5. BPO has been proven to be expressive enough to capture the semantics of all workflow patterns [AHKB03, MP07]. By using the π–calculus as a basis for representing the process behaviour, we are able to integrate existing tools and techniques for verification, simulation and substitution of processes in our framework [Puh06a, BP06]. More details on BPO are provided in Chapter 6.

The behavioral perspective could be seen as the core of a process representation and acts as glue (provides a connection point) [Wes07] for the other perspectives. Therefore, BPO imports the other framework ontologies (cf. Figure 3.5), which describe the process context (its business function, goal, involved actors/roles, resources used, etc.) [MHJS09].

The following three ontologies correspond to the remaining process perspectives defined in Fig. 3.2. The basic structure of these ontologies was defined as part of this thesis, while their refinement and detailed development is not our contribution. References for a deeper insight into their design are provided where appropriate.

3.3.4 Business Functions Ontology (BFO)

The BFO models the functional perspective and provides a basis for structuring and defining business functions. A business function is understood as a functional area of an enterprise such as e.g. Human Resources, Marketing, Finance, Sales Management, etc. Each business function consists of a set of business activities, which correspond to business process activities in Fig. 3.3. The Business Functions Ontology aims at providing a common vocabulary for describing business functions and activities within enterprises. The rich modeling content of the SAP Solution Composer [SAP05a] has been used as a basis in the development of the BFO. Its development and the application in business process modeling is described in [BFKM08].

3.3.5   Organizational Ontology (OO)

The OO contains concepts for representing organizational structure, units and roles within an enterprise[9]. It corresponds to the organizational perspective, discussed in Section 3.2.2. It is thus further divided into three sub-ontologies:

Organizational Structure Ontology (OSO). This ontology focuses on the organizational structure (hierarchy) of a company. The OSO shows how elements of an organization work together in order to achieve the organizational goals. It encompasses departments, employees, their responsibilities, resources used, etc. as well as relations among them.

Organizational Units Ontology (OUO). This ontology provides a common vocabulary for specification of typical units that may be found in a company. An organisational unit is defined as any recognized association (temporary or permanent) of people in the context of an enterprise. Along with the other ontologies (Business Functions, Business Roles, and Business Resources Ontology) it provides extensions to OSO.

Business Roles Ontology (BROnt). This ontology provides a common meaning of concepts related to roles featured by organizational members (i.e. actors). A business role is defined as a set of expected behaviours, prerogatives and obligations featured by an actor. Each actor may play more than one role and these roles may change depending on the context. The ontology allows for modeling both internal as well as external roles played by various actors. It includes relations for modeling role hierarchy (generalization, specialization) and reporting lines.

The development of OO and its sub-ontologies is described in [FKK+08, FHKM09].

3.3.6   Business Resources Ontology (BRO)

When formalizing knowledge about the business process space of an organization, we need a means for describing the tangible and abstract resources that are relevant in the respective operations. A resource is defined as "something that can be used or consumed in an activity" [UKH+98]. The BRO covers the informational perspective and defines the basic taxonomy of resource types, and associated notions of resource access, ownership, and consumption. The ontology can be imported and refined in more specific domain ontologies that define common types of business resources for specific application domains. More details on the development of BRO can be found in [FKK+08, FHKM09].

---

[9]For the reasons of clarity, the Organizational Ontology is not included in Fig. 3.5, rather only its sub-ontologies

3.3.7   Application of the Ontology Framework

The process-oriented enterprise ontology framework was applied within the telecommunication domain in the scope of the SUPER[10] project. In Fig. 3.6 we present the ontology layers used in SUPER.

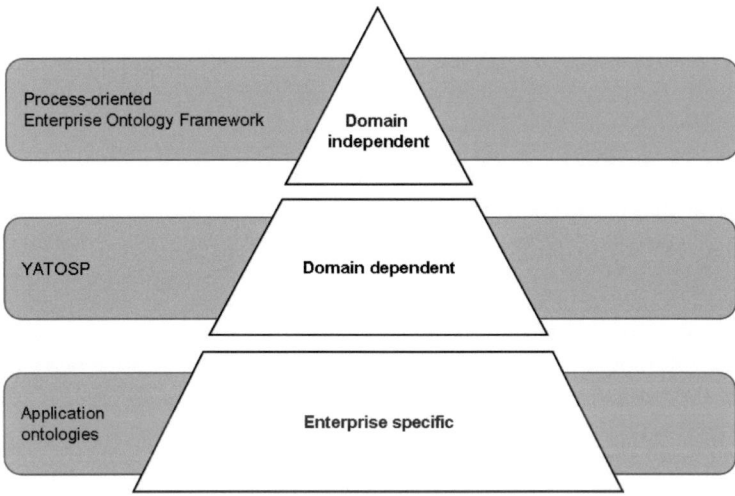

Figure 3.6: Ontology layers

On the top of the pyramid in Fig. 3.6 is the domain independent ontology layer, containing the set of ontologies which belong to the category of so called *core ontologies* [Gua97]. Core ontologies are application independent and generic over a set of domains. These are the ontologies constituting the process-oriented enterprise ontology framework (cf. Fig. 3.6). The ontology framework was used for guiding the design of *domain-dependent* and *application ontologies*, which were in turn used to describe various business scenarios in the telecommunication industry [FKRS08]. The domain-dependent (specific) ontology layer in Fig. 3.6 has been built on the basis of the NGOSS framework [CR05], a set of *de facto* telecommunication standards aiming at facilitating the design of business support systems in the service industries. The knowledge contained in the NGOSS framework was semantically lifted with the help and guidance of the process-oriented enterprise ontology framework, resulting in the YATOSP (Yet Another Telecommunication Ontology Services and Processes) framework [YAT07] (cf. Fig. 3.6). Hence, YATOSP defines a set of ontologies which capture the knowledge from the NGOSS framework. The application ontologies (bottom layer in Fig. 3.6) extend YATOSP in order to introduce vocabulary which adapts the ontologies form the previous two layers to a concrete application scenario.

After introducing the core ontologies from the process-oriented enterprise ontology framework, in the next section we focus on providing methodological guidance for the usage of ontologies in modeling conceptual business processes.

---

[10]www.ip-super.org

3.3.8   Related Work

In this section we give an overview of related efforts. We start with the conventional approaches and continue with the semantic-based ones.

ARIS (Architecture of Integrated Information Systems) is a method for analyzing processes and taking a holistic view of process design, management, workflow, and application processing [DB07]. ARIS consists of five views: organizational view, data view, control view, function view, and product/service view. However, the conceptual model of ARIS does not provide formal semantics which allows only for syntax-based analysis of models.

The Object Management Group (OMG) has been developing a set of business modeling standards for enabling business flexibility. Business Process Modeling Notation (BPMN) [Obj09] specification aims to define a standard modeling notation for business process models. Business Motivation Model (BMM) [OMG08a] standard provides a schema for modeling business plans. However, these standards do not cover all the relevant aspects and do not define the formal semantics of the concepts, attributes and relations defined in the specifications. This makes it impossible to perform automated analysis on models created using these specifications.

One of the earliest initiatives within the enterprise ontology approaches was the TOVE project [Fox92] that aimed at development of a set of integrated ontologies for modeling all kinds of enterprises. The model of an enterprise created in this approach, namely Common Sense Model of Enterprise, distinguished three levels: reference model with typical business functions (finance, sales, distribution, and administration), generic model (with such concepts as time, causality, space, resources), and concept model (e.g. role, property, structure). However, the granularity of developed ontologies may be perceived inconsistent what hampers their potential application. Also, an important drawback of the TOVE initiative is the lack of a contemporary ontology language the proposed concepts are expressed in.

Enterprise Ontology (EO) [UKH+98] is a collection of terms and definitions relevant to business enterprises. It was developed as part of the Enterprise Project, with the aim to provide a framework for enterprise modeling. EO is divided into five parts: i) terms related to processes and planning, ii) terms related to organizational structure, iii) terms related to high-level planning for an enterprise, iv) terms relating to marketing and sales of goods and services and v) terms used to define the terms of the ontology together with a few terms related to time. It was first completed in natural language format and afterwards ported to Ontolingua [UKH+98]. The lack of the formal version (expressed using one of the ontology languages) of the ontology hampers its practical application.

Finally, in [HR07], a set of ontologies for Semantic Business Process Management (cf. Section 2.4) is proposed. This work gives a rather high-level overview of an ontology stack covering the full BPM lifecycle, based on the ARIS [DB07] methodology. Due to its broad scope, the proposed stack remains on an informative level. In addition, the authors fail to recognize and position the central role of a *process* in the ontology stack.

In summary, the conventional approaches do not cover all perspectives of process description (e.g. business motivation) and do not define formal semantics for the models, while enterprise ontology works fail to provide a process-oriented view on the organization. Enterprise ontologies are also not available in any contemporarily recognized ontology language standard for which an efficient reasoner exists. Common weakness of all the works is that they do not support different process abstraction levels in order to reduce modeling complexity.

3.4 Semantic Business Process Modeling Methodology

We will now revisit the definition of a business process modeling framework provided in Section 2.2 in order to position and discuss the main contribution of this thesis - semantic business process modeling framework[11]. Our SBPM framework consists of three *modeling techniques* and their instantiating *modeling tools*. The modeling techniques include: *business motivation modeling*, *business policy and rule modeling* and *business process modeling* (cf. Fig. 3.7). Each modeling technique consists of a corresponding *modeling language* and a *modeling method*, which we present in detail in Chapters 4,5 and 6, respectively.

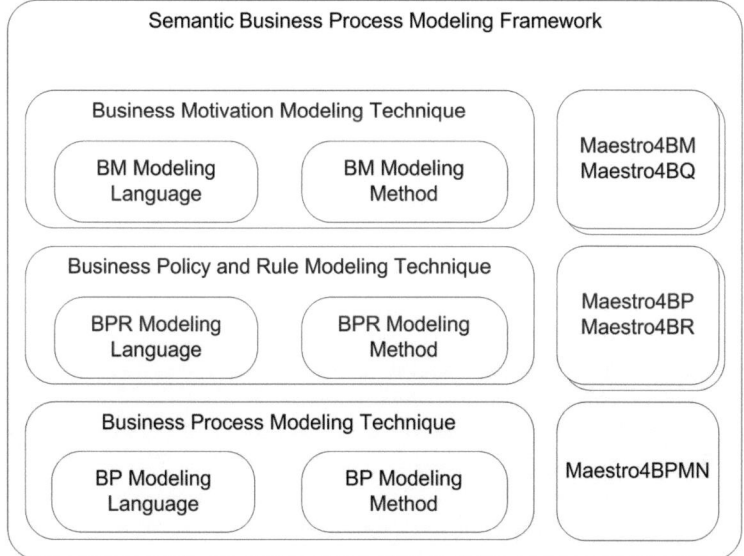

Figure 3.7: Semantic business process modeling framework – Fig. 2.3 revisited

Prototype instantiations of the modeling techniques are provided in the form of components of an integrated modeling tool – Maestro. The respective components which instantiate the modeling techniques are: *Maestro4BM* and *Maestro4BQ* for business motivation modeling, *Maestro4BP* and *Maestro4BR* for business policy and rule modeling, and *Maestro4BPMN* for business process modeling (cf. Fig. 3.7).

The introduction of semantic technologies in business process modeling has certain implications on how the modeling of processes is done. In order to provide guidance and direct *how* SBP modeling framework should be used, we define a semantic business process modeling methodology[12]. The SBPM methodology is presented in the form of a lifecycle, defining the activities, artifacts and tools involved

---

[11]We will use the term SBPM framework in the following.
[12]SBPM methodology in the following

in semantic business process modeling. We discuss the different activities, their ordering, purpose and dependencies in the following.

The SBPM lifecycle, shown in Fig. 3.8, is based on the spiral lifecycle model first proposed by Boehm [Boe88]. This spiral approach is widely adopted in the BPM community due to the dynamic nature of business processes and their consequent redesign cycle. Activities, depicted as the inner ring, and the sub-activities in the next ring are partly inspired by the current business process modeling and software engineering lifecycles [Pre05]. The major contribution of this lifecycle in comparison with existing ones is twofold. First, a strong emphasis is put on the early stages of business process definition - specifying the process purpose, metrics, constraints, etc. Ontologies provide the means for seamless integration of such notions in process descriptions. This is reflected in the first two activities within the lifecycle: *Motivation Modeling* and *Policy and Rule Modeling*. Ontologies thus allow for a unified modeling method on different levels of processes[13]. Second, the formal representation of different aspects of processes achieved through the usage of ontologies enables further advantages, such as: i) analysis of specifications on a semantic level, ii) context-based matchmaking, iii) querying/reuse of modeling artifacts, iv) modeling guidance and v) verification. The advantages are enabled through the usage of inferencing engines (reasoners) which provide the means for automated interpretation of such formal specifications. Different types of these advantages are illustrated in all of the activities within the SBPM lifecycle (cf. Fig. 3.8).

The lifecycle in Fig. 3.8 consists of four main activities: *Business Motivation Modeling*, *Policy and Rule Modeling*, *Process Modeling* and *Process Verification*. Each of the activities is subdivided into several sub-activities which are depicted in the second ring of Fig. 3.8. In the third ring we indicate the ontologies used (triangle symbol) and the methods supporting the respective activities (hammer symbol). Although it is beyond the scope of this methodology to provide the definition of a continuous evaluation and improvement process (such as CMMI [SEI09]), the usage of such processes in order to define the procedures to ensure the quality of any artifact produced during SBP modeling (ontologies, process models, scenarios, etc.) is strongly recommended and thus depicted in the outer ring of the Fig. 3.8. In the following subsections we present each of the activities and sub-activities of the lifecycle.

3.4.1   Business Motivation Modeling

This activity deals with formal specification of an organization's business motivation. With business motivation we subsume the ends a company wants to achieve, the means which are put in place to achieve them, the metrics for measuring the success in the achievement of the ends and influencers which may impact the redefinition of ends, means or metrics. The activity is divided into two sub-activities: *Visual Modeling* and *Analysis* (cf. Fig. 3.8).

Visual modeling sub-activity comprises the design of a graphical model of the business motivation, supported by the business motivation modeling notation and the Business Motivation Ontology (BMO)[14]. This includes the annotation of the created business motivation model with application ontologies, e.g. assigning existing

---

[13]Levels in process modeling were discussed in Sections 2.1 and 3.2.3

[14]The BMO and its visual notation are discussed in Chapter 4

processes to support the achievement of the defined goals, assigning existing organizational units as responsible for the implementation of a specified tactic, etc.

Analysis sub-activity is performed once the business motivation model is created. It supports various types of model analysis such as i) detection of conflicts, ii) consistency check, iii) evaluation of alternatives (what-if analysis) and iv) querying[15].

The ontologies used in this activity include the BMO and application ontologies, built on the basis of the process-oriented enterprise ontology framework. There are two methods supporting the activity: business motivation modeling method and the querying method, which supports all of the analysis types. The methods are described in detail in Chapter 4.

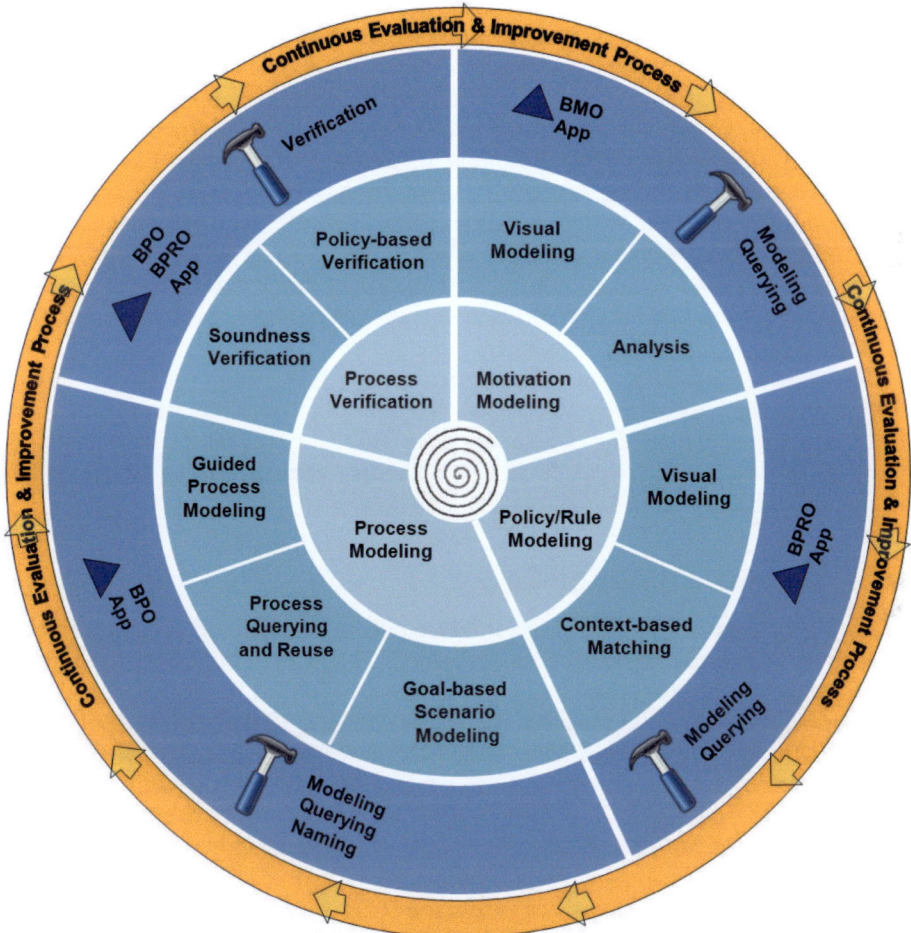

Figure 3.8: Semantic business process modeling lifecycle

---

[15]The types of analysis are discussed in detail in Chapter 4

3.4.2   Business Policy and Rule Modeling

This activity builds upon the previous one in that it precisely specifies the directives (business policies and rules) which need to be followed in the achievement of the desired ends. Business policies pose constraints on how an enterprise realizes its course of action, in a declarative manner. They can be defined based on external requirements (e.g. laws) as well as internal ones (e.g. cost-saving) and are usually implemented by a set of business rules. The activity is divided into two sub-activities: *Visual Modeling* and *Context-based Matching*.

Visual modeling sub-activity includes the design of a graphical model of the business policies and rules, based on the business policy and rule modeling notation[16] and the Business Policy and Rule Ontology (BPRO), which are further discussed in Chapter 5. For the formal specification of business policies and rules, the elements defined in the application ontologies are used (BPRO imports all the ontologies in Fig. 3.5). The specification of a policy involves the assignment of rules that implement it, as well as defining a context[17] in which a policy applies. When modeling rules, we capture what is *not* allowed to occur in the form of a constraint. Also, it is possible to specify the dependencies between one or more business rules.

Context-based matching sub-activity is performed based on the contextual information assigned to a modeled business policy. The policy context aims to capture as precisely as possible the application situation in which a policy should be triggered. Based on the formal specification of the policy context and that of a process context, context-based matching refers to finding all applicable business policies for an observed business process model.

The ontologies used in this activity include the BPRO and application ontologies, built on the basis of the process-oriented enterprise ontology framework. Two methods support the activity: business policy and rule modeling method and the querying method, which supports the context-based matching activity. The methods are described in detail in Chapter 5.

3.4.3   Business Process Modeling

Following the previous two activities and the specification of business requirements, the activity of designing process models begins. The process models created herein should refine the high-level strategy and tactics captured in the motivation modeling activity and follow the business directives specified in the business policy and rule modeling activity. This activity is divided into three sub-activities: *Goal-based Scenario Modeling*, *Process Querying and Reuse* and *Guided Process Modeling*.

Goal-based Business Scenario Modeling sub-activity starts with the refinement of goals and objectives set during motivation modeling and assigning the target values for their corresponding metrics. Consequently, a coherent subset of objectives is selected and arranged in a sequence so that they define milestones for a business scenario which aims at their fulfillment. Business scenarios are abstract business processes which are not fully defined in terms of concrete tasks, and thus are not complete models. The scenarios capture the first draft of a process, with an emphasis on

---

[16]The visual notation closely follows the underlying formal language used in our work, WSML-Flight

[17]The notion of context is discussed in more detail in Chapter 5

the business objectives while leaving the concrete definition of processes to a subsequent step. They represent a solution to a well known problem and a base to enable the extension to a concrete problem (similar to software design patterns [GHJV95]), providing best modeling practices. High-level scenario steps (subprocesses) within the business scenario are defined for the achievement of each of the specified milestones. Modeling of business scenarios includes the annotation of such high-level steps with their contextual information coming from application ontologies, e.g. the responsible organizational unit, consumed resources, corresponding business function, etc.

Business Process Querying and Reuse sub-activity enables the process modeler to query the process space of an organization in order to facilitate decision making or improve reuse of process artifacts (scenarios, processes) in modeling. Querying of the process space can be done by posing restrictions on one or more perspectives of process description (see Fig. 3.2). A special case of querying occurs when the modeler wants to find a more detailed process for reuse in the specification of a high-level scenario step. Here, the contextual annotations of that particular step are used as query criteria for finding the matching processes.

Guided Business Process Modeling sub-activity provides further support in the design of process models. There are two basic types of guidance provided to the modeler. The need for the first type of guidance stems from the fact that the process modelers do not have any support in naming (labeling) the process activities. This results in process models which are difficult to compare, reuse and evaluate due to common problems in naming such as i) use of the same term with a different meaning (homonym), ii) use of different terms for the same concept (synonym) and iii) use of inappropriate expressions. We argue that the labeling of process activities can be improved by a controlled vocabulary recommendation mechanism. In our case, the controlled vocabulary content comes from the Business Function Ontology (BFO), which was designed on the basis of the rich process modeling content provided by the SAP Solution Composer [SAP05a]. The BFO contains standardized terms for business functions and their constituting process activities. With the help of well-known string- and schema–matching methods [CRF03, RB01], we are able to provide naming suggestions to the process modeler based on the expression he started to enter or a resource label assigned to a particular process activity. The approach is similar to the Google search string autocompletion mechanism. This part is not covered in this thesis in further detail, rather we refer the avid reader to the respective publication [BFKM08]. The approach aims to enable process modelers to achieve consistency in naming of business process artifacts when modeling a process and thus also improve the readability, reuse and degree of comparison between business process models.

The second type of guidance is an automated suggestion of the subsequent process activities during modeling. Namely, the current process modeling approaches and tools do not provide any support in terms of recommendation of the next possible modeling steps in a similar way to how it is done in the IDEs for programming support. By using the contextual annotations of a modeled process, the process artifact repository can be filtered in each modeling step to find potentially reusable artifacts. In fact, this is again a special case of querying where it is triggered either after each modeling step or by the modeler invocation. There are multiple strategies for the automated completion of the modeled process [BBM+08]. This approach aims at improving the reuse of best practices and thus reducing the amount of errors in process modeling. Similarly to the previous one, this approach is not covered in further detail here. The reader is invited to consult the respective publication [BBM$^+$08] for additional information.

The ontologies used in this activity include the BPO and application ontologies, built on the basis of the process-oriented enterprise ontology framework. Three methods support the activity: business process modeling method, the querying method (which supports the retrieval of matching process artifacts), and the process activity naming method. The first two methods are described in detail in Chapter 6.

3.4.4 Business Process Verification

Verification of business process models (cf. Fig. 3.8, top left) is an important activity where it is ensured that the created business process model effectively covers the requirements captured in the prior activities from both a functional and a business perspective. This activity is divided into two sub-activities: *Soundness Verification* and *Policy-based Verification*, which we discuss in the following.

Soundness Verification sub-activity profits from the π–calculus based process flow representation. Since the BPO, which models the behavioral perspective of processes in the process-oriented enterprise ontology framework, is based on the π–calculus algebra we have provided the means to compile the process descriptions from BPO representation to the plain π–calculus format. This fact allows us to reuse the existing reasoning engines [VM94] and tooling [Puh06a, BP06] built for the π–calculus. Therefore, the soundness verification as well as simulation of processes are supported in our methodology based on previously existing technologies. More details are provided in Chapter 6.

Policy-based Verification sub-activity supports the verification of process models from the business perspective. As previously argued, business processes do not only have to accomplish certain functional requirements, but are also governed and guided by business policies and rules which are derived from the company strategy. In order to assure that a process model adheres to the organization's business policies and rules, we build on their formal specification described in the *Business Policy and Rule Modeling* activity (see Section 3.4.2). After the context-based policy matching is performed, the process modeler can select the business policies for verification from the matching list. The verification itself is performed as a consistency check on the knowledge base which includes the rules implementing a selected business policy. If the knowledge base proves consistent, it follows that the process model adheres to the verified policy and otherwise not.

The ontologies used in this activity include the BPO, BPRO and application ontologies, built on the basis of the process-oriented enterprise ontology framework. The activity is supported by the verification method which is described in detail in Chapter 5.

After introducing the activities constituting the semantic business process modeling lifecycle, in the following section we contrast our approach to the existing ones.

3.4.5   Related Work

BPM Systems usually follow BPM methodologies, such as the widely used ARIS [Sch00a, Sch00b], IBM [WAM⁺07, IBM06], or methodologies related to modeling tools such as Savvion [Sav05] or Ultimus [Ult06]. The BPM lifecycle of these method-ologies is mainly composed of the following activities: i) modeling: from business requirements to process model [Sch00a], ii) configuration: executable business pro-cess model preparation [IBM06], iii) execution: deployment of the process in an execution engine, and iv) analysis: analyzing the process execution. Our method-ological proposal, and therefore the related work analysis focuses on the modeling activity, where a big gap in the translation between business requirements to process models still exists [HLD⁺05].

BP modeling is covered by most of the methodologies, e.g. ARIS, IBM, Savvion, Ultimus. The modeling lifecycle is mainly formed by: requirement analysis from business analysts, process modeling by using a formal language, simulation and re-design [IBM06]. In addition, ARIS defines the five views of the knowledge (mainly focused on IT level) used during BP modeling activities [Sch00a]: data (information objects and their relationships), organization (organizational structures and their relations), function (activities), product (input and output produced by activities) and control (process flow). The knowledge related to BP modeling is broader than current methodologies and languages can represent [MCZ04]. Extending the rep-resentable knowledge of current methodologies and languages as presented in Sec-tions 3.2 and 3.3 provide several advantages which are discussed previously in this section.

In [WHMN07], the authors present a methodology for semantic business process modeling and configuration. However, they mainly focus on deriving the so called execution-level business process models out of conceptual ones. The execution-level models are introduced as an intermediary level between levels 4 and 5 in Fig. 2.2 for the purpose of mediating between purely conceptual models from the business perspective, and the technical models containing a lot of execution-relevant infor-mation. In other words, the work does not consider the early activities involved in creating a conceptual business process model. Hence, this work and our methodol-ogy can be seen as complementary.

Within the SUPER project[18], a methodology which covers the complete SBP management lifecycle (from modeling to execution and analysis) has been defined [FSM⁺06]. However, due to its broad scope, it stays on a rather superficial level when it comes to the definition of the semantic business process modeling activ-ity. Therefore, our SBP modeling methodology refines this activity with a focus on creation of conceptual business process models. Indeed, the SBPM methodology presented here has been incorporated in the later version of the project deliverables [FSK⁺09].

3.5   Conclusion

In this chapter, we have presented the concepts which serve as the foundations for our semantic business process modeling framework. We start with an analysis of

---

[18]www.ip-super.org

process knowledge captured in conceptual business process models in order to better understand and categorize it. We discuss the discovered knowledge in terms of six process perspectives and three process modeling abstraction levels. Based on the insights gained from this analysis, we define a process-oriented enterprise ontology framework which identifies the structure and building blocks necessary for the formal representation of relevant process knowledge. We further discuss the mapping of the ontology framework to process perspectives and abstraction levels defined previously, and present its application in the telecommunication domain. Finally, we introduce the semantic business process modeling methodology which provides methodological guidelines for the usage of ontologies and reasoning in business process modeling. The guidelines are discussed on the basis of a lifecycle where the role of semantic technologies is discussed in each of the lifecycle activities. Based on the framework foundations presented here, we present the first part of the semantic business process modeling framework - a modeling technique and tool for business motivation modeling.

Chapter 4

Modeling of Business Motivation

4.1 Introduction

If an enterprise prescribes a certain approach for its business activity, it ought to be able to say *why* i.e. what results the approach is meant to achieve. This is referred to as the motivational perspective of processes in Section 3.2.2. The motivational perspective (business strategy, goals, KPIs) aims to see a business process in its wider enterprise context. A business process is not just there for some isolated purpose, i.e. the intention why a business process is performed is not and should not be decoupled from what an enterprise intends to do as a whole. Thus, the motivation on the one hand provides an explanation, why structured activities, i.e. business processes, are performed and on the other hand suggests what is needed to become what an enterprise wants to become.

The problem of not integrating the motivational perspective in process descriptions is illustrated best in the fable "The Blind Men and the Elephant" by J.G. Saxe [Lin78]. In his fable, Saxe talks about six blind men who went to "see" the elephant and since each of them could only touch a part of the elephant, they all had different interpretations of what they "saw". A blind man who touched the elephant's foot "saw" a tree; the other who touched the elephant's trunk "saw" a snake; the third who touched the elephant's tusk "saw" a spear, and so on. Since none of the blind men had the vision to see the entire animal, they all grabbed hold of some part or the other and created their own different interpretations of it [MLA05]. In our case, the strategy is represented by the elephant and the blind men are employees of a company.

On the other hand, since the ancient times people have used models to communicate and share their design. More recently, models have been used in engineering disciplines (mechanical, civil, electrical engineering, architecture) to share designs, but also to perform various types of analysis on the models. For example, static analysis in building construction is widely used in civil engineering, circuit analysis in electrical engineering, material distortion analysis in mechanical engineering, etc. Thus, engineering models do not only serve communication purposes but are also executable and may be used to discover design errors much before an engineering artifact (car, bridge, microchip) is actually built. In order to profit from lessons learned in engineering disciplines, we take the engineering approach to process-oriented enterprise design. This implies the development of appropriate models and techniques for analyzing such models, so that the design can be communicated and shared among stakeholders and also analyzed for errors before it is implemented.

For creating the models in process-oriented enterprise design, the users first need to be provided with a modeling language. In addition, a modeling method which defines procedures and guidelines of using the language needs to be designed. Finally, a modeling tool that allows for the use of language in accordance with the appropriate method needs to be provided[1].

In this chapter, we aim to provide a modeling language, method and a tool for modeling business motivation. By doing so, we want to enable all employees to have the same interpretation of the elephant.This work represents the first part of the semantic business process modeling framework, as defined in Fig. 3.7. Visual modeling and analysis of business motivation are also the first activities within the semantic business process modeling lifecycle depicted in Fig. 3.8.

The chapter is structured as follows. Section 4.2 introduces a Core Ontology for Business Process Analysis which was used as a lightweight ontological foundation in creating a language for business motivation modeling. In Section 4.3 we provide a list of requirements which the modeling technique and a tool for business motivation modeling need to fulfill. Section 4.4 presents the modeling language and a method for business motivation modeling. The syntax and semantics of the modeling language are provided by means of Business Motivation Ontology (BMO) (see Fig. 3.5). In Section 4.5, we discuss the prototypical implementation of a business motivation modeling tool. Section 4.6 contrasts our work to related efforts and finally Section 4.7 summarizes our contributions in this chapter.

4.2   Core Ontology for Business pRocess Analysis

The Core Ontology for Business pRocess Analysis (COBRA) has been developed within the SUPER project in order to support business process analysis (BPA) activities [PDdM08]. COBRA, partly depicted in Fig. 4.1[2], was designed to provide a pluggable framework based on the core conceptualizations required for supporting BPA and defines the appropriate hooks for further extensions in order to cope with the wide-range of aspects involved in analysing business processes. In defining the core conceptualizations for BPA, the development of COBRA was informed and guided by existing ontologies, such as DOLCE [MBG+03], CIDOC [ICO07], Enterprise Ontology [UKH+98] and TOVE [Fox92]. COBRA thus provides a lightweight foundational basis by reusing the basic categorizations specified in existing foundational ontologies, such as the distinction between *Temporal Entities*[3] and *Persistent Entities* (see Fig. 4.1). These two categories are disjoint, where the former subsumes entities that have a temporal extent and the latter subsumes entities that are independent of time.

Persistent Entities are further categorized into *Physical* and *Non-Physical Entities*, where the former is used to represent entities that have a mass [PDdM08]. Both

---

[1]See definition of the modeling framework provided in Section 2.2

[2]Arrows represent *isA* relation, dashed arrows denote the *instanceOf* relation and lines represent custom relations.

[3]We focus here on the notions important for developing the core ontology for modeling business motivation. Temporal Entities are thus not shown in the figure. For detailed overview of COBRA, we refer the reader to [PDdM08].

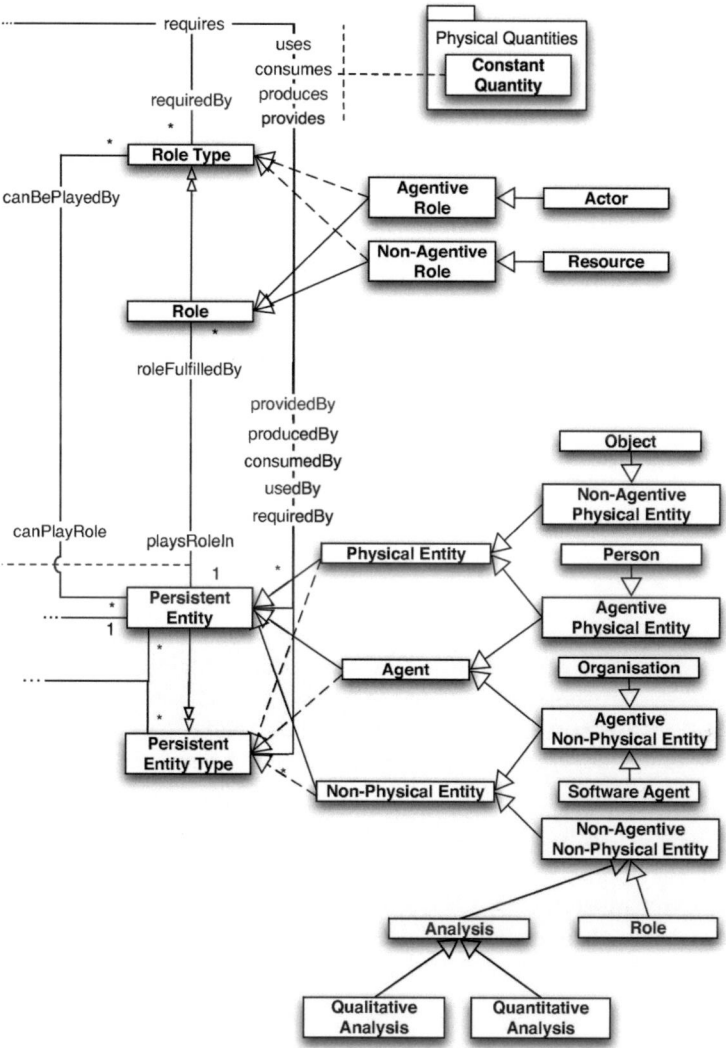

Figure 4.1: A fragment of Core Ontology for Business pRocess Analysis. Source: [PDdM08]

categories are further refined into *Agentive* and *Non-Agentive* (see Fig. 4.1), where Agentive Entities can take an active part in a certain activity. An *Agent* is defined as the union of Agentive Physical (e.g. Person) and Non-Physical Entities (e.g. Organization).

Two categories of Non-Agentive Non-Physical Entity are of particular interest for our work: *Role*[4] and *Analysis*. COBRA borrows the notion of Role from the Descriptions and Situations ontology [GBCL04], where Role is the function assumed or part played by an entity in a particular situation. It is used for capturing the context dependency of an entity (cf. Section 4.4.1). Role subsumes two categories: Agentive (e.g. Actor) and Non-Agentive Role (e.g. Resource), where the former denotes Role that can only be played by an Agent (see Fig. 4.1). The second category of Non-Agentive Non-Physical Entity, Analysis, provides the means for defining analysis specifications (e.g. metrics) which are used for all sorts of analysis tasks. The concept Analysis is refined into *Qualitative Analysis* (e.g., "is the process critical?") and *Quantitative Analysis* (e.g., "process execution time"), based on the type of analysis result it produces (see Fig. 4.1).

4.3   Requirements Analysis

In this section, we give an overview of a set of requirements elicited through relevant literature reviews, analysis of available commercial tooling and unstructured interviews with strategy management professionals at SAP. The requirements refer to all aspects of the modeling framework: language, method and a tool for business motivation modeling.

Req. 1. Identify relevant concepts and relations for business motivation modeling: In order to introduce the motivational perspective of business processes, the users need a shared vocabulary which they can use to talk about business motivation. This vocabulary subsumes concepts, attributes and relations relevant for the business motivation domain.

Req. 2. Establish the linkage to process space: One of the major issues in BPM today, as identified by [BIS+07], is the missing link between organizational strategy and BPM efforts. In order to address this, the motivational perspective must be properly integrated in process descriptions. This requires a proper conceptualization of the notion of strategy and its relation to organizational business processes.

Req. 3. Provide formal semantics for business motivation modeling constructs: **Req. 1** indicates the need for defining a vocabulary for business motivation. This requirement refers to the machine-processable specification of such vocabulary, with unambiguous meanings provided for the terms in it. In other words, providing logical statements that describe what the terms are, how they relate to each other, and rules that specify how the terms and their relations can be combined in order to extend the vocabulary [GDDS06].

---

[4]Note that Role is duplicated in the figure for the sake of clarity

Req. 4. Provide support for visual modeling of business motivation: The importance of graphical representation is widely acknowledged in existing modeling languages such as UML [Obj07], EPC [KNS92], BPMN [Obj09], which
are all based on a diagramming technique [And00] where language concepts, relations and constraints have their corresponding graphical symbols. Thus, a modeling language for business motivation also requires the
specification of a graphical modeling notation.

Req. 5. Ontology-driven design support: Using the formal semantics of the business motivation modeling language (**Req. 3**), further functionalities can
be provided in order to support the users in creating motivation models.
Namely, the modeling tools can now understand a model being created
on a semantic level and thus provide intelligent design support. This requires the specification of adequate procedures and algorithms that allow
for modeling guidance and thus reduction of modeling errors.

Req. 6. Automated transformation from visual to formal representation: Having
a graphical modeling notation for creating business motivation models on
the one hand, and the formal semantics for the motivation modeling constructs on the other hand, led to the requirement for providing support in
the automatic transformation from visual to formal representation.

Req. 7. Visual query specification: In order to introduce support for advanced
types of analysis on business motivation models, the users need to be provided with means for the formal specification of analysis to be performed.
As presented in Section 2.3.4, all reasoning (analysis) tasks for our underlying formal language of choice, WSML-Flight, are realized by Datalog
queries [Dah97]. Hence, the users require a query specification method
and tool.

Req. 8. Analysis methods: Based on the query specification from **Req. 7**, analysis
methods need to be defined that perform the desired analysis (gap analysis, evaluation of alternatives, conflict detection) on motivation models in
order to detect errors early in the design.

4.4 Approach

In the previous section we presented a list of requirements for user support in visual
modeling and analysis of formal business motivation specifications. This section
shows how we address those requirements through our approach which includes
the design of a modeling language and method for business motivation modeling.
We start with presenting the Business Motivation Ontology and show how it is used
to define the business motivation modeling language.

4.4.1 Business Motivation Ontology

The syntax and semantics of the business motivation modeling language is provided by the Business Motivation Ontology (BMO). The graphical notation for the
modeling constructs defined in BMO is given in Appendix C. This section describes

the BMO - its domain coverage as well as modeling decisions that were made. We will use Fig. 4.2[5], which represents a sample business motivation model, in order to discuss the BMO modeling elements.

Domain Capture

Ends   *Ends* refer to any aspiration concept (cf. Fig. 4.3, upper right). They state, *what* an enterprise wants to accomplish. This could be about changing what the enterprise is, as well as maintaining the actual position. The definition of an End, however, does not say *how* it will be achieved. Ends subsume the concepts *Vision* (an abstract End) and *Desired Outcome* (a concrete End).

A Vision represents an overall image of what an organization wants to be or become. It describes a future, ultimate, possibly unattainable state, an enterprise as a whole wants to achieve. A Vision often encompasses the entire organization, rather than being focused towards one particular aspect of a business problem. In Fig. 4.2, the vision modeling construct (see Appendix C) is named "Our Vision". Attribute *hasDescription* of the vision element provides more detailed description of the company vision: "be the car rental brand of choice in the countries in which we operate".

A Desired Outcome is an attainable state or target that an enterprise, or some part of it, intends to achieve. It can often be evaluated to assess whether it has been attained or not, in contrast to Vision. Desired outcomes are established for a certain time interval spanning the period of time for which a Desired Outcome holds. We distinguish between outcomes that need to be achieved at the end of the period, and those that have a periodic check by means of which one can define what we refer to as *continuous* desired outcomes. These outcomes have the particularity that they specify outcomes that are continuously desired during a given interval and that will be checked periodically. This allows to express things like "sales should increase by 1 percent per month for the next year" as well as "increase sales by 5 percent by the end of the year" in a simple and concise way.

Given the high-level of abstraction that Desired Outcomes can have, it is particularly difficult to assess the level of achievement currently attained, and decide how to map these desires into concrete enterprise-wide actions and decisions. In consequence, we support the decomposition of Desired Outcomes into finer grained ones, as a gradual process that takes us from purely strategic outcomes to the operational level where one can perform measures and contrast the achieved results with those desired. This gradual refinement of desired outcomes is supported through their refinement into less specific *Goals* or more specific *Objectives*, and by using what we refer to as *Logical Decomposition* constructs. Goals amplify the Vision (see "Meet customer expectation" goal in Fig. 4.2). They tend to be longer term, qualitative, and ongoing in comparison to Objectives. Objective is considered as a step along the way towards achieving a Goal. More precisely, an Objective is a measurable, time-targeted Goal. In Fig. 4.2, objective "Car availability" is measured by metric[6] "Percentage of requests fulfilled". The following axiom from BMO infers an Objective when a Goal is assigned a Metric (becomes measurable):

---

[5]The sample model is based on the fictitious car rental company, EU-Rent, which is often used in OMG business modeling specifications [OMG08a, Obj08]

[6]The notion of *Metric* is discussed later in this section

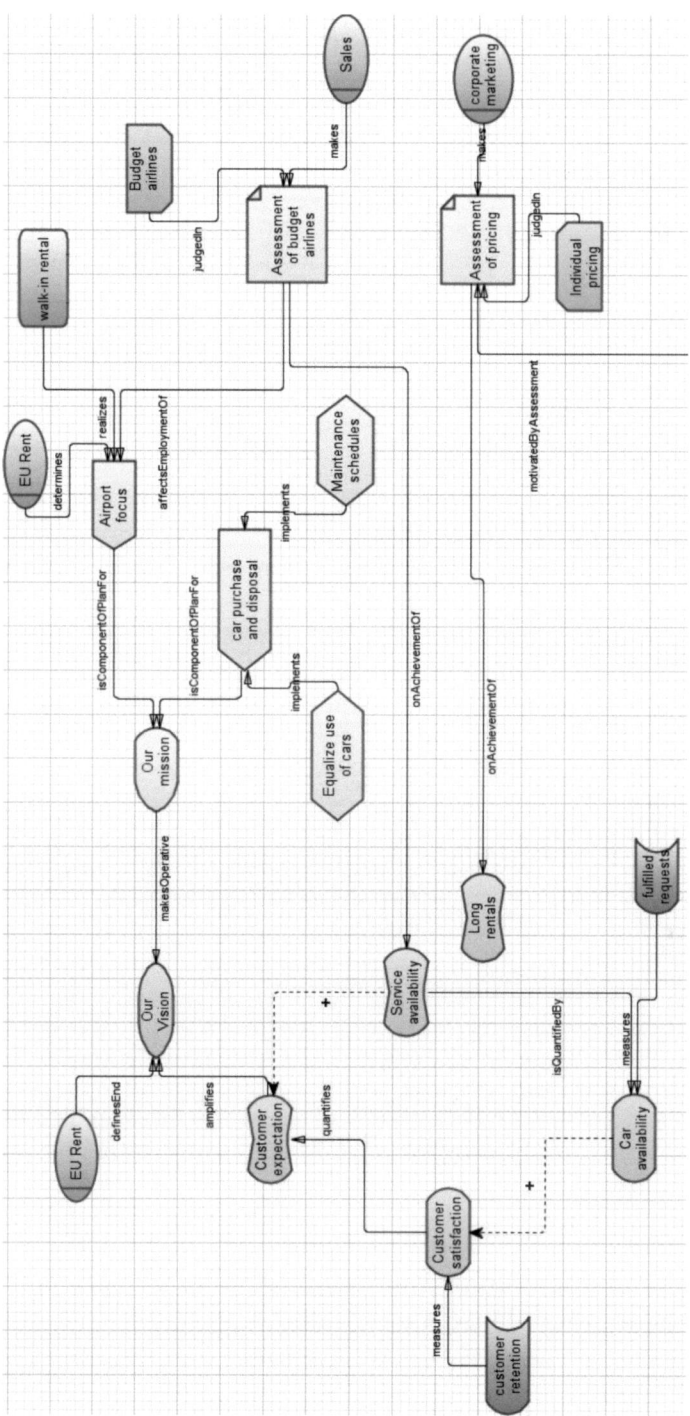

Figure 4.2: Sample business motivation model

?x **memberOf** Objective :− ?x **memberOf** Goal **and** ?y **memberOf** Metric **and** hasMetric(?x,?y).

In order to support the assessment of Desired Outcomes, BMO follows COBRA in distinguishing Analyses and Analyses Results. Hence, BMO allows for representing the assessment of Desired Outcomes using the concept DesiredOutcomeAssessment[7], which specializes COBRA Qualitative Analysis. Further, for storing the results of the assessments BMO provides the concept DesiredOutcomeAssessmentResult, which specializes COBRA QualitativeAnalysisResult. Finally, the ternary relation DesiredOutcomeAssessmentHasResult connects the type of Assessment performed, its Result and the Desired Outcome for which it was performed.

We consider a number of relations between Goals in BMO, which we detail in the following section.

Modeling Goal Relations: It is said that a goal quantifies another, if it is an objective and is its direct subgoal:

?x[quantifies **hasValue** ?y] :− ?x **memberOf** Objective **and** ?y **memberOf** Goal **and** ?x[
hasParentGoal **hasValue** ?y].

A goal is part of another, if it is subgoal of another. This is expressed using the axiom:

?x[partOf **hasValue** ?y] :− ?x **memberOf** Goal **and** ?y **memberOf** Goal **and** ?x[hasParentGoal
hasValue ?y].

Goals can have priorities, which allows us to order the goal set according to their importance. Relations *higherPriority(?x,?y)* and *lowerPriority(?x,?y)* are used to denote priority constraints between two goals. Goals are prioritized according to the value of their *hasPriority* attribute. The following axiom formalizes the notions of higher and lower priority:

higherPriority (?x,?y) :− ?x[hasPriority **hasValue** ?a] **and** ?y[hasPriority **hasValue** ?b] **and** ?x
memberOf Goal **and** ?y **memberOf** Goal **and** wsml#greaterThan(?a,?b).
lowerPriority (?x,?y) :− higherPriority (?y,?x).

Prioritization focuses attention on key areas, while allowing the modeler to describe goals which are currently perceived as less important or out of scope. Analysts can choose to show only those goals that are in scope. This can be achieved visually by filtering on the level of priority. The goal hierarchy approach thus makes clear the effects of scoping decisions, and allows trade-offs to be evaluated.

Goals can also conflict with each other. The conflicting situation between two goals occurs if one goal hinders the other (has negative contribution) and they are of the same priority:

conflicts (?x,?y) :− (WeakNegativeContribution(?x,?y) **or** StrongNegativeContribution(?x,?y))
and naf higherPriority(?x,?y) **and naf** lowerPriority(?x,?y).

BMO also provides a definition of all goals which are not a root goal. This serves as a helper axiom when defining a root goal in the next step.

isNotRootGoal(?y) :− ?y **memberOf** Goal **and** ?x **memberOf** Goal **and** isSubGoalOf(?y,?x) **and**
naf isSubGoalOf(?x,?y).

The following axiom states that a root goal is a goal, which has no parent goals:

---

[7]For the sake of clarity, the notions related to Desired Outcome assessment are not shown in Fig. 4.3. The reader is referred to Appendix B for details

isRootGoal(?y) :− ?y **memberOf** Goal **and naf** isNotRootGoal(?y).

All goals in the goal hierarchy apart from leaf goals and the root goal are called intermediate goals. An intermediate goal is therefore defined as a goal which is a subgoal of another and has subgoals itself:

isIntermediateGoal(?y) :− ?x **memberOf** Goal **and** ?y **memberOf** Goal **and** ?z **memberOf** Goal
    and isSubGoalOf(?x,?y) **and** isSubGoalOf(?y,?z).

A leaf goal is a goal that can not be further subdivided into subgoals. This type of goals occurs at the lowest level of goal decomposition hierarchy. We use the two previously specified axioms for the formalization in saying that a leaf goal is a goal, which is not known to be a root goal nor is it known to be an intermediate goal:

isLeafGoal(?x) :− ?x **memberOf** Goal **and naf** isRootGoal(?x) **and naf** isIntermediateGoal(?x).

Two goals which are known to be in the subgoal relation are inferred to be parent and subgoal, respectively:

?x[hasParentGoal **hasValue** ?y] :− ?x **memberOf** Goal **and** ?y **memberOf** Goal **and** isSubGoalOf(
    ?x,?y).
isSubGoalOf(?x,?y) :− ?x **memberOf** Goal **and** ?y **memberOf** Goal **and** ?x[hasParentGoal
    hasValue ?y].

Goals can be decomposed into Objectives and/or other Goals (subgoals). Decomposition of goals into subgoals and objectives can be done through an AND- or OR-decomposition [GMNS03]. If a goal x is AND-decomposed (OR-decomposed) into subgoals, then if all (at least one) of the subgoals are satisfied, so is goal x.

The hierarchy of goals is built using the relation *isSubGoalOf*. The relation *isSubGoalOf* is transitive, i.e. if a goal x is a subgoal of a goal y which is a subgoal of a goal z, then x is a subgoal of z:

isSubGoalOf(?x,?z) :− ?x **memberOf** Goal **and** ?y **memberOf** Goal **and** ?z **memberOf** Goal **and**
    isSubGoalOf(?x,?y) **and** isSubGoalOf(?y,?z).

The relation *isSubGoalOf* is also non-reflexive (a goal x can not be its own subgoal) and anti-symmetric (if x is a subgoal of y, then y is not a subgoal of x), as defined in the following statements:

!− isSubGoalOf(?x,?x) **and** ?x **memberOf** Goal.
!− isSubGoalOf(?x,?y) **and** isSubGoalOf(?y,?x) **and** ?x **memberOf** Goal **and** ?y **memberOf** Goal.

There must be no cycles in the goal hierarchy. This is ensured by specifying the following constraint:

!− isAncGoalOf(?x,?x).

A goal is another goal's ancestor, if there is link via the subgoal relation. The following axiom defines the ancestor goal relation:

isAncGoalOf(?x,?y) :− isSubGoalOf(?x,?y).
isAncGoalOf(?x,?z) :− isSubGoalOf(?x,?y) **and** isSubGoalOf(?y,?z).

Means *Means* (cf. Figure 4.3, upper left) are counterparts of Ends - they state *how* an enterprise intends to achieve its Ends. A Means may be either a *Mission*, a *Course of Action* or a *Directive*. A Mission describes a long-term approach which is focused on achieving the Vision. Its definition should be broad enough to cover all possible strategies and the complete area of enterprise operations. An example is given in Fig. 4.2, where the mission modeling construct (see Appendix C) is named "Our

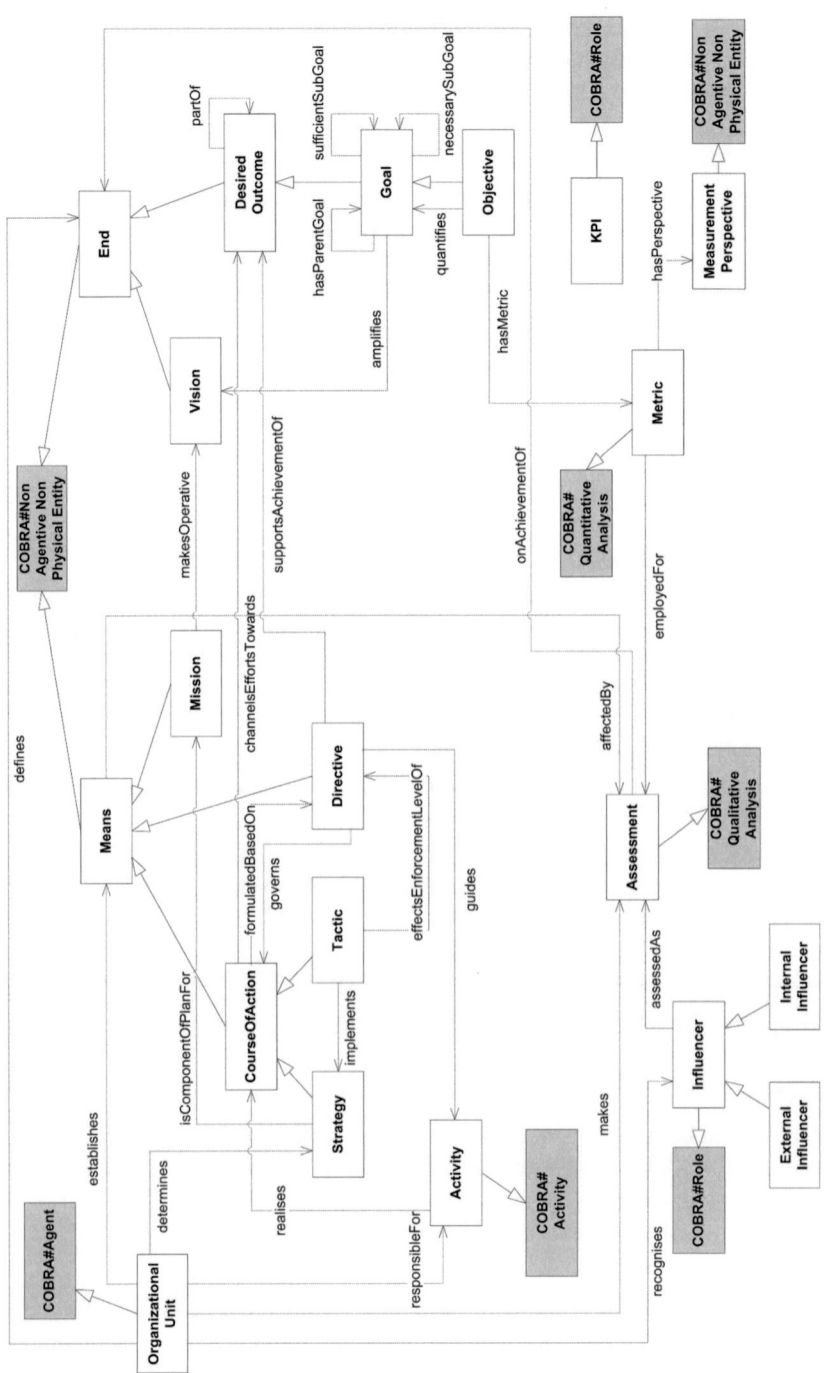

Figure 4.3: Business Motivation Ontology

Mission". A natural language description of the company mission is provided in the attribute *hasDescription*: "Provide car rental service across Europe and North America for both business and personal customers".

A Course of Action is an approach (plan) for configuring some aspect of the enterprise, based on available resources and capabilities, undertaken to achieve its Desired Outcomes. It includes the subconcepts *Strategy* and *Tactic* (see Fig. 4.3). Strategy is defined as a long term plan of action designed to achieve a particular goal or to win. It is differentiated from tactics or immediate actions with resources at hand by its nature of being extensively premeditated, and often practically rehearsed. The word derives from the Greek word strategos, which stems from two words: stratos (army) and ago (ancient Greek for leading). A Strategy is accepted by the enterprise as the right approach to achieve its Goals. In Fig. 4.2, a strategy "Car purchase and disposal" is depicted using the corresponding graphical symbol from Appendix C. As before, the *hasDescription* attribute provides more details: "Manage car purchase and disposal at the local area level, using national guidance". Each Strategy is implemented by Tactics, which tend to be shorter term and narrower in scope in comparison to Strategies. A Strategy may be implemented by several Tactics and a Tactic may contribute to the implementation of more than one Strategy. Two tactics implement the mentioned strategy in Fig. 4.2. First, "Equalize use of cars" tactic is set up to equalize the use of cars across rentals so that mileage is similar for cars of the same car group and age. Second, "Maintenance schedules" tactic is set up to ensure the compliance with manufacturer's maintenance schedules. To clarify the distinction, we say Strategies channel efforts towards Goals and Tactics channel efforts towards Objectives. Thus, the two concepts establish an analogy for concepts on different level of abstraction on the complementary sides of Ends (the *what*) and Means (the *how*). A Course of Action is realized by *Activities* (see Fig. 4.3). Activity refers to any type of activity within an enterprise - process or task. An activity "Walk-in rental", which enables the customers to book the rentals directly at major airports, is set up to realize the "Airport focus" strategy in Fig. 4.2.

Directives are set up to guide the Courses of Action (see Fig. 4.3). A Directive defines or constrains some aspect of an enterprise and can be either a Business Policy or Business Rule, which is further specified in the *Business Policy and Rule Ontology* presented in Chapter 5.

Metrics   You can only control what you can measure [DeM82]. Besides the fact that metrics play an important role in business process analysis, setting targets is crucial to the motivational perspective of an enterprise's process space. BMO follows the Balanced Scorecard approach [KN92] here, and assigns performance measures to the company's aspirations in order to control the progress of their achievement.

The concept Metric in BMO (see Fig. 4.3) may be characterized using the following metric *types*: leading, lagging, quantitative, qualitative, input, output, outcome. In the following, we discuss the meaning of each of these types. A *leading* metric is forward-looking in nature and drives future performance, e.g. *Employee turnover rate*. Improved performance in a leading metric is assumed to drive better performance in a *lagging* metric. Lagging metrics are backward-looking and represent the results of previous actions, e.g. *Employee satisfaction rating*. As such, they characterize historical performance and focus on the results at the end of a given time period. A Metric can also be *quantitative* or *qualitative*. Quantitative metrics represent empirical indicators of performance, e.g. *Throughput time*, whereas qualitative metrics are defined as perceptions and evaluations of major customers and stake-holders, e.g. *Customer complaints received as a percentage of total customers served*. A third categorization of metrics divides them into *input*, *output* and *outcome* metrics. Input metrics refer to the amount of investements, assets, equipment, labor hours or budget used; e.g. *Number of staff*. Output metrics represent units of a product or service provided, e.g. *Number of orders fulfilled*. Outcome metrics represent resulting effects (benefits) of using or applying a product or service, e.g. *Customer satisfaction rating*. In the example in Fig. 4.2, the metric "Percentage of requests fulfilled" can be characterized as lagging, quantitative and outcome metric.

The *hasDescription* attribute of a Metric provides textual description of a metric definition, while the *hasCalculation* attribute describes the formula which is used for calculating the *current* value of a metric. The *hasTarget* attribute contains the *desired* value of a metric and is often used when specifying actions to be triggered when reaching a certain treshold value.

A Metric is considered a Key Performance Indicator (KPI) for an Objective, if it is applied to indicate the performance for a particular Objective. Hence, being a KPI is a *role* that the Metric plays and not a subtype of a Metric. BMO allows for modeling this as a relationship `playsKPIRole(ofType Metric, ofType KPI, ofType Objective)`. KPI is modeled as a COBRA *Role* (see Fig. 4.3). A Metric is also usu-ally associated with one of four measurement perspectives: Financial, Customer, Process and Intangible (sometimes called Innovation and Learning) perspective, fol-lowing [KN92].

Influencers   Neither the enterprise's setup of goals, nor the ways they attempt the achievement is independent from the environment. Indeed, setting up strategies, defining tactics that detail those strategies, issuing directives and so forth is com-pletely within the control of the enterprise. However, control is not free from influ-ences. Thus, an *Influencer* is something that can cause changes that affect the enter-prise in the employment of its Means or achievement of its Ends. Almost anything within or outside a company could act as an Influencer in some situation. Accord-ingly, an Influencer is categorized as Internal or External. An *Assessment* is the pro-cedure of judging the impact of an Influencer on an enterprise. It is usually based on a set of defined *qualitative metrics* which are assigned to the influencers (see Fig. 4.3). Various *methods* can be used for performing an assessment. Consider an ex-ample method of SWOT analysis [Ans65], where the result of an assessment can fall in the following categories: Strength, Weakness, Opportunity and Threat. The first two categories indicate positive and negative effect for Internal Influencers, while the last two do the same for External Influencers. As a result of the assessment, an agent which is observed is assigned the corresponding influencer role. This is de-fined by the ternary relation `playsInfluencerRole(ofType cobra#Agent, ofType Influencer, ofType Assessment)`.

The following axiom specifies that an influencer can not be both, internal (strength or weaknesses) and external (opportunity or threat) at the same time:

!– ?x **memberOf** Influencer **and** ?y **memberOf** Influencer **and** ?x **memberOf** InternalInfluencer
    and ?y **memberOf** ExternalInfluencer **and** ?x != ?y.

BMO defines a number of additional relations and axioms for the aforemen-tioned concepts. For further details, the reader is referred to Appendix B.

Main Modeling Decisions

There are a number of approaches that deal with motivational issues. Most of them concentrate on software requirements or autonomous agents. Examples for those approaches are i* [Yu95], KAOS [KG] and TROPOS [FLM+04]. Those models rely heavily on the concept of goals and add concepts such as actors and roles, dependencies and others but leave the integration between high level goals and concrete activities rather unspecified. The core modeling decision for BMO is the separation in ends, i.e. where an enterprise wants to be, and means, i.e. how an enterprise intends to get there. Why means are in place depends on the ends - especially the concept of goals and the assessment of influences that are of impact on the enterprise. The Enterprise Ontology (EO) [UKH+98] takes similar modeling decisions regarding the distinction between means and ends. The top concepts there are Activity and Strategy. A plan is "an activity specification with an intended purpose" and a business process is a special kind of plan, i.e. it can be executed several times. In EO a strategy is "a plan to achieve a strategic purpose".

To define BMO, the decision was made to use the BMM motivation modeling approach [OMG08a] as a guidance, since it originated from practitioners (business rules community). The original proposal underwent the Object Management Group (OMG) standardization process and can thus be seen as being shared to a certain extent. BMO inherits some modeling decisions from the OMG specification. Concepts are developed from a business perspective, instead of the software engineering perspective taken for instance in TROPOS. Enterprises do not act randomly, but consciously. Thus, motivation is expressed as a state of affairs to reach (goals), as well as the judgment of influencers on the business (assessment). The behavior of an enterprise is not driven by change, but by how it decides to react to change. The separation of concerns principle is adhered at several points in the modeling, e.g. where to be vs. how to go there (means-ends distinction) and decomposition of concepts.

The OMG standard underlines method independence and thus advocates not including links to specific strategy theories. However, this is given up in certain points and the specification adopts certain approaches implicitly. BMO in contrast, aims to uncover those implicit assumptions originating from strategy research. Strategic thinking is reflected at several points in the ontology, referring to accepted ideas such as the Strength, Weakness, Opportunity, Threat Analysis advocated by Ansoff [Ans65] and the analysis that enterprises react to influences, sometimes called PEST factors (political/regulatory, economic, social, technological). The Balance Scorecard [KN92] is a way to express company strategy and relies on assigning performance indicators to goals while allowing for several perspectives on performance.

Further, one of the design goals was to ground each of the BMO top level concepts in the COBRA ontology, for it provides the necessary foundational basis. This significantly helped in making informed ontological choices and performing conceptual reengineering of the BMM metamodel. The grey boxes in Fig. 4.3 represent the concepts imported from COBRA.

4.4.2 BMO-driven Strategic Analysis

This section describes the procedure of the assessment of Desired Outcomes and provides the building blocks necessary for the formalization of the assessment procedure. The approach presented here is inspired by the work in the area of software requirements engineering [GMNS03]. In their paper, Giorgini et al. [GMNS03] describe both a qualitative and a quantitative model for evaluating goal models defined as AND/OR decompositions. Their model includes the formalisation of a set of propagation rules and a label propagation algorithm which is sound and complete. Additionally they include an extensive set of relations between goals that can capture typical situations such as the fact that Goals contribute or hinder each other, or even mutually impede or ensure the achievement of each other. The reader is referred to [GMNS03] for concrete details of their approach.

There are some important differences when comparing the work in [GMNS03] to our approach. First, [GMNS03] only focuses on modeling goals, without consideration of the broader context of strategic concerns in business modeling and its linkage to the organizational process space, which we refer to as business motivation. Second, the quantitative goal reasoning is not applicable in the assessment of Desired Outcomes since the influencer relations can not be straightforwardly quantified as proposed in [GMNS03]. Third, the advancement of semantic technologies has provided scalable tools for processing ontologies. In our case, usage of WSML-Flight formalism allows for application of a very good operational infrastructure. E.g. the currently available version of WSML2Reasoner uses the IRIS reasoner as a back-end reasoning engine. [BF08] reports that the functionality and performance of IRIS compare favourably with similar systems. Fourth, our concept of Objective being directly linked to measurable aspects, can be used as what the Giorgini et al. refer to as initial nodes and allow us to directly apply the evaluation of goals over monitored data without the need for users to introduce any data manually. As a consequence, our conceptual model i) supports the operationalisation of desired outcomes into a graph that can automatically be evaluated; and ii) allows for directing the analysis of processes and organisations based on those aspects which are known to be of strategic importance.

In the following, we will illustrate the formal machinery necessary to support strategic analysis using an illustrative example shown in Fig. 4.4. The example is an extension of the EU-Rent business motivation model depicted in Fig. 4.2.

Following [Nil71], we introduce four unary relations (properties) characterizing the level of evidence of satisfaction or denial of Goals. The level of evidence may be *full* or *partial*:

```
relation  fullSatisfaction  ( ofType Goal )
relation  partialSatisfaction  ( ofType Goal )
relation  fullDenial  ( ofType Goal )
relation  partialDenial ( ofType Goal )
```

The first two relations state respectively that there is at least[8] full and at least partial evidence that a goal is satisfied. Similarly, the following two relations state respectively that there is at least full and at least partial evidence that a goal is denied.

The following axioms represent the basic (ground) axioms for the four relations:

```
partialSatisfaction (?x) :− fullSatisfaction (?x).
partialDenial (?x) :− fullDenial (?x).
```

---

[8]We say *at least*, since in the goal tree there may be multiple sources of evidence for the satisfaction/denial of a particular goal.

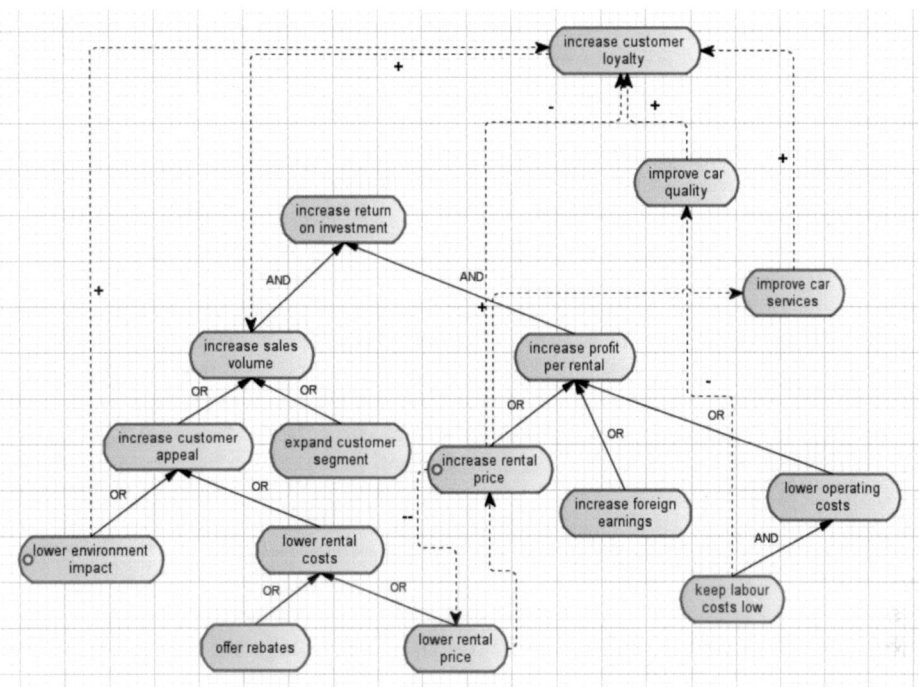

Figure 4.4: Strategic analysis – sample model

The two inference rules capture the indended meaning that a full evidence implies a partial evidence for a goal x.

As previously mentioned, goals can be decomposed using AND or OR constructs. We now define how the levels of evidence for goals propagate in such decompositions. We start by providing a set of axioms for the case of AND goal decomposition:

fullSatisfaction (?z) :− necessaryGoals(?x,?y,?z) **and** fullSatisfaction(?x) **and** fullSatisfaction (?y)
partialSatisfaction (?z) :− necessaryGoals(?x,?y,?z) **and** partialSatisfaction(?x) **and**
   partialSatisfaction (?y).
fullDenial (?z) :− necessaryGoals(?x,?y,?z) **and** (fullDenial(?x) **or** fullDenial (?y)).
partialDenial (?z) :− necessaryGoals(?x,?y,?z) **and** (partialDenial(?x) **or** partialDenial(?y)).

The `necessaryGoals (?x,?y,?z)` relation captures the situation where a goal z is AND decomposed into goals x and y. The four inference rules define the propagation mechanism for each of the goal evidence levels.

Similarly, a set of corresponding axioms is provided for the OR goal decomposition. The `sufficientGoals(?x,?y,?z)` relation captures the situation where a goal z is OR decomposed into goals x and y:

fullSatisfaction (?z) :− sufficientGoals(?x,?y,?z) **and** (fullSatisfaction (?x) **or** fullSatisfaction (
   ?y)).
partialSatisfaction (?z) :− sufficientGoals(?x,?y,?z) **and** (partialSatisfaction (?x) **or**
   partialSatisfaction (?y)).
fullDenial (?z) :− sufficientGoals(?x,?y,?z) **and** (fullDenial (?x) **and** fullDenial(?y)).
partialDenial (?z) :− sufficientGoals(?x,?y,?z) **and** (partialDenial (?x) **and** partialDenial(?y)).

Consider that we have a full satisfaction of the objective "lower rental price" in Fig. 4.4. The first rule will propagate the full satisfaction to the objective "lower rental costs". Similarly, this is further propagated to objectives "increase customer appeal" and "increase customer sales".

In addition to the goal evidence levels and AND/OR decomposition relations, following [GMNS03] we also consider the *contribution* relations between goals. The contribution relations may indicate a positive or negative influence of one goal to the satisfaction/denial of another. They provide means to capture more qualitative relations between goals when compared to AND/OR relations. In addition, they allow to accomodate the situations where there are contradictory contributions to a goal. This is important in cases when there are multiple decompositions of a goal, where some of them suggest satisfaction while others suggest denial of the decomposed goal. In fact, such cases occur often in practice and it is desired to have the possibility of evaluating alternative goal decompositions in order to detect conflicting situations. We discuss the goal contribution relations and define their formal semantics in the following.

Four variants of contribution relations are considered: weak positive ("+"), weak negative ("-"), strong positive ("++") and strong negative ("−") contribution [GMNS03]. These four variants are available both for satisfaction and denial.

In case of the weak positive contribution of goal x (for which a partial satisfaction evidence exists) to goal y, the following axiom infers the partial satisfaction evidence for goal y:

partialSatisfaction (?y) :− WeakPositiveSatisfactionContribution(?x,?y) **and** partialSatisfaction (?x)

In case of the weak negative contribution of goal x (for which a partial satisfaction evidence exists) to goal y, the following axiom infers the partial denial evidence for goal y:

partialDenial (?y) :− WeakNegativeSatisfactionContribution(?x,?y) **and** partialSatisfaction(?x).

For the strong positive contribution of goal x to goal y, the evidence levels of goal x are propagated to those of goal y:

fullSatisfaction (?y) :− StrongPositiveSatisfactionContribution (?x,?y) **and** fullSatisfaction (?x).
partialSatisfaction (?y) :− StrongPositiveSatisfactionContribution (?x,?y) **and** partialSatisfaction (?x).

For the strong negative contribution of goal x to goal y, the opposite evidence levels of goal x are propagated to those of goal y:

fullDenial (?y) :− StrongNegativeSatisfactionContribution(?x,?y) **and** fullSatisfaction (?x).
partialDenial (?y) :− StrongNegativeSatisfactionContribution(?x,?y) **and** partialSatisfaction (?x).

The semantics of the denial contribution relations is defined in a similar way, see Appendix B for details.

As previously mentioned, contribution relations allow for situations where there are contradictory contributions to a goal, i.e. conflicts. We distinguish two types of conflicting situations, namely *weak* and *strong* conflict. Their semantics is defined using the following two inference rules:

WeakConflict(?x) :− partialSatisfaction (?x) **and** partialDenial(?x).
StrongConflict(?x) :− fullSatisfaction (?x) **and** fullDenial(?x).

Weak conflict is inferred if both partial satisfaction and denial beliefs are suggested for a single goal. Strong conflict occurs when both full satisfaction and denial beliefs are suggested for a single goal.

Consider that the objectives "increase rental price" and "lower environment impact" in Fig. 4.4 are fully satisfied. Based on AND/OR-decomposition propagation rules, the objectives "increase customer appeal", "increase profit per rental", "increase return on investment" and "increase sales volume" are inferred as fully satisfied. Further, based on the weak positive contribution relation between "increase rental price" and "improve car services" as well as "improve car services" and "increase customer loyalty", and the satisfaction ground axiom, partial satisfaction is inferred for the latter two. The weak negative contribution relation between "increase rental price" and "increase customer loyalty" will result in inferring partial denial for the latter objective. This partial denial will be propagated due to weak positive influence to "increase sales volume" and AND-decomposition to "increase return on investment" objective, respectively. Finally, using the ground axioms and the newly propagated values, the weak conflict is inferred for the objectives "increase customer loyalty", "increase return on investment" and "increase sales volume".

The previous example illustrates how we can evaluate different alternatives by assigning different starting values for the objectives. This type of analysis (what-if analysis) allows for simulating different model configurations and detecting conflicting situations and is therefore considered very important in business modeling [Smi07].

Based on the provided formalizations, in the following axioms we define how the values for satisfaction and denial attributes of goals are inferred:

?x[denial **hasValue** full] :− fullDenial (?x) **and naf** WeakConflict(?x).
?x[denial **hasValue** partial] :− partialDenial (?x) **and naf** fullDenial (?x) **and naf** WeakConflict(?x).
?x[satisfaction **hasValue** full] :− fullSatisfaction (?x) **and naf** WeakConflict(?x).
?x[satisfaction **hasValue** partial] :− partialSatisfaction (?x) **and naf** fullSatisfaction (?x) **and naf** WeakConflict(?x).
?x[denial **hasValue** none] :− ?x **memberOf** Goal **and naf** partialDenial(?x) **and naf** WeakConflict(?x).
?x[satisfaction **hasValue** none] :− ?x **memberOf** Goal **and naf** partialSatisfaction(?x) **and naf** WeakConflict(?x).

For instance the first rule infers the value "full" for the goal attribute denial, if it is believed that the goal is fully denied and no weak conflict is inferred for the goal.

4.5 Implementation

In this section we discuss the implementation of two modeling tools: *Maestro for Business Motivation* and *Maestro for Business Queries*, based on the modeling technique presented above. We present the functionalities provided by the tools, following the business motivation modeling sub-activities depicted in Fig. 3.8.

4.5.1 Maestro for Business Motivation Modeling

Maestro for Business Motivation is a visual modeling application based on *Maestro*. Fig. 4.5 shows the screenshot of *Maestro for Business Motivation* with its several different *views*. The views are:

1. **Shapes view**: Provides the graphical notation for the business motivation modeling language as defined in Appendix C.

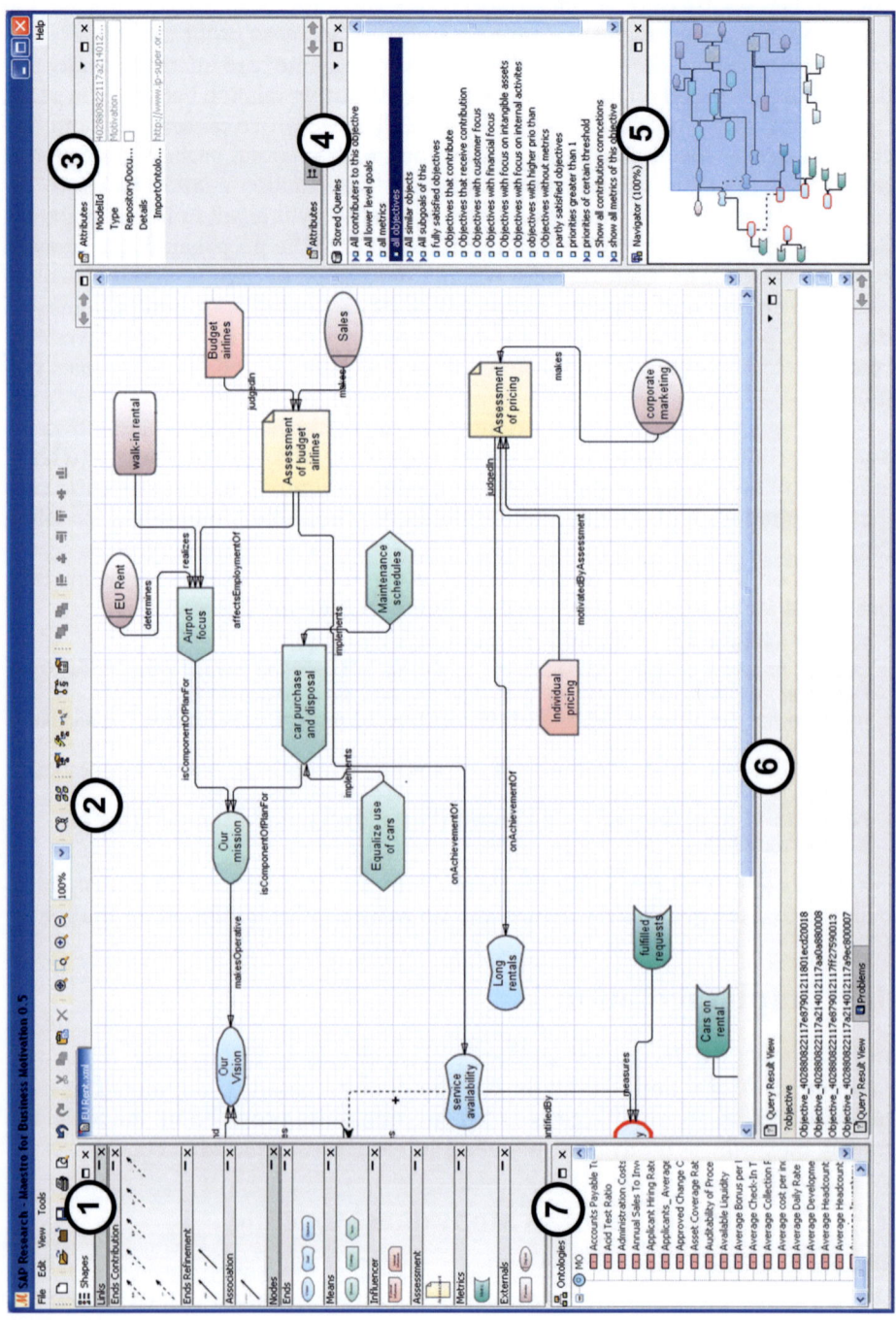

Figure 4.5: Maestro4BM

2. **Modeling view**: Provides the modeling pane in which visual elements from the *Shapes view* can be dropped in order to create business motivation models.

3. **Attributes view**: By using the attributes view, users can specify the values for attributes available for a particular modeling element. The attributes of a selected visual element are directly read from the BMO.

4. **Stored Queries view**: Stores the predefined queries which can be fired against the target motivation model. Queries are divided in two basic types: i) plain queries, which can be fired by double-click and ii) parameterizable queries, which require input parameters (these queries are marked with a small prefix symbol in Fig. 4.5). Input parameters are usually visual elements in the target motivation model.

5. **Navigator view**: It often happens that the motivation models become large. This view provides functionality to navigate to the part of the model which is currently of interest.

6. **Query Result view**: Lists the results of the queries fired from the *Stored Queries view*. Each of the results can be selected individually and the corresponding visual element in the model is highlighted in the *Modeling view* for improved understanding and analysis support.

7. **Ontology Browser**: Provides the functionality of browsing the desired ontologies required for business motivation modeling. It hierarchically displays elements of an ontology and these elements can be dragged and dropped in the *modeling view*.

Shapes, *modeling* and *attribute* views are standard Maestro views which are adapted to support the visual elements specific for business motivation modeling based on the modeling constructs defined in BMO (see Appendix C).

4.5.2 Ontology-driven Design Support

Using the BMO as an underlying metamodel for Maestro4BM offers further advantages. When selecting a modeling element from the *Shapes view*, a query is fired against BMO to retrieve all relations defined in it for the selected element. When dragging the modeling element to the Modeling view, a series of events is fired in order to detect the dropping position of the element. If the modeling element is dropped on another modeling element (as in Fig. 4.6(a)), an Overlay event is fired and the relation between the two modeling elements is created automatically through a simple query against the BMO. In the case shown in Fig. 4.6(b), the overlaying modeling elements are Mission and Vision, therefore the retrieved connecting relation is *makesOperative* (see Fig. 4.3). The order of the overlayed elements also plays a role, i.e. if we would drop Vision on Mission the created relation would be *madeOperativeBy* (see Appendix C).

This type of modeling support allows the user to focus his attention on what he wants to model rather than worrying about how to model it correctly. Further, it makes the modeling tool more flexible as both relations and attributes available in BMO are read on-the-fly for a selected visual element. In this way it also improves the quality of the models created through reducing the amount of modeling errors.

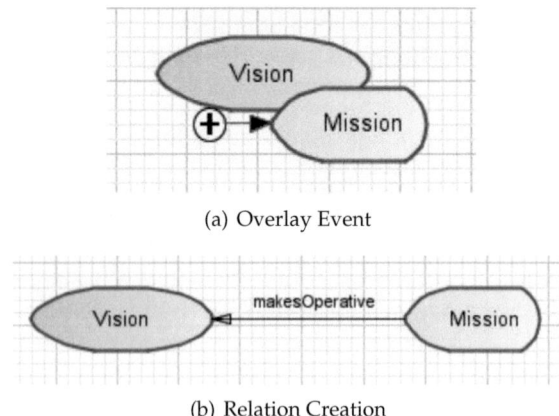

(a) Overlay Event

(b) Relation Creation

Figure 4.6: Maestro4BM modeling support

4.5.3 Gap Analysis

Constraints may be defined in order to perform gap analysis on the business motivation model specifications. WSML-Flight language provides us with the means for expressing such constraints. Consider the following example of checking whether all objectives have corresponding metrics assigned:

Objectives_with_metrics(?objective) :− bmo#measures(?metric,?objective) **and** ?objective
    memberOf bmo#Objective **and** ?metric **memberOf** bmo#Metric.
!− ?objective **memberOf** bmo#Objective **and naf** Objectives_with_metrics(?objective).

The constraint is violated if there is one or more objectives without an assigned metric in the model. The violation can be detected by the consistency check reasoning task, whereby the given constraint is loaded into the knowledge base in order to verify the model consistency. Similar constraints are defined for detecting other gaps in the model.

4.5.4 Maestro for Business Queries

In WSML, a query is equivalent to the body part of the WSML-Flight logical expression. Therefore, *Maestro4BQ* querying application (see Fig. 4.7) is a restricted version of the *Maestro for Business Rules* application (see Section 5.4.1) in which only conditional connectors are used to visually model the query. The visually modeled query is automatically transformed into its underlying WSML-Flight logical expression. The users can test the queries by selecting the finder button in the toolbar (see number 1 in Fig. 4.7), which results in the query being fired against the repository specified in the configuration options. The query results are shown in the *query result view* (see number 2 in Fig. 4.7). This view shows the results of a query in form of a dynamic table, whose number of columns depend on the number of variables used in the query. Once the user is finished with query design, she can store it for reuse in the repository which is read when loading the *Maestro4BM* application (see number 4 in Fig. 4.5).

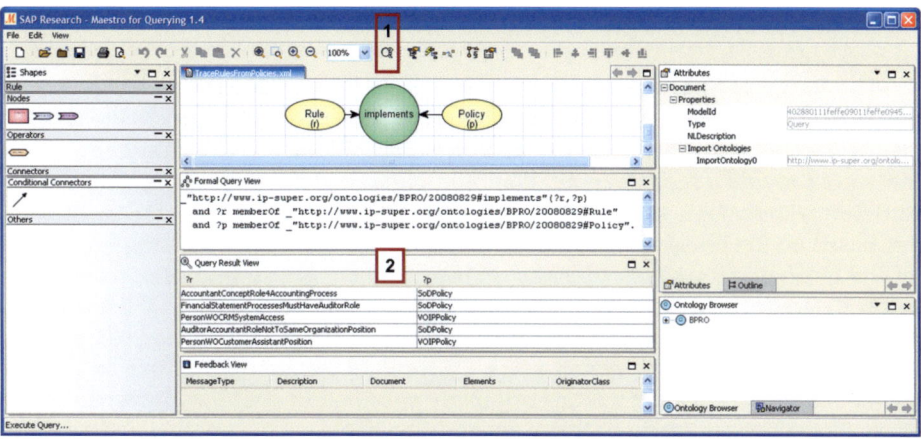

Figure 4.7: Maestro4BQ

4.6 Related Work

The i* framework originates from "early requirements" research [VL01, GMP+08] and is used to understand organizational processes, in terms of strategic relationships and goals in order to elicit the rationale for software requirements. Since i* is based on intentionality, the concept of an *actor*, i.e. any active entity, is central. The core work for i* [Yu95] proposes two types of diagrams, capturing the strategic dependency relationships among actors (SD model) and the strategic rationale model for expressing the rationale behind dependencies (SR model). Using SD and SR models, i* provides two levels of granularity: The former focusing on the relation between actors, using dependency links and actor aggregations. The latter connects hard goals to tasks and softgoals (non-functional goals) to contributing entities, thereby capturing the agent's intentions and abilities. i* has been extended by a number of research efforts[9]. A formal description for i* has been proposed, using temporal logic and model checking for analysis [FLM+04]. The approach can detect self-contradictory specifications, over- and under-specification using a graphical modeling tool[10] with a model checker interface. To check the satisfiability of i*-like goal models, label propagation techniques and a SAT solver are applied [SGM04].

We now contrast the most important differences of the i* framework when compared to our approach. Although the concept of goal is rather detailed, there is no concept of strategy or functional decomposition. Resources and tasks stay on an abstract level, without consideration of the notion central to our work - *process*. Since the notion of actors is fairly general it provides no specific means for modeling organizational structures. Although tasks are important elements of SR modeling, there is no sequential connection (flow) between them. There are no means for expressing priorities or measures for goals, although that sort of information would be required on the enterprise level. The absence of policies/rules and performance

---

[9]http://www.troposproject.org/
[10]http://www.dit.unitn.it/~ft

indicators underline that process-oriented enterprise modeling is not the main goal of the i* approach.

The Business Motivation Model (BMM) is an OMG standard accepted in 2006 [OMG08a], originating from the business rules community. Central to BMM is the distinction between means, ends, directives, assessments and influencers. BMM does not provide a modeling notation but defines a metamodel containing classes, subclass relationships and associations. The terms forming the vocabulary of BMO are based on the BMM specification, in order to foster the shared conceptualization of the business motivation domain. However, there are several important differences between the two. First, BMO development was guided by COBRA ontological foundation which resulted in significant conceptual reengineering of the BMM metamodel (discussed in Section 4.4.1). Conceptual reengineering came as a consequence of sharpening the notions originally specified in BMM, with respect to the basic distinctions made in COBRA. Second, the BMM set of concepts and relations was considerably extended, in particular regarding the notion of Metrics and influencer/refinement relationships between Desired Outcomes. Finally, BMO provides a formal specification of terms from the business motivation vocabulary, paving the way for various types of automated analysis on business motivation models. Apart from BMO, we also define a modeling method and a tool that demonstrate the benefits of the formal representation. This is considered out of scope in the BMM specification.

The "ARchitecture of Integrated Information Systems" (ARIS) is a mature, industry-adopted method for business modeling. The initial modeling notation [KNS92] was later updated to extended EPCs by adding elements such as *objectives*. However, those extensions similarly to the whole modeling approach do not have precise semantics. The objective modeling element presented can be attached to tasks only and their relation has a very open interpretation. Furthermore, it remains unclear if relations between objectives can be specified. ARIS adopts Value Chain Diagrams (VCD) [Por85] as a means of modeling high level processes. Although VCD capture functions which directly create corporate output, neither them, nor the EPC flow model with additional goals elements do capture the entire motivational process perspective (cf. Fig. 3.2). The toolset gradually evolved to several platforms for various modeling tasks. It was recently completed by a straightforward implementation of the Balanced Scorecard strategy approach [KN92] making use of cause-and-effect diagrams and KPIs. The current ARIS toolset is capable of checking certain model properties by using (predefined) macros written in a script language and output the results as a report. However, this approach is cumbersome as it requires programming effort even for metamodel consistency requirements such as the absence of cycles in tree structures.

The work in [Lin08] introduces a general process ontology and proposes annotation of business processes with instances from a goal ontology, in order to facilitate semantic search and reuse of heterogeneous process models. The goal ontology described in [Lin08] allows for modeling of notions commonly found in goal modeling languages such as the distinction between hard- and soft goals, but fails to incorporate relations between the goals, such as e.g. the conjunction of two goals in order to achieve the parent goal. Furthermore, the goal ontology is modeled rather as a mere taxonomy of concepts, where the semantics of the relationships between goals remains underspecified. The approach also does not consider other elements of the motivational process perspective (cf. Fig. 3.2) apart from goals. Besides, the approach is restricted to goals which are defined as operational goals and thus gives away the valuable insight on how processes contribute to the strategic goals of an enterprise. Finally, the focus of the work remains on the usage of ontologies for information integration in the context of business processes.

4.7 Conclusion

In this chapter, we have presented a modeling technique and a tool for business motivation modeling. This work is positioned in the motivational perspective of business processes, defined in Section 3.2.2. It also covers the first two activities of the SBP modeling methodology (see Fig. 3.8). We start with an overview of the COBRA ontology, which was used as an ontological foundation in designing a modeling language for business motivation modeling. Further, we have listed a set of eight requirements for comprehensive support in modeling and analysis of formal business motivation specifications. Based on these requirements, we have defined a modeling language for the formal modeling of business motivation, based on the Business Motivation Ontology (BMO). The syntax and semantics of this modeling language is provided by BMO, whereas the graphical notation for the modeling constructs defined in BMO is given in Appendix C. Based on the modeling language, we devise an approach (method) to formal specification and analysis of business motivation meeting the aforementioned requirements. Finally, we discuss an instantiation of our approach in form of the prototypical implementation within the SAP Research Maestro modeling tool. With our approach we establish an explicit linkage between organizational strategy and the process space, and pave the way for various types of analyses on formal business motivation specifications.

   This chapter presented the first part of the semantic business process modeling framework as depicted in Fig. 3.7. In the following chapter, we describe the second part of the framework: a modeling technique and tool for business policy and rule modeling.

Chapter 5

Modeling and Verification of Business Policies and Rules

5.1 Introduction

The compliance perspective within the *process-oriented enterprise ontology framework* (see Section 3.3) captures the notion of directives which govern and guide the business processes of an organization. Directives are categorized as business policies and business rules. According to OMG's Business Motivation Model (BMM) [OMG08a], a business policy is a high level directive that exists to control, guide and shape how an enterprise realizes its courses of action. Business policies define what is allowed or not allowed, and direct, or specify constraints on how it should be done. They may be formulated for internal requirements, e.g. domain constraints, or external requirements, e.g. legal regulations. Business rules on the other hand are derived from and implement business policies. They are structured more formally and focus on a single aspect of governance and guidance [OMG08a].

Usually enterprises either don't capture directives formally or they just document them in natural language. This makes the procedure of determining which directives apply to a certain process and the verification of their adherence within this process very costly and cumbersome. In order to support explicit specification and automated verification of business policies and rules against business processes, we have devised an approach supported by semantic technologies and the process-oriented ontology framework [MHJS09]. In our approach we semantically model business policy and business rules which implement a policy. The approach is based on the notion similar to anti-patterns of process models [KV07] i.e. explicitly capturing the violating scenario and looking for it in a process model rather than checking for the correctness of process models. Therefore, we explicitly capture violation of business policy in terms of formalized business rules which implement this policy and verify them as constraints against the process models. This approach refers to the policy-based verification phase of the semantic business process modeling lifecycle described in Section 3.4.

This chapter is structured as follows: Section 5.2 provides a set of requirements based on which the overall approach for the modeling and verification of business policies and rules was designed. Section 5.3 presents our approach on how to verify semantic process models against formally captured business policies. We discuss the prototypical implementation of our approach in the SAP Research Maestro modeling tool in Section 5.4. Section 5.5 gives an overview of related work and it contrasts our approach with the already existing ones. Finally, Section 5.6 summarizes our contributions in this chapter.

5.2   Requirements Analysis

Based on literature reviews and a series of internal workshops with process modelers at SAP[1], in this section we provide a list of requirements which need to be fulfilled by a policy-based verification approach to ensure that process models conform to business policies of an organization in the design phase of the business process management lifecycle (cf. Section 2.1).

Req. 1.   Graphical modeling of policies and rules: Breaux and Niehaus in [BN05] and Moore et al. in [MESW01] considered the balance between machine-enforceable and human-readable as one of the requirements for any policy-based system. This also stresses the need for an appropriate representation of policies as they are mostly modeled by business users [TBJ+03]. Therefore, the need and tool support for graphical modeling of policies [Bon06] and rules [NM07, Mai03] is of high importance [Bon06].

Req. 2.   Formal specification of policies and rules: The use of formal language for describing business policies and rules would provide formal semantics, reduce ambiguities, and enable a platform to perform formal analysis and automated processing [EKSMP08]. Therefore, formal specification of business processes and business policies is required in order to automate the verification of business process models against modeled business policies.

Req. 3.   Automated transformation from graphical to formal representation: Req. 2 indicates the need for use of formal machine-enforceable language in order to automate the verification process. On the other hand, **Req. 1** requires the use of a graphical and less formal approach for modeling of business policies and business rules. This led to the requirement for providing support in the automatic transformation from graphical to formal representation.

Req. 4.   Integration of business policies and rules in the enterprise model: An organization formulates its business policies for a purpose [OMG08a] and business rules are used to implement them. In order to get a holistic view of an enterprise, business policy and rule models need to be integrated with the other parts of the process-oriented enterprise model [KMS07, Kar08, MHJS09].

Req. 5.   Policy specification for the holistic enterprise model: In existing literature, large parts of investigations focus on specifying policies for the behavioral process perspective, e.g. [ADW08, FESS07, SPH03]. However, business policies apply to other process perspectives too, e.g. organizational or resource perspective. Therefore, it should be made possible to

---

[1]http://www.sap.com

specify policies and rules constraining any aspect of the process-oriented enterprise model [Kar08].

Req. 6. **Support for explicit specification of policy context information:** Business policies and rules, formulated based on the notion of process context, are less prone to changes compared to the ones formulated based on a particular process especially when a process change/deletion occurs frequently [LGRMD08]. An organization usually has a large number of business policies and not all of them are relevant to a particular business process. This emphasizes the importance of not only enriching process models but also policy models with its respective contextual information in order to indicate the situation in which a business policy is applicable.

Req. 7. **Support for finding relevant business policies for a given business process model:** Finding relevant business policies for a given process should be supported by a matchmaking approach between the process context and a policy context, which describes its applicability criteria. For example, a business policy concerned with business processes involved in a particular business function (e.g. financial management) does not need to be checked against business processes that are not performing any financial management activities. This would automate the manual effort of creating an inventory of applicable policies for a given process context (situation).

Req. 8. **Verification of semantic business process models against modeled business policies:** Semantically described business process models provide the formal basis required for the automation of the verification process. As discussed previously, verification at the time of process design helps to detect errors early in the BPM lifecycle [Boe81, Moo05]. Therefore, the verification of a semantic business process at the time of modeling is of high importance. Benefits of the verification of semantically enriched execution-level process models are presented in [Web09].

Req. 9. **Querying support:** The dynamics of today's world requires business processes, business policies and rules to change frequently. Therefore, it is desirable to know what is affected when a change occurs. For example, when changing a process model, one would like to know against which business policies it has to be verified again, similarly on change of a business policy, which processes need to be verified again. The user should be able to get answers for some common queries such as: *which policies are applicable for a business function x? which are applicable for an organizational unit y?*. Accordingly, in the case of business rules, the queries such as: *which rules are used for implementing a particular policy?*. This illustrates the importance of having an effective query mechanism.

5.3 Approach

In the previous section we presented a list of requirements for comprehensive support that a solution for the verification of process models against business policies of an enterprise must support. In this section we show how we address those requirements through our approach shown in Fig. 5.1. We start with a general overview of the approach and continue with describing each part of the approach in detail.

5.3.1   Overview

The overall approach is inspired by the notion of process *anti-patterns* [KV07]. In our approach, an anti-pattern captures a frequently occurring violation scenario in the design of process models. The violation scenarios are described (formalized) by means of business rules, and process models are checked to ensure that they do not model an occurrence of any violation scenario. A business policy is then modeled as a set of one or more of such business rules, which implement the policy. In this way, formal representation of business rules and business process models allows to automate the detection of violation scenarios in process models by enforcing business rules as constraints on process models.

The overall approach (see Fig. 5.1) is composed of five main components, namely *Business Policy/Rule Modeling*, *Business Process Modeling*, *Policy Matchmaker*, *Policy Verificator*, and *Repository* component which is used for storing graphical models and their formal representation. Our approach allows for modeling of business policies/rules separately from business processes as this enables better reuse and facilitates change, as described in [Ros03b]. This separation of concerns is also evident from independent components for business process modeling and business policies/rules modeling in Fig. 5.1.

The *Business Policy/Rule Modeling* component consists of two main layers, namely *Visual Business Policy/Rule Modeling Layer* and *Business Policy/Rule Formalization Layer*. A modeler interacts with the *Visual Business Policy/Rule Modeling Layer* to model a business policy/rule. *Business Policy/Rule Formalization Layer* formalizes the visually modeled business policy/rule into an ontology instance of *Business Policy & Rule Ontology* described in Section 5.3.2. A detailed description of *Business Policy/Rule Modeling* is given in Section 5.3.2.

Similar to *Business Policy & Rule Modeling*, the *Business Process Modeling* component consists of two layers, namely *Visual Business Process Modeling Layer* and *Business Process Formalization Layer*. The approach extends the standard *Visual Business Process Modeling Layer* in order to assist the process modeler in finding the relevant business policies during the modeling of a process, using the functionality provided by the *Policy Matchmaker* component (cf. Section 5.3.3). Process modelers can select business policies from the list of business policies relevant for verification (see Fig. 5.1, top right). The *Policy Verificator* (cf. Section 5.3.4) component functionality is used for the purpose of policy-based process verification. The *Business Process Formalization Layer* formalizes the modeled business process into an ontology instance of the *Business Process Ontology* (see Fig. 3.5). The *Business Process Modeling* component layers are described in detail in Chapter 6.

The context-based policy matching approach is used by the *Policy Matchmaker* to find the relevant business policies for the currently modeled business process. Here, the context of a business process is matched against the context of business policies in the *Business Policies & Rules* repository to check the relevance of a business policy for a process model. The list of relevant business policies is ranked and shown to

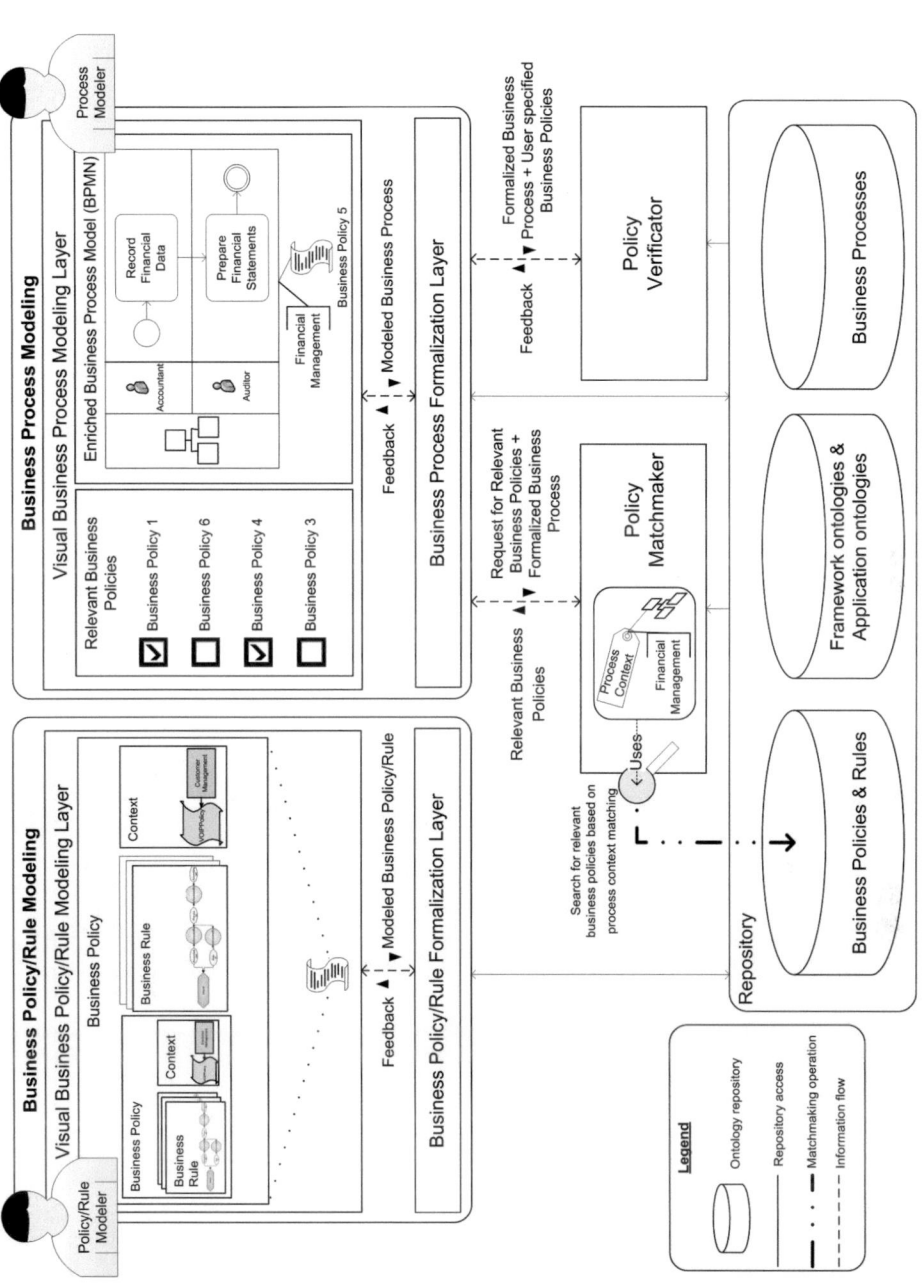

Figure 5.1: Approach

the process modeler through the *Visual Business Process Modeling Layer*. The context-based matching process is further described in Section 5.3.3.

The *Policy Verificator* checks the adherence of the selected business policies within a business process model. The knowledge base used for verification consists of ontologies corresponding to the business process model being verified, specified business policies, relevant application ontologies and the process-oriented enterprise ontology framework (cf. Section 3.3). A consistency check on this knowledge base is performed in order to check the presence of violation scenarios in the process model. The verification process is further explained in Section 5.3.4.

In the subsequent sections, the approaches for business policy/rule modeling, context-based policy matchmaking and policy verification are described in more detail.

5.3.2   Modeling of Business Policies and Rules

The *Visual Business Policy & Rule Modeling Layer* (see top left of Fig. 5.1) allows to model business policies and business rules using the process-oriented enterprise ontology framework [MHJS09] and application ontologies of an enterprise. Apart from describing business policies in natural language, this layer allows the users to model the context of a business policy using elements defined in application ontologies, and to define its implementation using available business rules and other business policies from the repository. Finally, this layer formalizes modeled business policies as instances of the Business Policy and Rule Ontology (BPRO) [MHJS09], which is discussed in the next section.

Business Policy and Rule Ontology

The most important concepts, attributes and relations in BPRO which are relevant to our work are shown in Fig. 5.2 as a class diagram using the stereotype extensibility mechanism of UML [Obj07].

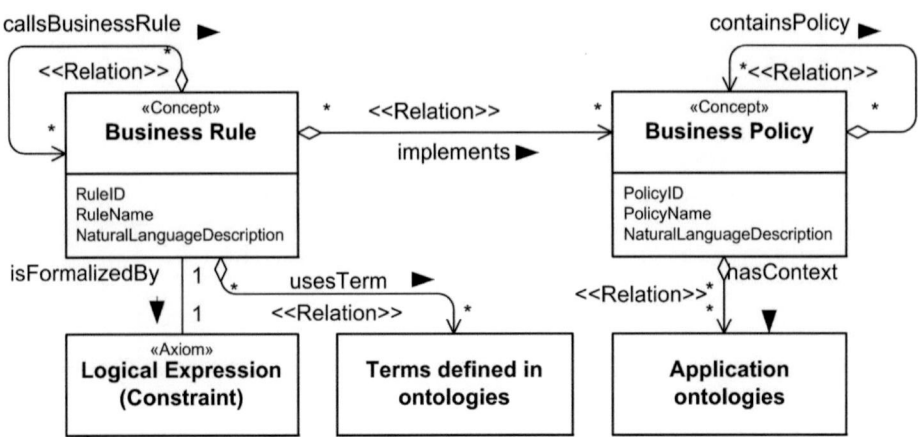

Figure 5.2: A fragment of Business Policy & Rule Ontology (BPRO)

In addition to standard attributes such as *PolicyName* and *NaturalLanguageDescription*, a business policy integrates with other enterprise sub-models using the *hasContext* relation (see right bottom of Fig. 5.2). Using this relation, one can capture rationale for existence of a business policy by connecting it to a goal or strategy defined in the motivational model of an enterprise. Similarly, by connecting to other enterprise sub-models one can capture the applicability situation for a business policy. For example, one can restrict the scope of a business policy's applicability by associating a business policy to a particular business function or organizational unit within an enterprise. This addresses the requirement (**Req. 4**) regarding the integration of business policy models with other enterprise sub-models. Requirement (**Req. 6**) regarding the capture of contextual information of business processes and business policies is addressed partially with respect to business policies and later we show how contextual information with respect to business processes is captured to fulfill the requirement completely.

A business policy can be composed of other business policies using the relation *containsPolicy* (see top right of Fig. 5.2) and/or business rules which implement it using relation *implements* (see center of Fig. 5.2). For example, a high level business policy can be composed of many low level operational business policies which are in turn implemented as business rules. Business rules are more formal compared to business policies and hence it is possible to automatically verify business policies in terms of business rules against business process models. Similarly, a business rule can trigger other dependent business rules using the relation *callsBusinessRule* when executing it (see top left of Fig. 5.2). The WSML representation of the BPRO ontology is provided in Appendix F.

Visual Modeling of Business Policies and Rules

Maier [Mai03] identified the need for a visual rule editor as one of the software tools to support ontology-based integration. Maier envisioned that a visual rule editor would allow for visual modeling of rules by dragging and dropping elements defined in an ontology. Following [Mai03], the *Visual Business Policy & Rule Modeling Layer* (see top left of Fig. 5.1) provides a set of visual elements (cf. Appendix H) for modeling a business policy/rule. As there is no restriction to building business rules using elements from any particular ontology, business rules constraining not only process models but also any other enterprise sub-model, can be built using elements defined in any ontology from the repository. Hence, the requirement (**Req. 5**) for supporting the specification of business rules for other enterprise sub-models is fulfilled. Therefore, a business rule can be formed involving concepts from multiple enterprise sub-models and similarly a business policy can include business rules constraining many enterprise and process models.

In the following two sections, we discuss the visual modeling of business policies and rules, respectively, in more detail.

Visual Modeling of Business Policies (see Fig. 5.3) involves three activities namely the modeling of its context, linking implementing business rules and linking lower level business policies. A policy modeler performs all of these three activities using the instances defined in various enterprise ontologies. The modeling layer finds the appropriate visualization construct (cf. Appendix H) for an instance via

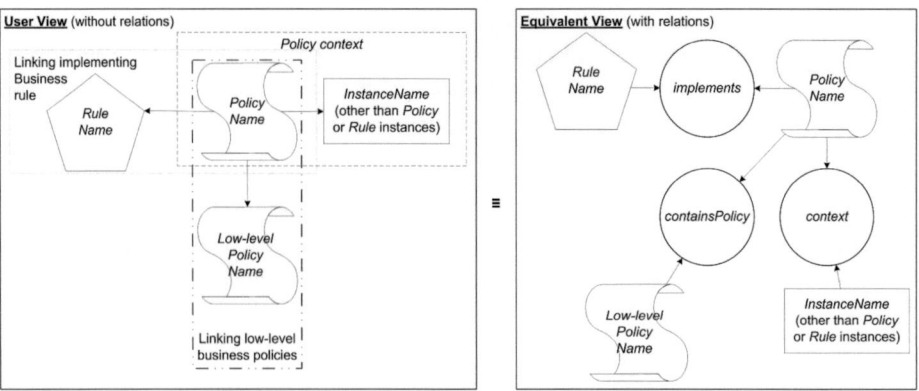

Figure 5.3: Business Policy Modeling

logical reasoning. For example, if the chosen element is an instance of the concept *Rule*, then the business rule visual construct is used. Instances which do not belong to the concepts *Policy* and *Rule* are considered as the context of the modeled policy (see Fig. 5.3). Therefore, the users do not have to explicitly specify the relation as it is inferred via logical reasoning based on the types of the connecting elements (see Fig. 5.3, right). The *connector* (cf. Appendix H) in the case of business policies modeling is used for connecting different visual elements, and there is no differentiation as in the case of business rules modeling in terms of *head* and *body* connectors. The modeled business policy is formalized in the form of an ontology instance of the *Business Policy & Rule Ontology*. The formalization process starts with checking for modeling errors such as isolated edges, isolated nodes, etc. If there are no modeling errors in the policy model, then the relation instances based on the elements used in the model (e.g. business rules, context etc.) are determined. Finally, a BPRO ontology instance is created with an instance of the concept *Policy*, representing the currently modeled policy and the relation instances determined in the previous step. The formalization process of a business policy addresses our requirement (**Req. 3**) regarding the need for automatic transformation of visually modeled business policies into a formal machine-readable representation. In the end, both the graphically modeled and the formalized business policy are persisted separately in the *Business Policies & Rules Repository*.

Visual Modeling of Business Rules   is similar to business policy modeling, the additional part being the visual formulation of business rules through the combination of the visual representation of an atomic expression (see Table H.2 in Appendix H) by using different visual connector constructs (see Table H.1 in Appendix H). Fig. 5.4 shows the visual modeling of a business rule corresponding to the following WSML-Flight inference rule:

worksIn(?e,?b) :− ?e **memberOf** Employee **and** ?a **memberOf** Activity **and** ?b **memberOf** BusinessFunction **and** performs(?e,?a) **and** belongsTo(?a,?b)

Constraint modeling is similar to inference rule modeling (see Fig. 5.4), with the difference that the constraints do not contain a conclusion part. Fig. 5.4 also shows the use of variables representing instances of the corresponding concepts.

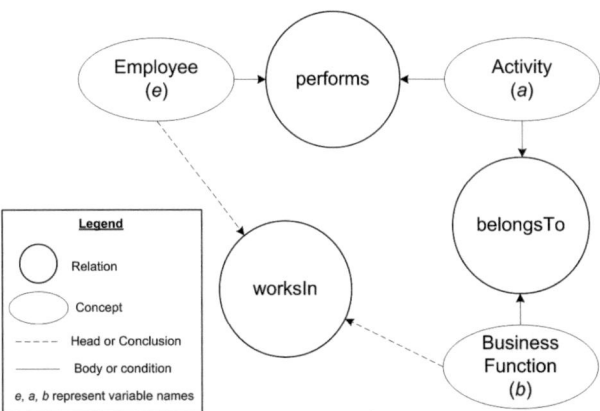

Figure 5.4: Business Rule Modeling

The formalization of business rule formulation as an axiom is done by the *Business Policy & Rule Formalization Layer* and starts with checking for modeling errors such as isolated edges, isolated nodes, etc. If the business rule formulation does not contain any modeling errors, the set of atomic expressions for the conditions represented as the body is determined, formulated and combined using the *conjunction* operator. The same procedure is repeated for the *head or conclusion* part provided that the rule is of type inference and not constraint. Finally, the WSML-Flight logical expression obtained as an axiom is checked against the WSML-Flight grammar. The formalization of a business rule model is similar to that of a business policy model except that the names of the relations are *callsBusinessRule* for the grouping of business rules and *usesElement* for the elements used in the formulation of a business rule. In addition, the formalization process involves the addition of the obtained axiom in the ontology. This finally completes our requirement (**Req. 3**) that addresses the need for automatic transformation of a visually modeled business rule into a formal machine-readable representation. The graphically modeled business rule and its formal representation are stored separately in the *Business Policies & Rules Repository*.

Note that the formal language specification for business policies and rules is provided by the underlying formal logics of the ontology language used to model them. As argued in Section 2.3.2, our ontology language of choice is WSML-Flight. Our approach allows to model business rules which result in inferring new knowledge, as well as to model constraint style business rules which would be verified against models. Therefore, WSML-Flight provides a formal basis as mentioned in requirement (**Req. 2**) for capturing information related to process and application ontologies in order to perform their formal analysis.

In the following sections we discuss the usage and advantages of the formalized business policies and rules in terms of assisting the process modeler by automating the process of finding the relevant business policies for a given process model and their automated verification.

5.3.3 Context-based Policy Matching

Our approach also shows how the process modeler can be assisted in process modeling with respect to business policies. The *Business Process Modeling Layer* (see top right of Fig. 5.1) allows to model processes using the Business Process Modeling Notation (BPMN) [Obj09]. *Business Process Formalization Layer* (see center right of Fig. 5.1) transforms the BPMN process model into an instance of Business Process Ontology (BPO) based on π-calculus formalization of workflow patterns [PW05, XLY07], as discussed in Chapter 6. Here we focus on supporting business policies during business process modeling phase in multiple ways. First, support in finding relevant business policies for a business process model based on its context information. Second, support in annotating business policies to business process models.Finally, support in verifying business policies against process models i.e. ensuring that the semantically enriched business process models adhere to business policies of an enterprise.

Business process models are enriched with process context information (e.g. the business function it performs, the organizational unit which performs it, the process goal, metric etc.) by means of semantic annotation (see Section 6.4.2). Similarly, business policies can also be attached to a business process model using semantic annotation. Therefore, requirement (**Req. 6**) regarding the representation of process context is fulfilled.

An enterprise usually has a large number of business policies corresponding to legal regulations, domain constraints, strategic requirements, etc. With increasing number of business policies it becomes a difficult task for the process modeler to find the relevant business policies for a given process model. Explicit capture of contextual information of processes and policies can be useful to assist the process modeler in finding relevant policies. The *Policy Matchmaker* component (see middle row of Fig. 5.1) helps to overcome this problem by providing a ranked matching list of business policies with respect to the currently modeled process. The process modeler then makes a final decision on their relevance.

The authors in [LH03] define matchmaking as a process that returns all advertisements that may potentially satisfy the requirements specified in a given request as input from a repository where those advertisements are published. In our case, business policies are advertisements which are published along with their contextual information in the business policies and rules repository. Context of the currently modeled process acts as a request and process modelers are interested in finding all potentially relevant business policies for it.

The automation of the matchmaking process is usually confronted with two main problems. The first one is the gap between humans and machines in understanding and interpretation of data [SHP03]. The second is the softer definition of "potentially relevant match" in order to support more flexible matches apart from using the restrictive criteria of looking for the exact use of instances, both in business policies and processes [PKPS02].

The use of semantic technologies for defining a common vocabulary in the form of ontologies (process-oriented enterprise ontology framework and application on-

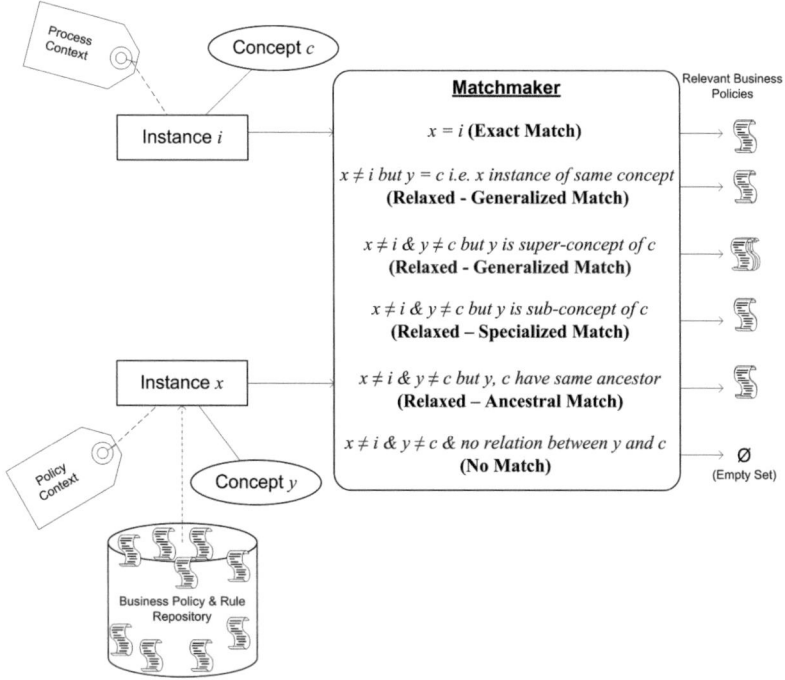

Figure 5.5: Matchmaking Algorithm

tologies) addresses the first issue. In order to address the second issue, we introduce different types of matches. The definition of different types of matches are adapted from [LH03]. The definitions are adapted with regard to the instance rather than the concept, as in our approach the process and policy context are defined in terms of instances. Fig. 5.5 shows the different types of matches used by the *Policy Match-maker*.

- *Exact Match* occurs when the same instance is used in both policy and process context.

- *Relaxed Match* can be one of three types that we distinguish:

  - *Generalized Match* occurs in two ways as shown in Fig. 5.5. First, if an instance in process context is matched to an instance of the same concept in the policy context[2]. Second, if a concept of the instance in the matched policy context is a generalization (i.e. super-concept) of a concept of the instance from the process context.

  - *Specialized Match* occurs if the concept of the instance in the matched policy context is a specialization (i.e. sub-concept) of the concept of the instance in the process context.

---

[2]Some may argue that instances of the same concept should be considered as an exact match, but since our approach is focused on the instance level rather than the concept level, it makes sense to consider it as a generalized match.

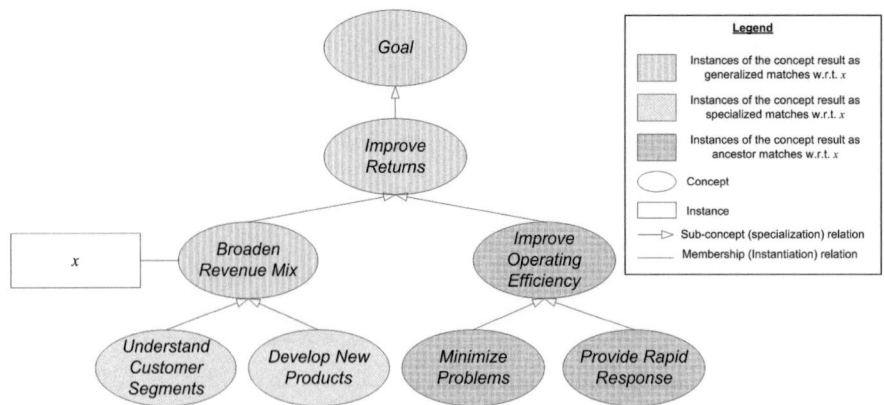

Figure 5.6: A fragment of the *Business Motivation Ontology* depicting different types of matches

> – *Ancestral Match* occurs if the concept of the instances in the policy and process context share a common ancestor in their concept hierarchy.

- *No Match* occurs if the instance of the process context cannot find matching instances in the policy context using the above defined types of matches.

The matchmaking logic is captured declaratively using a set of axioms in the *Policy Recommendation Ontology* (cf. Appendix G). We define the exact match in the following way:

```
match(?Pr, ?Po, ?x) :− bpdo#isAnnotatedBy(?Pr, ?x) and bpro#policyHasContext(?Po, ?x) and naf
    bpdo#isAnnotatedBy(?Pr, ?Po).
```

i.e. the exact match is recorded when process and policy are annotated with the same instance and the process is not already annotated with that policy[3].

Using `memberOf` in WSML-Flight we get the direct concept an instance belongs to as a result, but also all other concepts in the hierarchy that the direct concept is a specialization of. For example in Fig. 5.6, the query `?x memberOf ?c` would return the concepts: *Broaden Revenue Mix*, *Improve Returns* and *Goal*. As we need to get only the direct concept (*Broaden Revenue Mix*) of an instance, we defined the following two axioms which realize this:

```
memberOfSubConcept(?m, ?c, ?sc) :− ?m memberOf ?c and ?sc subConceptOf ?c and ?sc !=
    ?c and ?m memberOf ?sc.
directConceptOnly(?x, ?c) :− ?x memberOf ?c and naf memberOfSubConcept(?x, ?c, ?y).
```

The relation `memberOfSubConcept(?m, ?c, ?sc)` stores all the member concepts, but the direct concept (*Improve Returns* and *Goal*)[4]. Finally, the relation `directConceptOnly(?x, ?c)` stores only the direct concept (*Broaden Revenue Mix*). We use this relation to formally define the relaxed types of match, e.g. generalized match is defined in the following way:

---

[3]Policies which are already annotated to a process are automatically taken into account when performing policy verification

[4]Note that subConceptOf is reflexive in WSML-Flight

generalizedMatch(?pr, ?po, ?pa, ?poa) :− bpdo#isAnnotatedBy(?pr, ?pa) **and naf** match(?pr, ?po,
?pa) **and** bpro#policyHasContext(?po, ?poa) **and naf** bpdo#isAnnotatedBy(?pr, ?po) **and**
directConceptOnly(?pa, ?padc) **and** directConceptOnly(?poa, ?poadc) **and** ?padc
subConceptOf ?poadc.

The definition of other types of matches is done in a similar manner, see Appendix G.

When searching for relevant business policies, the matching results also need to be ranked. For ranking, exact match is the most desired compared to the relaxed match and no match. In the case of relaxed match, we consider the generalized match as the next most relevant compared to specialized and ancestral matches. For example, consider the concept hierarchy depicted in Fig. 5.6. A process contributing to *Broaden Revenue Mix* goal will be more likely to follow the policies of *Improve Returns* than more specific goals such as *Understand Customer Segments*. Similarly, in the case of specialized and ancestral matches, the specialized match is preferable to the ancestral match.

In ranking, the *Policy Matchmaker* also takes into account that the increase in the number of instances in the process context increases the scope of the search. For example, a process context containing instance *x* of the *Broaden Revenue Mix* goal (see Fig. 5.6) and an instance of an *Organizational Unit* from *Organizational Unit Ontology* (cf. Section 3.3), might need to be validated against the business policies containing either the instance *x* corresponding to the *Broaden Revenue Mix* goal or the *Organizational Unit* instance. Business policies with both instances are ranked higher compared to business policies with only one instance match. Hence, while ranking, the *Policy Matchmaker* also takes into account the number of instances matched with the particular match type. The *Policy Matchmaker* thus fulfills the requirement (**Req. 7**) for the support in finding relevant business policies for a process model. After the matching is performed, a process modeler makes the final decision for selecting the appropriate business policies for the verification process, which is the focus of the next section.

5.3.4   Policy Verification

In the previous section, we have demonstrated how formally captured context information of business policies and process models can be used for finding relevant policies for a given process model. In this section, we show how the formally modeled business policies and rules discussed in Section 5.3.2 can be used for the automated verification of process models.

The process modeler can select business policies from the ranked list for verification against a process model. The verification is performed by the *Policy Verificator* component (see lower right of Fig. 5.1). The violation of any business rules which are specified as constraint axioms inside business policies is automatically detected by logical reasoning, i.e. performing a consistency check on the knowledge base formed of all relevant ontologies. The knowledge base consists of the following ontologies: a formalized business process model as an instance of the Business Process Ontology; ontologies corresponding to user specified business policies and rules in the business process model; ontologies corresponding to additional business policies and rules which the process modeler has selected from the ranked list provided by the *Policy Matchmaker*; ontologies of process-oriented enterprise framework and application ontologies which are used either in the business process model, business policies, or business rules. During verification of processes with multiple modeling abstraction levels, the formal definition of the `contains` relation in the *Business Process Ontology* is used to propagate the specified business policies through lower process abstraction levels. After the verification is performed, the *Policy Verificator* component provides feedback to the process modeler (see lower right of Fig. 5.1) depending on the status of the consistency check. If the consistency check fails, the feedback is provided in the form of natural language description of the violated business rule(s). The natural language description of a violated business rule provides the process modeler with enough information regarding the reason for failure and how to overcome it.

5.4   Implementation

As a proof of concept of the approach described in section 5.3 we extended Maestro [DKZD06, Dör07], a business process modeling tool from SAP Research. In this section we present how we implemented Maestro extensions to allow the users to i) visually model business policies and rules, ii) match relevant policies based on their process context, and iii) perform policy-based process verification.

5.4.1   Maestro for Business Policies and Rules

Maestro for Business Policies/Rules is a visual modeling application based on *Maestro*. The visual modeling component of Maestro was extended to support modeling of business policies and rules. The extended component provides the visual elements (see Appendix H.1) based on the metamodel shown in Appendix H.1. It also provides additional views like *ontology browser*, *formal rule view* (in the case of business rule modeling) apart from the traditional Maestro views. The extension also transforms the visually modeled business policy/rule into a BPRO ontology instance. Finally, both the ontology and the visual model are persisted in the repository. The ontology is persisted in the human-readable syntax of the WSML language through the serialize functionality provided by the WSMO4J API [5]. The visual model is serialized as XML file using the Maestro serializing functionality.

Modeling Business Rules with Maestro

Fig. 5.7 shows the screenshot of *Maestro for Business Rules* with its several different views. The views are:

1. **Ontology Browser**: Provides the functionality of browsing the desired ontologies required for modeling a business rule. It hierarchically displays elements of an ontology and these elements can be dragged and dropped in the modeling view to model a business rule.

2. **Shapes view**: Provides the additional visual elements like *connectors*, WSML built-in data types and predicates, apart from the visual elements correspond-

---
[5]http://wsmo4j.sourceforge.net/

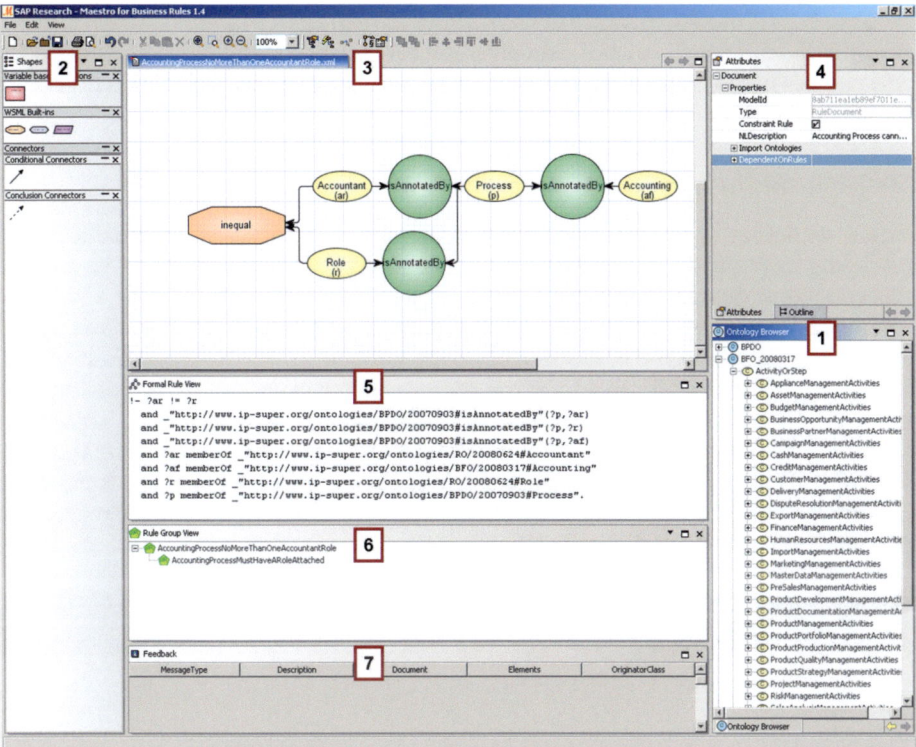

Figure 5.7: Maestro for Business Rules

ing to ontological constructs (concepts, relations, instances) used from the ontology browser.

3. **Modeling view**: Provides the modeling pane in which visual elements corresponding to elements of ontologies from the ontology browser and from the shapes view can be dropped in order to model a business rule.

4. **Attributes view**: By using the attributes view, users can specify natural language description and other properties of the modeled business rule such as type of the rule (inference or constraint). In addition, this view is also used to specify properties of some of the visual elements, e.g. setting parameters for a relation.

5. **Formal rule view**: The visually modeled business rule is automatically transformed to WSML-Flight logical expressions in the background. The generated expression is shown in this view.

6. **Rule Group view**: This view helps users to group other related business rules which need to be verified along with the currently modeled one.

7. **Feedback view**: It assists users by providing them feedback while modeling a business rule.

The shapes, modeling, and attribute views are standard Maestro views which are adapted to support the visual elements specific for the modeling of business rules and policies based on the underlying metamodel for these visual elements described in Appendix H.

Modeling Business Policies with Maestro

Visual modeling of business policies can be seen as a subset of the business rule modeling in terms of the provided tool functionality. The *formal rule view* and the *rule group view* described in the previous section are specific to modeling a business rule, and are not available in the case of modeling business policies. The visual elements are also specific in the case of policy modeling. WSML-Flight built-in constructs are not available, and only the *body connector* from logical expression constructs is available for modeling business policies (see Appendix H.1). This holds since the policy modeler needs only the ontological constructs (concept, relation, instance) and means of connecting them (via the *body connector*) in order to model a business policy. The modeling view for modeling business policies and an example of a modeled policy are shown in the Fig. 5.8.

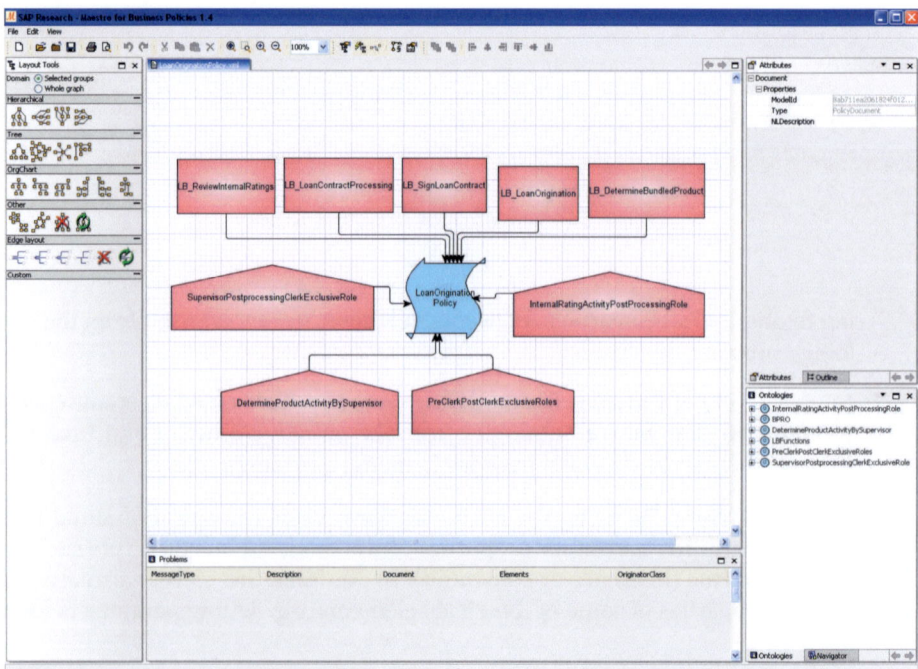

Figure 5.8: Maestro for Business Policies

5.4.2   Policy Matchmaker

Fig. 5.9 shows the *Policy Recommendation* option available to users through the Tools menu in the *Maestro for BPMN* application. The *Policy Recommendation* command

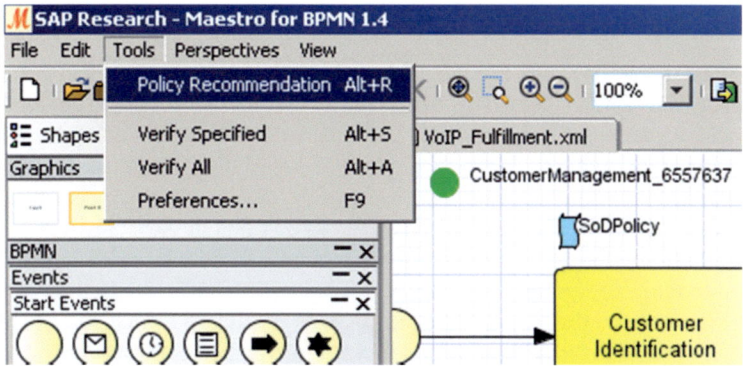

Figure 5.9: Policy Recommendation Menu

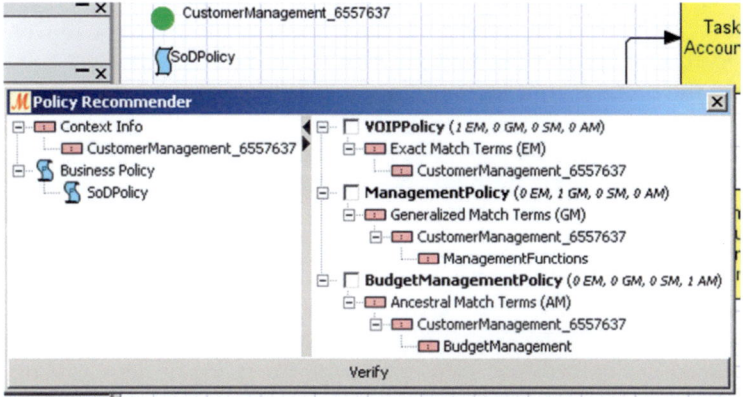

Figure 5.10: Policy Recommender UI

exposes the underlying context-based policy matching functionality provided by the *Policy Matchmaker*.

The *Policy Recommendation* option sends a request to the *PolicyRecommender* component for finding the relevant business policies matching the context[6].

The *PolicyRecommender* component then obtains a formal representation of the current process, extracts the contextual process information from it and use that to query the reasoner for matching business policies. The results obtained from the reasoner are unranked matching business policies. Our ranking algorithm then ranks the policies by relevance and presents them together with the contextual process information through the *Policy Recommender UI* (see Fig. 5.10). In the left pane of Fig. 5.10, the extracted contextual information of the process model is shown, while the right pane lists the matched policies along with the types of matches (exact, generalized, ancestral).

---

[6]The context of a process is defined by annotating it with the elements of the ontologies (see small circle in the modeling view above the *Policy Recommender* menu in Fig. 5.9). The business process model in Fig. 5.9 is also enriched with a business policy (see business policy notation for SoD Policy in Fig. 5.9)

5.4.3   Policy Verificator

The Maestro modeling tool has also been extended to integrate the functionality of the *Policy Verificator*. The *Policy Verificator* component provides the functionality of verifying a process model against the business policies of an enterprise. In a more precise way, it checks for the presence of a violating scenario depicted by the implementing business rules of a business policy in a business process model.

The *Policy Verificator* supports three different options of verifying a business process model. The first option is to verify the business process model against all business policies from the business policy repository (see *Verify All* option of the Tools menu in Fig. 5.9). In the second option, process modelers enrich the business process model with the desired business policies through semantic annotation (see Section 6.4.2). The *Policy Verificator* then verifies the business process model against the annotated business policies (see *Verify Specified* option of the Tools menu in Fig. 5.9). The third option for verification includes using the functionality of the *Policy Matchmaker* described earlier for finding the relevant business policies. In this way, the issue of manual search for relevant policies is resolved. The process modelers can then select the desired policies from the ranked list of policies for verification (see Fig. 5.10).

For all three options, the way business policies are specified for the verification process is different. Apart from this difference, the rest of the verification process remains the same. The *PolicyVerificator* checks the satisfiability and consistency of the knowledge base by invoking *checkConsistency* method of the WSML-Flight reasoner. If any of the implementing business rules of business policies are violated, the consistency check fails and returns the name of the violating business rule. If the natural language description attribute is specified for the violated business rule, it is displayed in the feedback view, otherwise the name of the violating business rule is displayed.

5.5   Related Work

OntoStudio® [Ont] is a commercial development environment for modeling ontologies. Its Graphical Rule Editor (see Fig. 5.11) allows users to visually model rules as envisioned in [Mai03]. Concepts can be dragged from the ontology view and dropped into the modeling view to construct a rule, as shown in Fig. 5.11. Different edge types are used to represent the condition and conclusion part of the rule. Edges also indicate a relationship between two concepts. Visually modeled rules are formalized into F-Logic [KLW95] expressions using a language which is to our knowledge not WWW compliant. Also, in our approach, WSML-Flight allows for n-ary relations (in contrast to binary relations in OntoStudio®), since visually modeled rules are formalized as WSML-Flight logical expressions.

In [GMS06, SGN07], the authors present an approach to compliance checking of business processes based on a specialized modal logic. The proposed approach focuses on behavioral descriptions associated with compliance requirements and processes. We argue that the behavioral perspective of processes is only one aspect of the problem. In order to fully address the problem of ensuring compliance of business processes, one must consider the constraints stemming from the organizational, resource, functional and motivational perspectives of business processes

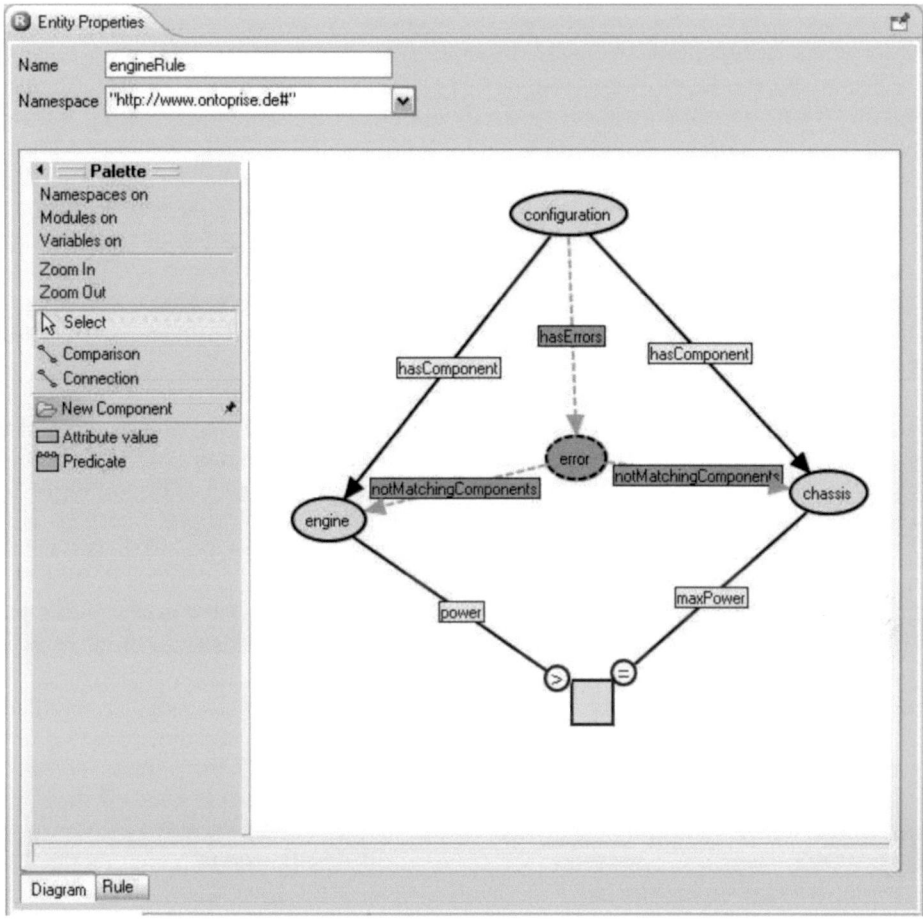

Figure 5.11: Graphical Rule Editor in OntoStudio® [Ont]

[MH09]. It is not shown how the complex nature of business processes (i.e. multiple abstraction levels) is supported by the approach. In addition, the expressiveness and processing scalability of the proposed logic have not been thoroughly investigated. The extension of this work in [GHSW08] includes semantic annotations of process activities in the form of postconditions (effects). It allows to (i) identify the regulatory obligations that will definitely arise in a given business process and (ii) determine which of those obligations are definitely fulfilled, violated or remain unfulfilled. This extension is considered out of the scope for our work since it deals with execution-level business processes, but can be seen as complimentary.

Further related efforts include [LMX07, RK07, ADW08], however the works target solely the behavioral (temporal) aspects of business processes and therefore do not cover compliance requirements concerned with the other process perspectives. The work in [GV06] presents a declarative, rule-based approach to modeling business processes. It is shown how business rules can be used to capture the semantics of business policies and regulations. The approach however lacks formal foundations which would allow for its operationalization.

The authors in [HS06] present a prototypical implementation of a system for automatic detection of errors in semantically enriched business process models using compliance regulations expressed in SWRL language [HPSB$^+$04]. Domain and process ontologies are built using OWL language [Wor04], while the regulations are modeled textually as SWRL rules. A similar approach is also described in [NS06]. When compared to our approach, the system lacks the possibility of visual modeling of rules and does not show how the multiple process abstraction levels are handled. Furthermore, as the system has only been tested with a very specific set of e-government regulations, there is no evidence of its general application in other domains.

The work in [Lam07] presents an ontology-based Web service market infrastructure, where the automation of a policy-based contracting process, that includes the matching of service offers and requests, is investigated in detail. First, an ontology framework is proposed to allow for the formal specification of offers, requests and contracts in SWS markets. Second, a mechanism is developed to enable the automation of the contracting and contract monitoring process [Lam07]. The automated monitoring of contracts is done by performing SPARQL queries in order to find out if a particular contract has been correctly fulfilled. If the query result set is empty, there is at least one violation of the contract obligations. In order to find out which obligation was violated, an additional (refined) set of queries needs to be defined. In contrast to this, our approach captures policies as constraints which depict the violation scenario. Using the consistency check reasoning task, we can automatically determine which policy is not adhered to within the process, without making further queries. The modeling of policies as constraints is allowed through the closed world assumption followed by the LP paradigm of ontology languages (e.g. WSML-Flight), as opposed to the open world assumption followed by the DL paradigm and used in [Lam07].

5.6   Conclusion

In this chapter, we have presented an approach to modeling and verification of business policies and rules against business process models. This work is positioned in the compliance perspective of business processes in Section 3.2.2. First, we have listed a set of eleven requirements for comprehensive support in modeling and verification of business policies and rules on semantically enriched process models. Based on these requirements, we have defined modeling languages for the formal modeling of business policies and rules, where the rule modeling language is based on the metamodel of WSML-Flight. The syntax and semantics of these modeling languages are provided by the BPRO (see Appendix F) and WSML itself, whereas the language modeling notation is provided in Appendix H. Further, we devise an approach (method) for the formal specification and verification of business policies and rules meeting the aforementioned requirements. Finally, we discuss the prototypical implementation of our approach within the SAP Research Maestro modeling tool, completing the design of the policy and rule modeling framework (see Section 2.2). With our approach we support the automation in ensuring compliance of organization's business process models with the established business policies and rules which improves the quality of process models.

Chapter 6

Modeling, Annotation and Querying of Business Processes

6.1 Introduction

Business process (BP) modeling is the first and most important phase in the business process engineering chain. BP models are created by business analysts with the objective to capture business requirements, enable a better understanding of business processes, facilitate communication between business analysts and IT experts, identify process improvement options and serve as a basis for the derivation of executable business processes.

Current modeling tools offer poor support to the process modelers. In fact, the most commonly used process modeling tools are MS Visio, Excel and PowerPoint which are merely drawing tools. As a consequence, the process models created using such tools contain formal errors [Men08], are disconnected from other process artifacts created on higher process levels (cf. Fig. 3.3) and do not foster reuse of best practices.

The problem of formal errors in process models was recognized by the research community and soon a number of formal languages for modeling business processes evolved [vdA98, AH05, DtH01]. However, all of these languages focus only on a single aspect of process description - the behavioral perspective, as defined in Section 3.2.2. In order to integrate other relevant perspectives of process description, in the previous section we have proposed the process-oriented enterprise ontology framework.

In this section, we present how the behavioral process perspective is modeled in this ontology framework and provide further details on how we managed to integrate the other process perspectives. We also describe a modeling method for creating semantically rich process descriptions and using such descriptions to improve current modeling practices. Finally, we provide a modeling tool which instantiates the modeling technique and enables semantic modeling, annotation and querying of business processes. We demonstrate what benefits this brings in terms of tooling support for process modeling.

The remainder of this chapter is organized as follows. In Section 6.2 we present a requirements analysis for creating a modeling technique and tool which supports the modeling and querying of processes on a semantic level. To make the chapter self-contained, Section 6.3 gives a short introduction to the formal foundations used herein. Section 6.4 reports on our approach for modeling, annotating and querying of business processes. In Section 6.5, we discuss the prototypical implementation of our approach within the SAP Research Maestro modeling tool. Section 6.6 discusses the related work. We summarize our contributions in Section 6.7.

6.2 Requirements Analysis

In order to support the business process modeling activity of the semantic business process modeling lifecycle (cf. Fig. 3.8), we need to provide a modeling technique and a modeling tool (cf. Fig. 3.7). In this section, we describe a list of requirements that a modeling technique and tool designed for semantic modeling, annotation and querying of business processes should fulfill. These requirements were partly elicited based on the interviews conducted with business experts concerned with process modeling at SAP.

Req. 1. **Rich process description** The process model needs to be formally described to enable automatic matchmaking of user requests (queries) against process descriptions. In order to support the user to expressively search the process repository, we need a rich process description.

Req. 2. **Intuitive user request specification** The user must be provided with a user-friendly query interface for specifying his requests. The user must be able to query for processes based on multiple aspects of their description (see Section 3.2.2).

Req. 3. **Query language** There needs to be a query language with expressive power that is sufficient to formally describe the user requests.

Req. 4. **Querying mechanism** There needs to be a mechanism that will perform expressive matchmaking of user requests against process descriptions. The algorithm should take a user request as an input and return a ranked list of results that match the request.

Req. 5. **Flexibility** The framework must provide support for relaxation and refinement of user queries. In the case that we get too few results matching the query, we can relax the query, i.e. incrementally abstract elements of the query, e.g. by using subsumption hierarchy. Similarly, if we get too many results, the user needs to be provided with a possibility to refine his request.

Req. 6. **Ranking** To increase the usability of matching results, the list of results should be ordered with respect to the level of match.

Req. 7. **Computational efficiency** The underlying querying mechanism must be computationally tractable and efficient to provide the required design-time user support.

6.3 Preliminaries

In order to solve the first of the aforementioned requirements, we have selected the π-calculus for capturing the behavioral aspect of business processes. This section gives a brief overview of the π-calculus and provides a rationale for its usage.

6.3.1 π-calculus

The mathematical foundation which we use to describe the behavior of business processes was created by Milner, Parrow and Walker, published in [MPW89]. The π-calculus is a process algebra for specifying mobile systems, where communication and change play crucial roles. Communication takes place between π-calculus processes by means of communication channels. Central to the π-calculus is the notion of a *name*. One of the cornerstones of the calculus is the dual role that names play in communication: they can be both communication channels (links) and transferred objects (variables).

We now briefly explain the syntax of the π-calculus and the notation used in our work:

(6.1)
$$P ::= M \mid P|P \mid vzP \mid !P$$

(6.2)
$$M ::= 0 \mid \pi.P \mid M + M$$

(6.3)
$$\pi ::= \overline{x}\langle y\rangle \mid x(z) \mid \tau \mid [x = y]\pi$$

Basically, the π-calculus consists of processes and names. Equation 6.1 is the definition of a **process** and it defines the following: $P|P$ is a composition where processes P and P run in parallel – **concurrent** execution. vzP represents a **restriction** of the name z to P. $!P$ is the notation for a **replication**, where multiple instances of P run in parallel. The replication operator also satisfies the equation: $!P = P \mid !P$.

Equation 6.2 gives the summations behind M: 0 is the **inaction**, a process that can do nothing. $M + M$ is the **exclusive choice** between M and M. The π is a prefix.

Finally, equation 6.3 defines the **prefix** π: $\overline{x}\langle y\rangle$ is the **output** prefix, which sends the name y over the name x and then continues as P. On the other hand, $x(z)$ is the **input** prefix receiving any name over x, and then continues as P with z replaced by the received name. τ is an unobservable **internal action** of the process. The last symbol, the **match** prefix $[x = y]\pi.P$ behaves as $\pi.P$, if x is equal to y.

The syntax of π-calculus is used as a basis for creating the grammar of the Business Process Ontology explained in Section 6.4.2.

6.3.2 Why π-calculus?

There has been an emerging paradigm shift in Business Process Management research in the recent years where business processes are not seen anymore as static, predefined control flows, but rather as dynamic, flexible flows where there is no absolute control of the process execution [Puh06b]. These dynamic flows are centered around the notion of *events* which can trigger activities and can also be produced by the activities. The event-driven paradigm allows for flexible integration of distributed activities which makes the business processes more adaptable.

The existing works on formal foundations for BPM [vdAvH02] fail to capture the event-driven, distributed nature of modern business processes. On the other hand, it has been argued that the π-calculus possesses the necessary ingredients to become a formal foundation for modern BPM systems [SF06, Puh06b]. Indeed, in [PW05] it has been shown that the π-calculus in combination with the *Event, Condition, Action* (ECA) approach [DHL90] can be used to capture the formal semantics of all workflow patterns reported in [AHKB03]. The combined approach enables declarative, flexible, rule-based specification of process flow. We adopt this approach in our work to provide a basis for describing the behavioral perspective in our process-centric enterprise ontology framework (see Section 3.3).

6.3.3 Workflow Patterns

Aalst et al. in [AHKB03] introduced *workflow*[1] *patterns*, based on the notion of a pattern defined in [RZ96]. The authors in [RZ96] defined a pattern as "the abstraction from a concrete form which keeps recurring in specific nonarbitrary contexts". In [AHKB03], later revised and extended in [RtHvdAM06], a set of 43 workflow patterns was formulated. Workflow patterns consequently became the requirement and evaluation criteria for workflow languages because they represent the most frequently found patterns in workflows and are independent of any particular language. The formalizations of workflow patterns have thus been provided in several workflow modeling languages, e.g. using Petri Nets [vdA98], YAWL [AH05] and UML activity diagrams [DtH01]. The authors in [AHKB03] further argue that the patterns provide the basis for a comparison of commercially available workflow management systems. For the same reasons, *workflow patterns* are used to compare the expressiveness of different business process modeling languages (such as BPMN, EPCs), based on the number of workflow patterns supported by the language [Whi04].

Börger in [Bör07] provides an interesting critical analysis of workflow patterns, mainly driven by the deficiencies in existing formalizations of the patterns and their ill classification. The streamlined classification presented in this work turns the set of 43 workflow patterns into 13 basic ones with simple refinements. It is also shown that 7 out of these 13 patterns are in fact versions of standard programming constructs [Bör07]. We use these insights when providing a formal representation of workflow patterns in the Business Process Ontology, presented in the following section.

6.4 Approach

In Section 6.2 we presented a list of requirements for user support in semantic modeling, annotation and querying of process artefacts. In this section we show how we address those requirements through our approach shown in Fig. 6.1. We start with a general overview of the approach and continue with describing each part of the approach in detail.

---

[1]Workflow Management Coalition in [WfM99] defined workflow as "the automation of a business process, in whole or part, during which documents, information or tasks are passed from one participant to another for action, according to a set of procedural rules."

6.4.1 Overview

The overall approach consists of three main components, namely *Business Process Modeling, Query Engine, Parser/Serializer* and *Repository* component (see Fig. 6.1).

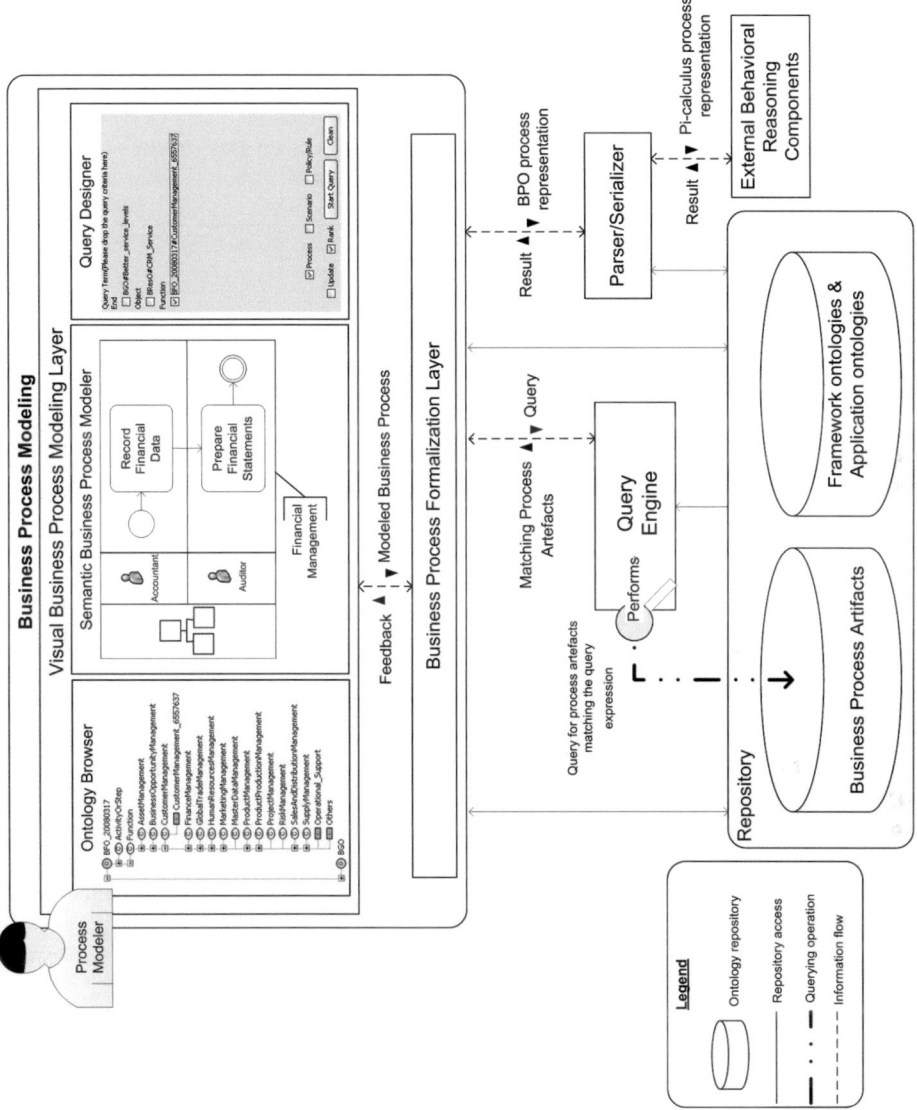

Figure 6.1: Approach

The Business Process Modeling component consists of two layers: *Visual Business Process Modeling Layer* and *Business Process Formalization Layer*. The Visual BP Modeling Layer is further divided into subcomponents: Semantic BP Modeler, Query Designer and Ontology Browser, as depicted in Fig. 6.1. A *Process Modeler* uses the *Semantic BP Modeler* to design a business process. She can annotate the created process model using the metadata available in the *Ontology Browser*. The *Query Designer* is used to build queries for searching the process space for existing artifacts which could be reused in the design.

The *Business Process Formalization Layer* serializes the visual process model representation into a machine-processable instance of the Business Process Ontology. We describe the ontology in detail in Section 6.4.2.

The *Parser/Serializer* component has the role of providing the round trip transformation between the WSML ontological representation and plain *pi*-calculus representation describing the behavioral perspective of a process.

The *Query Engine* receives the query expressions from the modeling tool and performs queries on the repository of process artifacts.

The *Repository* component stores descriptions of various types of process artifacts as well as the process-oriented enterprise ontology framework extended with domain and application ontologies.

6.4.2   Modeling of Business Processes

The *Visual Business Process Modeling Layer* (see Fig. 6.1) allows to model business processes using the process-oriented enterprise ontology framework [MHJS09] and application ontologies of an enterprise. Apart from creating process models using standard modeling notations, this layer allows the users to annotate and enrich a process model with metadata describing a process from the functional, organizational, resource, motivational and compliance perspective. Further, this layer allows the users to specify queries for searching the process artifact repository. Finally, this layer formalizes modeled business processes as instances of the Business Process Ontology (BPO) [MP07], which is discussed in the next section.

Business Process Ontology (BPO)

In order to represent the behavioral (dynamic) perspective of a process, we use a process algebra, the π-calculus. The π-calculus was introduced in Section 6.3 with its syntax and constructors. The language is quite simple and suitable to constitute the foundation for the BPO.

The concepts in BPO are visualized in Figure 6.2, using WSMO Studio[2]. Our conceptualization closely follows the π-calculus constructs given in Equations 6.1,6.2,6.3 in Section 6.3.1. Thus, the two top-level concepts of the BPO are the basic elements of π-calculus: *Process* and *Name*.

A π-process can have a *hasDefinition* attribute (defining a π-process), and/or it can have a *hasNext* attribute, which corresponds to "." symbol in Equation 6.2 and represents a sequence. For the process definition we adopt the ECA approach, where each process activity is mapped to an independent π-process. Each *pi*-process has pre- and postconditions. A precondition for a π-process P could be that it can only start after a π-process Q has finished (executed). The preconditions correspond to the event and conditional part of the ECA rules. Hence, a π-process which has no event part represents a starting process activity. The events are mapped to input prefixes in π-calculus. Once an input prefix is triggered (an event occured), a condition needs to be checked (optional), which is represented by a match prefix.

---

[2]http://www.wsmostudio.org/

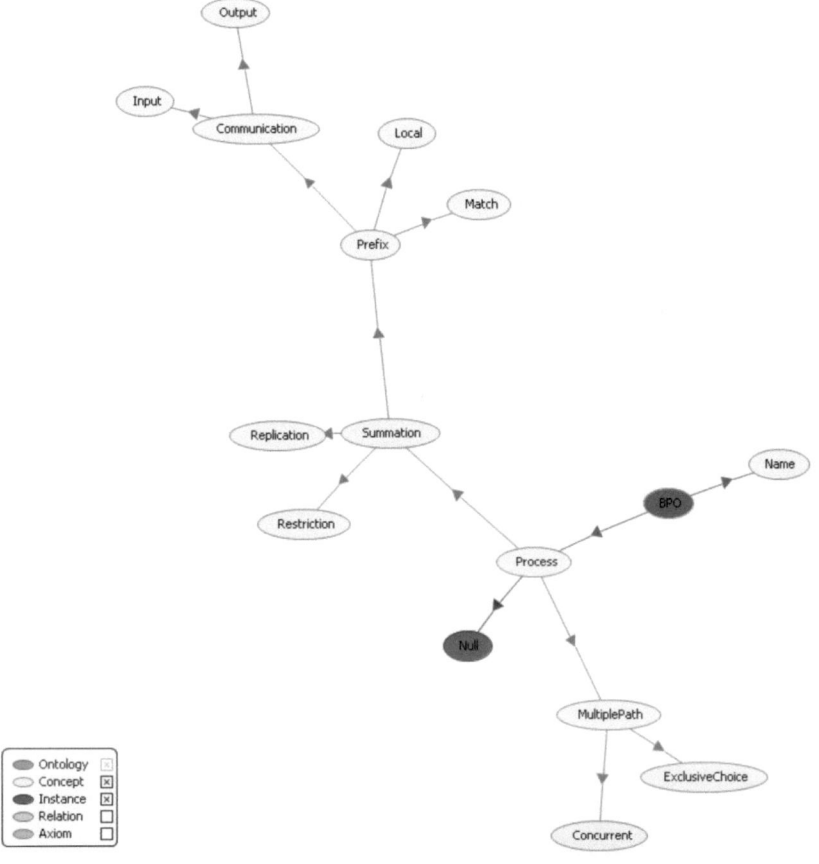

Figure 6.2: BPO – Concepts

The action part is modeled using two building blocks. The performing action of an activity is represented via internal action τ and the output prefix is used for representing the fact that a π-process triggers other π-processes. Output prefixes are in fact postconditions. A postcondition for Q can be that upon its execution, it signals this information to other *pi*-processes. In case a π-process does not have an output prefix, it is an ending process activity.

We summarize this discussion through a complete definition for a single process activity:

$$x.[a = b].\tau.\bar{y}.0$$

where a π-process receives a trigger x (event), does a comparison $[a = b]$ (condition), performs internal work τ and triggers another process through $\bar{y}$ (action). The *hasDefinition* attribute in BPO is in fact a placeholder for this ECA-style π-process definition.

The main π-process can be either a business process or scenario, which is marked by the *hasType* attribute. All π-processes within the main π-process use this attribute to store the corresponding type of modeling construct used in their graphical representation: Event, Activity or Gateway. The attribute *hasLabel* stores the label of the modeling element, while the attribute *hasDescription* stores the natural language description of the process.

The concept Process has two sub-concepts: *MultiplePath* and *Summation* (see Fig. 6.2). *MultiplePath* subsumes two flow branching possibilities: i) concurrent execution of π-processes (all paths executed in parallel) and ii) exclusive choice, where only one of the multiple paths is chosen. Corresponding concepts are *Concurrent* and *ExclusiveChoice*, which map directly to the π-calculus elements defined in Equations 6.1 and 6.2. The attribute *subdivide* contains the π-process identifiers which participate in branching.

Summation has the sub-concepts explained directly by the π-calculus syntax: *Replication*, *Restriction* and *Prefix*. *Replication* is used for specifying that a π-process has multiple instances running in parallel. *Restriction* is used to list the names which are scoped within the overall process definition. *Prefix* maps directly to the π-calculus element defined in Equation 6.3. It subsumes the unobservable action τ (concept *Local*), the match prefix (concept *Match*) and *Input* and *Output* prefix. The latter two are grouped into a super concept *Communication*.

In addition to the process constructs, BPO allows for the modeling of names (connections) contained in the process diagram using the concept *Name*. The complete serialization of BPO in WSML-Flight language is given in the Appendix D.

Visual Modeling of Business Processes

We will now illustrate the usage of BPO in formal representation of the behavioral perspective for the Customer Order Fulfillment process shown in Fig. 6.3. The process is composed of simple tasks (receiving a message, checking an order, sending a message), an exclusive choice for sending the correct message back, and the merge for synchronization.

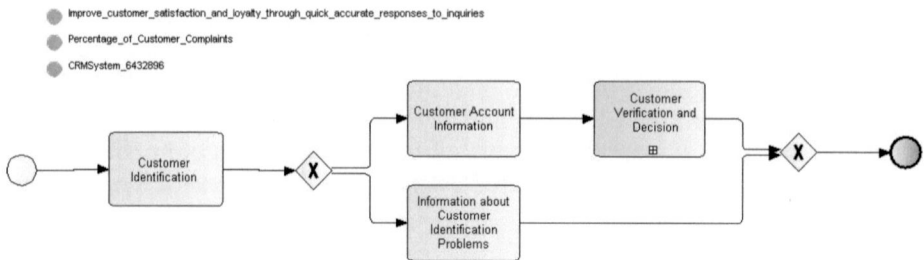

Figure 6.3: Customer Order Fulfillment Process

The main π-process, *InstanceProcess*, which consists all other process elements is defined in Listing 6.1. The content of the InstanceProcess is defined using the *hasDefinition* attribute: the instance *InstanceRestrict* scopes all the names[3] which belong to this process definition. Further, the instance *InstanceAND* (see listing 6.1) defines

---

[3]The seven names in the *onNames* attribute definition of the InstanceRestrict represent the connecting links shown in Fig. 6.3

all π-processes which run in parallel within the main π-process[4]. This part defines the constituents of the main π-process. We now turn attention to the definition of the individual names and π-processes.

```
instance InstanceProcess memberOf bpo#Process
    bpo#hasID hasValue "ModelInstance"
    bpo#hasDefinition hasValue InstanceRestrict

instance InstanceRestrict memberOf bpo#Restriction
    bpo#onNames hasValue {a8ab71071210c101301210c1041be0005,
        a8ab71071210c101301210c11ec810013, a8ab71071210c101301210c120d170019,
        a8ab71071210c101301210c107dd5000b, a8ab71071210c101301210c11d2e1000f,
        a8ab71071210c101301210c1203130017, a8ab71071210c101301210c1228e8001d }
    bpo#hasNext hasValue InstanceAND

instance InstanceAND memberOf bpo#Concurrent
    bpo#hasID hasValue "ParallelProcessing"
    bpo#subdivide hasValue {a8ab71071210c101301210c102e2f0001Process,
        a8ab71071210c101301210c11ec310011Process,
        a8ab71071210c101301210c107d8f0009Process,
        a8ab71071210c101301210c1202cd0015Process,
        a8ab71071210c101301210c11d291000dProcess,
        a8ab71071210c101301210c122897001bProcess,
        a8ab71071210c101301210c103c4e0003Process }
```

Listing 6.1: The main π-process definition for the process in Fig. 6.3

All names (connections) in the main process are defined as instances[5] of the BPO concept *Name*:

```
instance a8ab71071210c101301210c1041be0005 memberOf bpo#Name
    bpo#hasID hasValue "a8ab71071210c101301210c1041be0005"
```

Listing 6.2: Definition of a name

Listing 6.3 provides the ECA-style definition of a process activity, as previously discussed. The π-process definition starts with instance *a8ab71071210c101301210c103c4e00030Receive*, which is in fact an input prefix (event) and belongs to process control flow as indicated in its definition. After the event occurs, the *hasNext* attribute indicates that the internal action follows (activity is executed) and finally the π-process terminates.

```
instance a8ab71071210c101301210c103c4e0003Process memberOf bpo#Process
    bpo#hasID hasValue "Check Ordera8ab71071210c101301210c103c4e0003"
    bpo#hasType hasValue "Activity"
    bpo#hasNames hasValue {a8ab71071210c101301210c1041be0005,
        a8ab71071210c101301210c107dd5000b }
    bpo#hasDefinition hasValue a8ab71071210c101301210c103c4e00030Receive

instance a8ab71071210c101301210c103c4e00030Receive memberOf bpo#Input
    bpo#hasName hasValue a8ab71071210c101301210c1041be0005
    bpo#hasNext hasValue a8ab71071210c101301210c103c4e0003Tau

instance a8ab71071210c101301210c103c4e0003Tau memberOf bpo#Local
    bpo#hasID hasValue "tau"
```

---

[4]Note that the Start and End Event as well as the XOR split and merge constructs are mapped to π-processes

[5]Note that a unique identifier for each *Name* and *Process* from the example business process in Fig. 6.3 is automatically generated by the Maestro modeling tool

```
       bpo#hasNext hasValue a8ab71071210c101301210c103c4e00031Send

instance a8ab71071210c101301210c103c4e00031Send memberOf bpo#Output
       bpo#hasName hasValue a8ab71071210c101301210c107dd5000b
       bpo#hasNext hasValue bpo#Null
```

Listing 6.3: Customer Identification Task from Fig. 6.3

In listing 6.4, we provide the BPO definition of the Exclusive Choice Pattern (XOR Gateway) in Fig. 6.3. First, the XOR gateway itself is modeled as a π-process. Its incoming and outgoing gateway links are defined through the *hasNames* attribute. The exclusive choice between two paths is modeled using the π-calculus operator $+$, which is represented by the *ExclusiveChoice* concept in BPO.

```
instance a8ab71071210c101301210c107d8f0009Process memberOf bpo#Process
       bpo#hasID hasValue "XorGatewaya8ab71071210c101301210c107d8f0009"
       bpo#hasType hasValue "Gateway"
       bpo#hasNames hasValue {a8ab71071210c101301210c107dd5000b,
           a8ab71071210c101301210c11d2e1000f, a8ab71071210c101301210c11ec810013 }
       bpo#hasDefinition hasValue a8ab71071210c101301210c107d8f00090Receive

instance a8ab71071210c101301210c107d8f00090Receive memberOf bpo#Input
       bpo#hasName hasValue a8ab71071210c101301210c107dd5000b
       bpo#hasNext hasValue a8ab71071210c101301210c107d8f0009Tau

instance a8ab71071210c101301210c107d8f0009Tau memberOf bpo#Local
       bpo#hasID hasValue "tau"
       bpo#hasNext hasValue a8ab71071210c101301210c107d8f0009XOR

instance a8ab71071210c101301210c107d8f0009XOR memberOf bpo#ExclusiveChoice
       bpo#hasID hasValue "ExclusiveChoice"
       bpo#subdivide hasValue {a8ab71071210c101301210c107d8f00091Send,
           a8ab71071210c101301210c107d8f00092Send }

instance a8ab71071210c101301210c107d8f00091Send memberOf bpo#Output
       bpo#hasName hasValue a8ab71071210c101301210c11d2e1000f
       bpo#hasNext hasValue bpo#Null

instance a8ab71071210c101301210c107d8f00092Send memberOf bpo#Output
       bpo#hasName hasValue a8ab71071210c101301210c11ec810013
       bpo#hasNext hasValue bpo#Null
```

Listing 6.4: Exclusive Choice Pattern from Fig. 6.3

The BPO representation of the *Simple Merge* pattern in Fig. 6.3 is given in Appendix E.

After creating the BPO, we had to show that it allows for expressing the semantics of all workflow patterns. Therefore, all representations from [AHKB03] were carefully modeled using BPO concepts.

Note that we do not reason on behavioral properties of processes using ontological reasoning due to the fact that WSML-Flight inferencing engines do not support behavioral reasoning. Rather, the behavioral semantics of process models is translated into plain *pi*-calculus syntax for which several reasoners based on bisimulation theory [San96] are available [VM94, Bri03]. The possibility of behavioral reasoning allows for soundness verification in process models [PW06, vdAvH02, vdA97], which detects modeling errors leading to deadlocks and livelocks. A deadlock leads to processes stopping their execution and interaction with the environment, whereas a livelock leads to the situation where a process is never finished. The soundness verification corresponds to the first process verification activity in our semantic business process modeling lifecycle shown in Fig. 3.8.

In some applications, e.g. the policy-based verification of processes, multiple process modeling abstraction levels need to be considered (see Section 5.3). To provide means in dealing with process abstraction levels, we define the following three axioms in the BPO. The first axiom defines the constituents of an observed process, i.e. the π-processes (activities) and names (connections) it consists of:

> contains(?x, ?r) :− ?x[hasDefinition **hasValue** ?y] **memberOf** Process **and** ?y[hasNext **hasValue** ?z] **memberOf** Restriction **and** ?z[subdivide **hasValue** ?r] **memberOf** Concurrent.

The second axiom adds the process definition at a lower abstraction level (subprocess) to the higher level process definition:

> contains(?x, ?y) :− ?x[hasSubprocessDefinition **hasValue** ?y] **memberOf** Process **and** ?y **memberOf** Process.

Finally, the third axiom specifies the transitivity of the `contains` relation to support multiple abstraction levels:

> contains(?x,?z) :− contains(?x,?y) **and** contains(?y,?z).

In order to integrate behavioral with other process perspectives, BPO imports concepts from several other ontologies, as discussed in Section 3.3.

The integration of other process perspectives is done by introducing a set of relations shown in Figure 6.4. The relation *isAnnotatedBy* subsumes the relations connecting the concept *Process* with top level concepts in other ontologies: Business Functions Ontology (relation *isAnnotatedByBusinessFunction*), Business Motivation Ontology (relation *isAnnotatedByBusinessObjective*), etc. We provide an example relation definition for an organizational unit responsible for a process (integrating the organizational perspective):

> **relation** isAnnotatedBy/2
>
> **relation** isAnnotatedByOrganizationalUnit(**ofType** Process, **ofType** ouo#OrganizationalUnit)
>   **subRelationOf** isAnnotatedBy
>
> **axiom** hasOrganizationalUnitRelDefn
> **definedBy**
> isAnnotatedByOrganizationalUnit(?x, ?y) :− isAnnotatedBy(?x,?y) **and** ?y **memberOf** ouo#OrganizationalUnit.

Definition of the remaining relations is done in a similar manner and provided in Appendix D. These relations are used extensively in semantic annotation and querying of process artifacts, as described in the following sections.

Annotation

Semantic annotation of processes is performed in order to enrich them with metadata which describe a process from multiple perspectives in addition to the behavioral one (see Figure 3.2). Thus, a process is annotated with the resources consumed or used by process activities (resource perspective), organizational units, roles and actors responsible for a process (organizational perspective), etc. As described in Section 3.3, we provide the process-oriented ontology framework which allows for modeling additional process perspectives.

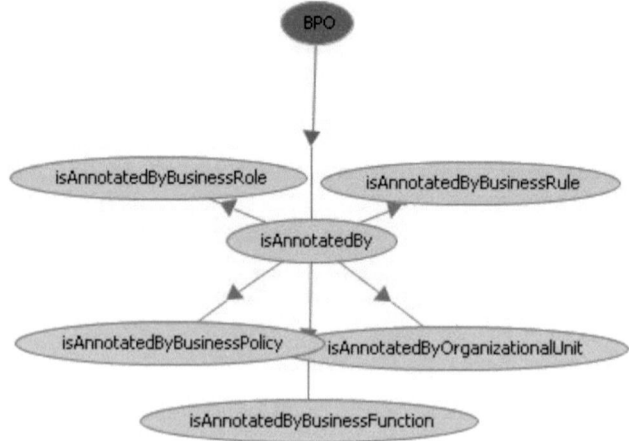

Figure 6.4: BPO – Relations

In order to annotate a process, the user needs to browse an ontology describing the relevant process perspective. Once she has found a desired instance for annotation, she can drag and drop the instance into the modeling panel as shown in Fig. 6.3. The instance can be placed either outside the process (which results in the whole process being annotated) or inside a particular part of the process (a task or a subprocess). If an annotated subprocess has a more detailed process attached, the annotations are propagated to the lower level process utilizing the `contains` relation in BPO. On the implementation level, individual visual modeling elements specify whether they are allowed to be annotated and with which types of annotations.

The process annotation is stored in the BPO instance using *isAnnotatedBy* relation instances. For example, for the annotation *CRMSystem_6432896*[6] in Fig. 6.3, we have the following relation instance:

relationInstance bpo#isAnnotatedBy(InstanceProcess, breso#CRMSystem_6432896)

Other process annotations are stored in a similar way. After loading into the knowledge base, the relation instances get materialized depending on the concept the annotated instance belongs to. In our example, since *CRMSystem_6432896* instance belongs to the concept *System* in the Business Resource Ontology, the relation is materialized into *isAnnotatedByBusinessResource*.

The semantic enrichment of process descriptions through annotation is pivotal for enabling the semantic querying of process artifacts, which will be our focus in the following sections. We start by discussing the query designer component.

Specification of Queries

The intended users of our framework are business experts. Therefore, they need to be provided with an intuitive and user-friendly interface to be able to specify their queries in an easy way, not much different from using the applications they are used

---

[6]The annotation marks that the process requires access to a particular instance of a CRM system

to. The complexity of ontologies and reasoning needs to be hidden from the user. In the following, we describe how we designed the query designer component (cf. Fig. 6.1) based on this requirement.

The query designer component and the ontology browser are presented in Fig. 6.5.

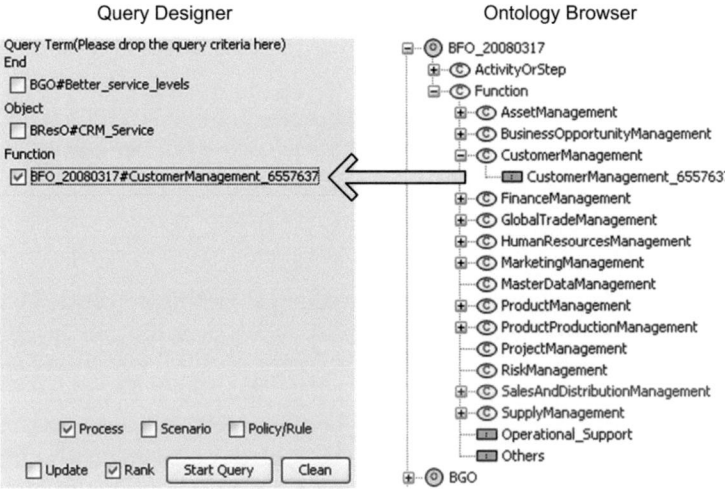

Figure 6.5: Query Designer and Ontology Browser

The query specification is performed in a similar manner to the process annotation. The user can navigate through the ontology browser for selecting semantic annotations (business goals, functions, roles, resources, etc.) of the process artifacts she wants to retrieve[7]. Desired annotations can be dragged as query arguments from the ontology browser to the query designer panel, as shown using the arrow in Fig. 6.5 for the *CustomerManagement_6557637* instance. The dragged instances are grouped by the top-level concept they are a member of in the corresponding ontology (*Business Function* in this case).

The dragged instances can be marked as required or optional (default) for querying. This is important for achieving flexibility in querying, since the concepts marked as optional can be omitted when constructing the query for retrieving more results. The user can also specify the type of artifacts he is looking for (process, scenario, business policy/rule), shown at the bottom of the query designer panel in Fig. 6.5.

The visual query specification is translated into WSML-Flight logical expressions in the background. The corresponding WSML expression generated from the example query shown in Fig. 6.5 is:

(bpo#isAnnotatedBy(?x, bfo#CustomerManagement_6557637)) **or** (bpo#isAnnotatedBy(?x, bfo#CustomerManagement_6557637) **and** bpo#isAnnotatedBy(?x, bgo#Better_service_levels)) **or** (bpo#isAnnotatedBy(?x, bfo#CustomerManagement_6557637) **and** bpo#isAnnotatedBy(?x, breso#CRM_Service))

---

[7]Note that these characterictics correspond to the process perspectives depicted in Fig. 3.2.

The query expression is built in the following way. The first part of the query comprises the required query criteria - in our example, the *Customer-Management_6557637* instance. Next, each optional criteria (*Better_service_levels*, *CRM_Service* instances) is grouped with the required criteria (*CustomerManagement_6557637* instance) into an aggregated optional criteria (see the following two query parts in the example expression above).

6.4.3   Query Engine

In this section, we discuss how the querying process operates within our approach. First, we shortly describe the mechanism for processing queries and continue with discussing its improvements in flexibility and ranking in querying.

Query Mechanism

The querying mechanism reuses the matchmaking algorithm for context-based business policy matching described in Section 5.3.3. In this case, the user specified query (as described in the previous section) acts as a request and it is matched against the process descriptions from *Business Process Artifact Repository*. The possible levels of matches are those defined in Section 5.3.3, i.e. *exact*, *relaxed* (*generalized*, *specialized*, *ancestral*) and *no match*. However, since in this case the user manually specifies the query, we slightly extended the matchmaking algorithm to deal with required and optional query criteria.

6.4.4   Soundness Verification

Ensuring that the resulting business process model is sound is an important aspect of the quality of conceptual process models. Since a plethora of work on soundness verification exists in literature (see e.g. [vdA97, vdA00, DR01, vdAvH02, Mar03]), we aimed at reusing these techniques and incorporating them into our modeling framework. In order to do that, a *Parser/Serializer* component which translates the BPO process descriptions to plain *pi*-calculus syntax was necessary, along with the integration of a *pi*-calculus reasoning engine (see Fig. 6.1). The soundness verification algorithm used for checking process models is given in [PW06].

6.5   Implementation

In this section we discuss the implementation of a modeling tool, Semantic Maestro4BPMN[8], based on the modeling technique presented above. Semantic Maestro4BPMN is an extension to the SAP Research Maestro modeling tool (cf. Section 5.4 for further technical details). We will now discuss the functionalities provided by the tool following the process modeling sub-activities depicted in Fig. 3.8.

Semantic Maestro4BPMN provides a modeling view with a simplified modeling notation for the manager modeling role (cf. Fig. 6.6). This notation is based on the

---

[8]Note that BPMN notation was selected for illustrative purposes due to its increasing popularity. The modeling technique is independent from the concrete modeling notation

most commonly used subset of the BPMN notation, defined through the analysis of over 100 process models from industry and academia in [MR08].

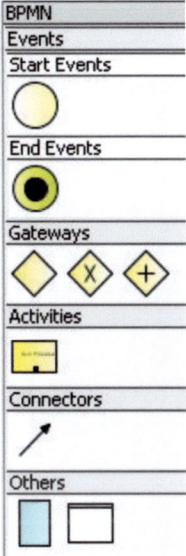

Figure 6.6: Most commonly used subset of BPMN constructs. Source: [MR08]

Using this notation, a business manager can design scenarios such as the one shown in Fig. 6.7. In the next step, she can annotate the scenario using the ontology instances from the ontology browser (lower right in Fig. 6.7). The annotations are visualized as circles in the modeling pane. For detailing each of the high-level scenario steps (subprocesses), the user can ask for recommendations (cf. *Get Process Recommendation* option for the *Provide Service* scenario step). Based on scenario annotations, the process artifact repository is queried for matching modeling artifacts. A list of matching results is shown in the query container on the left side of Fig. 6.7. The user can then drag-and-drop a query result to the scenario step in order to attach its detailed definition.

If a user wants to see the detailed subprocess definition that was attached, she can select the *View Process Definition* option for the desired scenario step (cf. Fig. 6.8).

Since the detailed process definition contains a richer set of modeling constructs, a new modeling view for the business analyst role is opened (see Fig. 6.9). The new view includes the additional constructs which allow for editing the target process model, while maintaining the linkage between two process modeling levels.

Finally, in the query view shown in Fig. 6.10, we show a ranked list of processes obtained as a result of the query built using the query designer. The user can browse the matching models from the process repository in order to reuse them in her design.

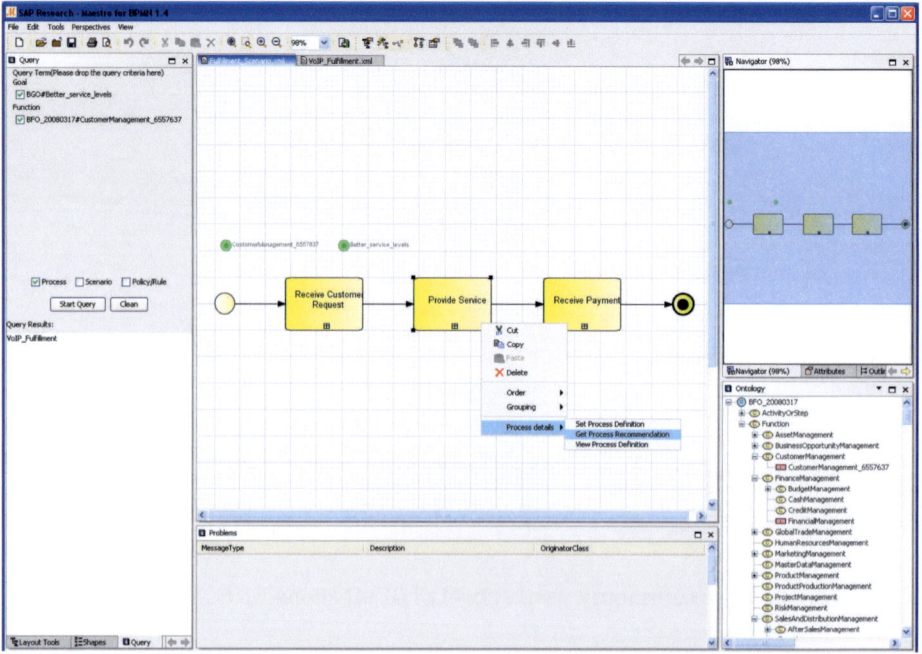

Figure 6.7: Scenario modeling and process recommendation

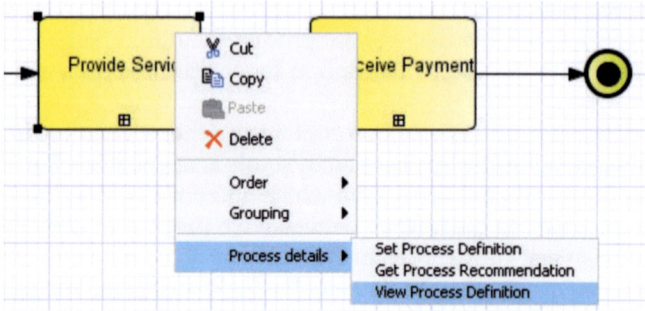

Figure 6.8: View Process Definition option

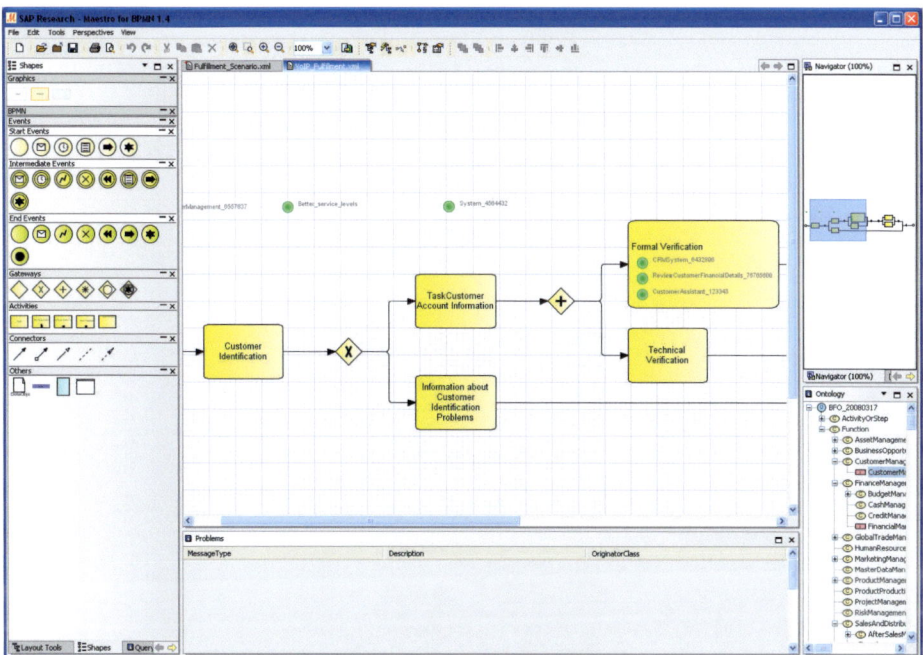

Figure 6.9: Business analyst view

6.6 Related Work

In [OSS94, LNO⁺89], the authors present INCOME approach for conceptual modeling of information systems. The approach uses Petri Nets [Pet62] as a uniform
specification framework for all design-relevant static and dynamic system aspects.
It includes a prototyping environment which allows for validation early in the system design process. When positioned in the context of this thesis, INCOME approach is placed between process levels 4 and 5 in Fig. 2.2, i.e. between the roles
of business analyst and process architect. It covers mainly the functional, resource
and behavioral perspective of processes, shown in Fig. 3.2. Compared to the IN-
COME approach, our SBP modeling framework abstracts from system-level aspects
and aims at providing modeling languages, methods and tools used earlier in the
system design process.

The approach in [AS06] presents matchmaking of Web services based on π-
calculus and description logics. The ontology is used for modeling input/output
data exchanged between service operations. In our case, we capture broader and
more high-level business knowledge in the ontology. Furthermore, with respect to
the behavioral process perspective, we are mainly interested in the soundness verification of process models. For this reason we needed to combine the *pi*-calculus
with the ECA approach in order to be able to represent the semantics of all workflow patterns. In contrast, the work in [AS06] does not consider the representation
of complex flow structures but rather focuses on service matchmaking and substitution mechanisms. In addition, the authors follow the DL knowledge representation

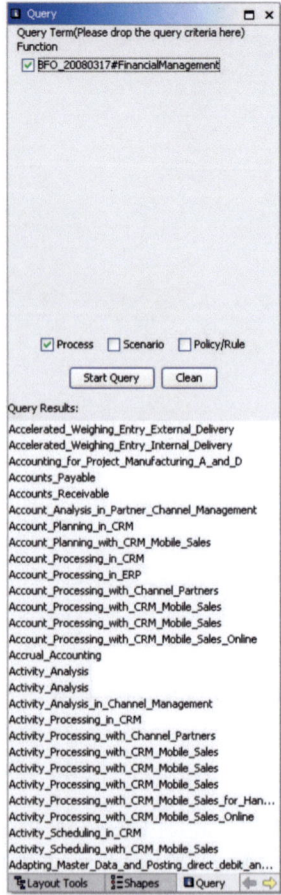

Figure 6.10: Process query view

paradigm (see Section 2.3.2) which is less suitable for querying large instance data sets (process descriptions) when compared to the LP paradigm used in our work.

Within the SUPER project, a Business Process Modeling Ontology (BPMO) is proposed for semantic representation of business processes. In the SBPM approach (see Section 2.4), the BPMO is supposed to model processes from the business perspective while ontologized BPEL [AAA+07] does so from the technical perspective. Since the main objective of SBPM approach is the automated mediation between the two perspectives, BPMO resulted in being a mere lightweight version of BPEL in order to enable the mapping between the two perspectives. Thus, it can be seen as rather an execution-level specification language than a business specification language. It fails to capture broad contextual business knowledge related to business processes. Furthermore, the BPMO does not allow for modeling behavioral semantics of processes which prevents the possibility of performing process soundness verification.

Related to this, the work in [Web09] presents an approach for supporting process modelers in designing execution-level business process models, using semantic technologies. The approach is based on describing the semantics of process activities in terms of their *change semantics*[9], i.e. annotating their pre- and postconditions. Such annotated process models are used to design two modeling techniques for the modeling support: task composition and verification. The verification of annotated process models here refers to checks such as i) are there any two activities executing in parallel that have conflicting effects, ii) are preconditions for all activities always satisfied and iii) can every activity in the process be reached [Web09]. This work thus focuses on providing modeling techniques for the execution-level business process models (in between levels 4 and 5 in Fig. 2.2) and can be seen as complementary to our work.

The significance of querying business processes has been acknowledged by BPMI[10] who launched a Business Process Query Language (BPQL) initiative [BPM]. However, no standard specification has been published yet.

In [BEKM06], the authors present a query language for querying business processes, BP-QL. The query language is designed based on the BPEL standard and thus focuses on querying executable processes. In addition, the language is graph-based and therefore only supports querying the process structure.

6.7 Conclusion

This chapter presents a modeling technique and tool for modeling and querying of business processes on a semantic level. After identifying a list of requirements, we start with discussing the modeling language to be used for semantic business process modeling. The syntax and semantics of this language is provided by means of the Business Process Ontology and for illustrating purposes we take the widely adopted BPMN as the modeling notation. Further, we present a modeling method which profits from a semantically rich process representation to provide the elements which introduce the benefits of its usage. Finally, we discuss the prototypical implementation of the modeling technique as an extension to the SAP Research modeling tool Maestro and contrast our contributions to the related efforts.

---

[9]This notion is well-known in the actions and change community within the field of artificial intelligence

[10]Business Process Management Initiative, http://www.bpmi.org/

Part III

Finale

Chapter 7

Evaluation

Evaluation of the quality of conceptual models, such as the ones presented in this thesis represents a challenge. This is due to the fact that there is no quality framework which is commonly accepted in practice, despite their proliferation in research literature, see e.g. [LSS94, BRvU00, VCM$^+$07]. Moody [Moo05] identifies several issues in the existing research on quality frameworks which led to this state: lack of testing and acceptance in practice, different levels of generality, lack of agreement on terminology, lack of evaluation procedures and improvement guidelines, etc. This is why conceptual modeling is still considered an art rather than an engineering discipline.

On the other hand, ensuring the quality of conceptual models is of high importance since the cost of errors increases exponentially over the system development lifecycle [Moo05]. Also, empirical studies show that more than half of the errors occurring during the system development are errors where requirements specifications do not match the actual user requirements [ER03].

In order to evaluate the quality of the proposed SBP modeling framework, we take a multi-viewpoint approach and perform the evaluation based on four different aspects. First, in Section 7.1 we compare the modeling framework to established and influential modeling approaches in the field based on several criteria. Second, in Section 7.2 we investigate the modeling content of one of the largest software providers to understand its conceptual model and map it to the process-oriented ontology framework for evaluating its representational completeness. We also test the performance and scalability of the process querying method using a large data set of business processes. In Section 7.3, we evaluate the applicability of the policy and rule modeling approach using two real-life business scenarios. Section 7.4 gives an overview of the application and impact of research results presented here within SAP projects. Finally, Section 7.5 concludes the chapter.

7.1 Comparison with Influential Modeling Approaches

Process-oriented modeling approaches in computer science received growing attention from the beginning of the 1990s onwards, strongly advocating to give up the purely functional structuring of enterprises in favor of a process-oriented view [HC93]. Some approaches to business process modeling using information systems even date back to the 1980s [Sch88]. Sections 3.2.2 and 3.2.3 motivated different viewpoints that business process modeling is concerned with. In this section we build upon these descriptions and define criteria for the comparison of common modeling approaches, both from academia and from industry.

7.1.1   Criteria

Section 3.2.2 gave an overview on information in process modeling and proposed six perspectives on knowledge involved in process modeling. As a first criterion, we are interested in comparing the parts of the knowledge related to processes that are covered by the various approaches. We refer to this criterion as *(1) process perspectives*. Section 3.2.3 introduced the notion of different *(2) levels of abstraction* bound to typical roles involved in process engineering. Therefore, we secondly investigate what viewpoints the approach supports. Thirdly we deal with what kind of models are produced. We refer to this as *(3) modeling business knowledge*. The last two criteria discuss the abilities of a framework to work with the captured knowledge. Under *(4) querying/reuse* we ask for what possibilities exist to retrieve the modeled information, while with *(5) analysis/inference* we tackle questions like: What can be deduced and is not explicitly modeled? What ways of detecting weaknesses are provided?

To date, there is no predominant modeling approach for neither enterprise modeling nor business process modeling. To give a brief survey on the abilities of today's modeling techniques, we selected the most influential approaches: ARIS [Sch88], BMM [OMG08a], i* [Yu95], TOVE enterprise ontology [Fox92]. By selecting a wide variety of approaches, we illustrate the broad spectrum that process-oriented enterprise modeling takes into account.

7.1.2   Comparative Description

i* framework

The i* framework originates from "early requirements" research and is used to understand organizational processes, in terms of strategic relationships and rationales in order to elicit the rationale (the "why") for software systems requirements (the "what"). Since i* is based on intentionality, the concept of an *actor*, i.e. any active entity, is central to the approach.

The core work for i* [Yu95] proposes two types of diagrams, capturing the strategic dependency relationships among actors (SD model) and the strategic rationale model for expressing the rationales behind dependencies (SR model). A dependency model is a graph stating which actor (*depender*) depends on which other actor by what element (*dependum*). The dependum could be either a goal, a task, a resource or a softgoal. A *strategic rationale model* focuses on the "inside" of one or more actors, i.e. their motivation. This takes into account that goals, plans and activities are intrinsic to actors. The framework defines a basic connection between goals and tasks, known as *means-end links*. There are a number of additional links, connecting so called *softgoals* (goals which have no clear cut criterion for their achievement) with other modeling elements, influencing the achievement of those goals. They can be supported ("help", "make") or hindered ("break", "hurt") more or less. A *task* can be decomposed into four types of elements: a subgoal, a subtask, a resource, and/or a softgoal. Using SD and SR models, i* provides two levels of granularity: The former focusing on the relation between actors, using dependency links and actor aggregations. The latter connects hard goals to tasks and softgoals to contributing entities, thereby capturing the agent's intentions and abilities.

i* has been extended by a number of research efforts, most notably the TROPOS project[1], proposing a software development methodology based on early requirements. A formal description for i* has been proposed by [FLM+04], using temporal logic and model checking for analysis purposes. By the means of a graphical modeling tool[2] interfacing a model checker, the methodology allows for *animation*, *consistency checks* (avoiding self-contradictory in the specification), *possibility checks* (avoiding over-specification) and *assertion checks* (avoiding under-specification). To check the satisfiability of i*-like goal models containing softgoals, [SGM04] apply label propagation techniques and a SAT solver.

The i* framework mainly captures information for the motivational perspective (cf. Fig. 3.2). Although the concept of goal and softgoals is rather detailed, there is no concept of strategy or functional decomposition. Resources and tasks stay on an abstract level. Since the notion of actors is fairly general, it provides no specific means for modeling organizational structures. The missing of important parts, such as policies/rules and performance indicators, underline that enterprise modeling is not the main goal of the i* approach. A number of tools, such as OME3[3] and openOME[4] amongst others, are provided by the i* community. None of the tools is capable of displaying only parts of the model, and could therefore be seen mainly as an aid for drawing models. Although tasks are important elements of SR modeling, there is no sequential connection between them (no notion of process).

BMM

The Business Motivation Model is an OMG standard accepted in 2006 [OMG08a]. While i* originates from the software requirements research, BMM has its roots in the business rules community.

OMG sees BMM as a blueprint for business planning which is neutral in respect to methodology. They provide, however, an exemplary progression through the model starting with the identification of influencers via the setup of directives governing the courses of action to the final assignment of organizational responsibilities. It is important to note that BMM is not a complete business model nor is it intended to be one, but should be supplemented by other standards such as BPMN and UML. Therefore, BMM deals mainly with the motivational perspective given in Fig. 3.2.

As a standardization organization, OMG does not provide any tooling itself, but encourages academia and industry to adopt the specification for individual tooling [OMG08a]. KnowGravity's[5] KnowEnterprise builds on an UML2 modeler framework and allows for integrated modeling of BMM compliant diagrams as well as business vocabulary, rules and BPMN diagrams. These tools mainly focus on implementing the specifications in terms of model visualization. Due to the lack of formality, there are no means for analysis or inference on BMM models so far.

---

[1]http://www.troposproject.org/
[2]http://www.dit.unitn.it/~ft
[3]http://www.cs.toronto.edu/km/ome/
[4]http://www.cs.toronto.edu/km/openome/
[5]http://www.knowgravity.com

Table 7.1: Comparison summary

	Process Perspectives	Abstraction Levels	Modeling of business knowledge	Querying / reuse	Analysis / inference
i* frame-work	motivational, organiza-tional, (resource)	coarse: actor dependen-cies, fine: actor's goals, tasks and resources	graphical models, formal	–	(soft)goal satisfiability, consistency checks, detecting over- and under-specification
BMM / KnowEn-terprise	motivational	–	graphical models	keyword search	–
TOVE	behavioral, functional, organiza-tional, resource, (motiva-tional)	–	non-graphical, formal models in first-order logic	formal, by the use of formulae	deduction capabilities model inherent
ARIS	behavioral, functional, organiza-tional, resource, compliance, (motiva-tional)	(executive), manager, analyst different granularity on functional, flow level. filters restrict modeling facilities	graphical models (VCD, eEPC, OrgCharts, ...)	report generation, query for model objects	–
SBPM frame-work	behavioral, functional, organiza-tional, resource, compliance, motivational	executive, manager, analyst	graphical models, formal	visual querying, formal	conflict detection, what-if analysis, gap analysis, process verification

TOVE

Parallel to the early days of BPM in the area of information systems [KNS92] and shortly after process orientation reached a wider audience in management [HC93], organizational modeling was approached from knowledge management communi-ties. One of the earliest efforts aiming at the development of an organizational on-tology is the TOVE initiative [Fox92]. Within TOVE, the authors aim at the creation of a shared representation of an enterprise, definition of semantics, development of a set of axioms in order to provide automatic deduction capabilities and finally at the definition of symbols depicting defined concepts. It is worth noticing that at least the early version of the ontology considered a typical functional paradigm of the business model. However, the ontology underwent a comprehensive evolution and the current versions focus on multidimensional enterprise modeling, and the ontology itself was converted into a set of tightly connected sub-ontologies (for details see [FG98]) describing many aspects and different aims (although preserving a non-specific perspective on the organization). Although the approach knows the concept of roles within the enterprise model, it does not provide different levels of abstraction for its usage.

The model of the enterprise created in this approach, namely Common Sense Model of Enterprise, distinguishes three levels: a reference model with typical business functions (finances, sales, distribution, and administration), i.e. the functional perspective; a generic model (with concepts such as time, causality, space, resources); and a concept model (e.g. role, property, structure), covering the organizational perspective. The behavioral perspective is formally described using a situation calculus. In later works of the authors, some additional aspects, such as quality related ones [KF94], aspects related to the organizations integration [FG94], costs (financial aspects) of actions and resources [TFG94], were identified. Due to underlying situation calculus [FG98], the models can answer some interesting competence questions, as for instance: when will a perishable resource spoil, given certain events or scenarios?; is it possible to prevent the spoilage?

The main impact of TOVE was the recognition of common problems for different models of enterprises and organizations as it was one of the first models at such large scale and with such advanced features. The main drawback of the TOVE initiative is the lack of a contemporary ontology language in which the proposed concepts are expressed. Although the authors give a rich axiomatization, tool support is another weak point.

ARIS

The ARIS (Architecture of Integrated Information Systems) approach is a mature, industry-adopted method for business process modeling. Central to the approach is the so-called *ARIS house*: It is an architecture for describing business processes [Sch99], provides modeling methods, builds the foundation for the toolset and acts within the ARIS house of business engineering (HOBE) as a computer-aided business process management lifecycle. The goal for the introduction of ARIS was to bridge the gap between business strategy, processes and information technology by supporting a holistic description of business concepts for the development of information systems.

To deal with complexity, the ARIS house describes different views on processes which are specialized on the levels of requirements definition, design definition and implementation definition within the mentioned lifecycle. We concentrate on the early process modeling only. Following [EW03] the views could be summarized as follows. *Organization view:* Who (e.g. organizations, departments, roles) is involved in the process? *Function view:* Which functions are carried out? *Data view:* Which objects represented by data are manipulated? *Output/Input view:* Which products or services are produced or consumed? *Control view:* How do the views mentioned before interoperate in a process?

The functional view deals with hierarchical decompositions of functions such as information-transforming or material-transforming functions. A connection between the former and goal decomposition diagrams is given in [Sch99]. The organizational view operates on organization charts. Links in these types of diagrams have no precise semantics, but can have several meanings such as *is technical superior to, is disciplinary superior to, is a component of.* The data view includes the description of data objects, manipulated by functions. Data objects can be modeled using Entity-Relationship-Diagrams. Product models, either as a decomposition of different types of product or as parts decomposition, are suggested in [Sch99] for the Output view.

Event-driven process chains (EPC) are the integrating notation linking the other views together within the control flow. EPCs consist of chains of events triggering activities, which in turn can result in an event, possibly split up for parallel or alternative execution. The initial notation was introduced in [KNS92] and later updated to extended EPCs (eEPC) by adding notation elements for *roles, objectives, technical terms, organizational units,* and others. So called *control points* are introduced to reflect compliance requirements and to associate appropriate activities ensuring compliance.

ARIS adopts Value Chain diagrams (VCD) [Por85] as a means of modeling high level processes. Porter's distinction between primary and supporting activities, however, centers on functional decomposition. Although VCD are used to capture functions which directly create corporate output and are essential for generating profit, neither value chain diagrams nor the extension of EPC with a model element for capturing business goals could be seen as modeling the entire motivational perspective (cf. Fig. 3.2). Tooling was initially tied to the ARIS house and later evolved to several platforms for various modeling tasks within BPM. The ARIS toolset was completed recently by an implementation for the Kaplan/Norton Balanced Scorecard approach making use of cause-and-effect diagrams as well as Key Performance Indicators [DB07].

The Designer tool helps modeling by filtering appropriate modeling elements for a selected model type. ARIS provides capabilities to generate reports from the process perspective, e.g. for usage in ISO 9000 compliance. Since all modeled elements are stored in a relational database the ARIS tools allow for querying for single or groups of model elements and their related objects. Simulation allows for analysis such as process cycle time and total process cost, as long as the required information is explicitly given as attributes in the model [DB07].

Notice in Table 7.1 that the ARIS method for business process modeling comes closest to our approach. Indeed, the SBP modeling framework presented in this thesis can to an extent be considered as "Semantic ARIS".

7.2   Enabling SBP Modeling with Solution Composer

SAP Business Maps comprise the business content provided by the SAP Solution Composer. The Solution Composer is a modeling tool for creating and browsing business related diagrams. These diagrams focus on multileveled process components and related business artifacts depicting how a business may create value for their customers and how the different software components provided by SAP and its partners may support these processes [SAP05a].

In conjunction, the Solution Composer and the Business Maps strive for the goal to allow different stakeholders to "work from the same page" [SAP05a]. The role of Business Maps here is to help shaping a common conceptualization of the domain SAP provides its solutions for. They provide communication means bringing together SAP prospects, customers, partners, sales and service representatives, product managers, marketers, and solution developers. By imposing a structure on the vast universe of SAP products they bridge the gap between the breadth of SAP's solution offering and the specific understanding of the different stakeholders' business contexts. By their multileveled composition the Business Maps provide a homogeneous, high level entry point to further, more detailed information reducing the perception of an option overflow.

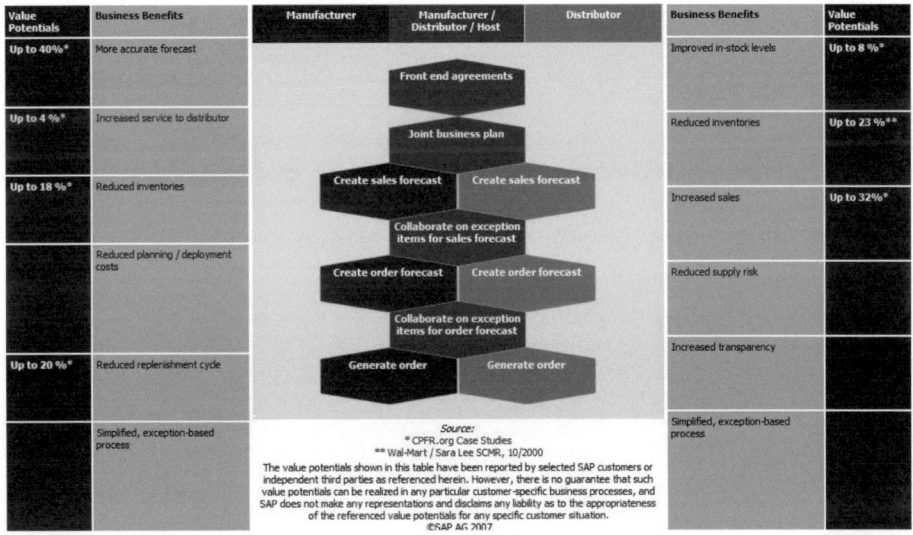

Figure 7.1: SAP Business Scenario Map - Collaborative Planning, Forecasting and Replenishment

There are two kinds of Business Maps delivered with the Solution Composer, each providing a different perspective on a company's business [SAP07]. First, SAP provides a detailed view of end-to-end business processes illustrated in the so called Business Scenario Maps (see Fig. 7.1). They are a graphical representation of key business scenarios - both industry specific and cross-industry. In addition to the process steps and process flow, participating roles and business partners as well as quantifiable business benefits, are illustrated in Fig. 7.1.

The second kind of Business Maps is called Solution Maps. Business diagrams of this type may be further subdivided into Industry Solution Maps (see Fig. 7.2) and Application Maps (see Fig. 7.3). Both provide a multileveled composition of business processes supporting the structured scoping of IT requirements [SAP05b]. They aid the realization of a customer specific information technology solution by

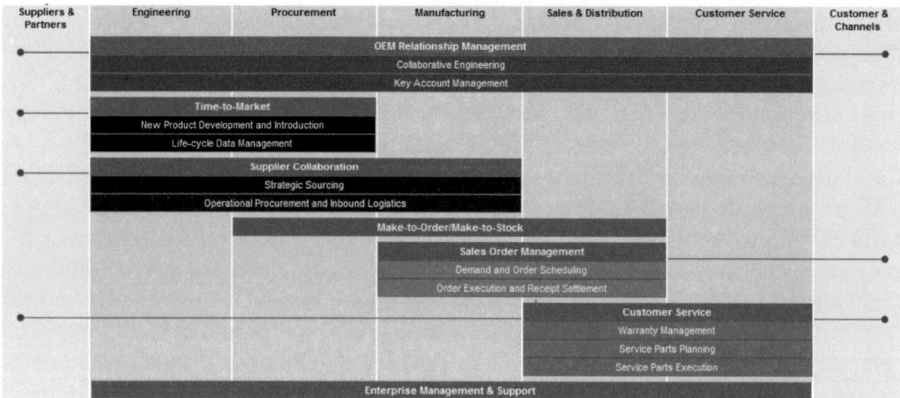

Figure 7.2: SAP Industry Solution Map - Automotive-Supplier

providing means of planning and illustrating customer needs in a coherent and integrated manner [SAP07]. At this, Industry Solution Maps structure the processes supported by SAP or partner products along a generic industry specific value chain of a typical enterprise and subdivide them into scenario groups and business scenarios. In contrast, Application Maps provide a multi-level blueprint of cross-industry processes categorized by process categories and main processes [SAP05a].

Demand & Supply Planning	Demand Planning & Forecasting	Safety Stock Planning	Supply Network Planning	Distribution Planning	Supply Network Collaboration
Service Parts Planning	Parts Demand Planning	Parts Inventory Planning	Parts Supply Planning	Parts Distribution Planning	Parts Monitoring
Procurement	Strategic Sourcing		Purchase Oder Processing		Invoicing
Manufacturing	Production Planning & Detailed Scheduling			Manufacturing Operations	
Warehousing	Inbound Processing & Receipt Confirmation	Outbound Processing	Cross Docking	Warehousing & Storage	Physical Inventory
Order Fulfillment	Sales Order Processing				Billing
Transportation	Transportation Planning		Transportation Execution		Freight Costing
SC Design & Analytics	Strategic Supply Chain Design			Supply Chain Analytics	

Figure 7.3: SAP Application Map - mySAP Supply Chain Management

In addition to the mere structuring of SAP supported business processes further information is annotated to the maps. For instance, the diagrams depict business documents transferred in a process. Key performance indicators, business objectives, and partner opportunities are visualized within the maps. Furthermore, details on technical implementation variants of supported processes are given.

In addition to the distinction between Business Scenario Maps, Industry Solution Maps, and Application Maps the Solution Composer's content is also classified according to its industry relation. At the top level the maps are grouped as Industry-Specific Business Maps, Cross-Industry Business Maps, and Infrastructure and Service Maps. All of the former kind are assigned to industries which themselves are grouped under industry sectors. For instance, the industry-specific Industry Solution Map "Wholesale Distribution" is assigned to the "Wholesale Distribution" industry which is part of the "Trading Industries" industry sector. Cross-Industry Business Maps are assigned to a one or two-leveled hierarchy of business segments. For example, the cross-industry Application Map 'mySAP Supply Chain Management is assigned to the top level business segment "Supply Chain Management" whereas the cross-industry Business Scenario Map "Inbound Logistics" is annotated to the "Supply Chain Coordination" business segment which is a sub segment of the former mentioned. There are merely three Infrastructure and Service Maps which are sub elements of the "Technology" business segment.

To understand the Business Maps' suitability for providing the basis for our evaluation, it is important to know about their evolutionary history. They do not provide a knowledge base SAP once developed out of the box but the outcome of an iterative process of adoptions and alignments in which many different parties have been involved over time. Aside from its rich navigation capabilities on the existing Business Maps, the Solution Composer provides easy to use creating and editing functionalities in the first place [SAP05b]. The tool's design focusing a high degree of usability and a set of diverse export options motivate the tool's extensive application in operative implementation and development projects of SAP products. The architecture of the Solution Composer and the underlying content repository affords a good degree of flexibility rather than imposing a nonelastic, dogmatic structure on the Business Maps. Focus is put on acquiring a rich and comprehensive knowledge repository rather than providing well structured but outdated information which is not updated frequently due to usability deficiencies. As a result of SAP's predominant market share and more than 35 years of experience, the available Business Maps offer a representative snapshot of the concepts and terminology perceived and applied in every-day business.

7.2.1 Conceptualization of Business Maps

In order to better understand the business knowledge captured in Business Maps, we have thoroughly analyzed and conceptualized the content delivered with SAP Solution Composer. Several sources provided input to the conceptualization of Business Maps. On the one hand, information material on the Solution Composer gave a rough overview of the major concepts and their intended meanings [SAP05a, SAP05b, SAP07]. On the other hand, and even more important, the Business Maps as such were analyzed on an instance level. Due to the flexibility that the Solution Composer offers in terms of editing options often merely a close look at the delivered Business Maps clarified the meaning of a concept and its relations. As almost all map elements may be interrelated with each other, only analyzing the delivered instances revealed which interconnections were regarded as meaningful by the map creators and thus have to be integrated into a "shared understanding" of the domain of discourse. Thus, this has to be understood as a conceptualization of the Business Maps in their current state. By virtue of the evolutionary process of map refinement further releases of the Business Maps may contain concepts and relations which are not considered in the conceptualization presented in the following.

The analysis of the Business Map content was conducted both on the basis of the graphical representations offered by the Solution Composer and on the basis of the structure of the flat XML files as which the maps are stored and exchanged. The latter was rather handy since technologies like XSLT[6] and XPath[7] allow for a comprehensive examination of several instance facets which the Solution Composer does not support in such detail. The evaluated set of Business Maps contains 410 maps in total: 339 Business Scenario Maps, 53 Industry Solution Maps, and 18 Application Maps. 152 Business Scenario Maps are classified industry-specific, 115 maps of this kind are assigned to the cross-industry Business Map branch, and 2 Business Scenario Maps have been considered being both. 74 Business Scenario Maps are neither linked to an industry nor to a business segment. There are 53 industry-specific Solution Maps, 13 cross-industry Solution Maps, and 3 Solution Maps which may be found under the Infrastructure and Service Map branch.

For illustrating the conceptualizations, graphical models of the included concepts (ovals) and relations (directed arrows) are presented. For the sake of clarity the graphical models do not illustrate the set of attributes defined for the concepts. Also, most of the relations between two concepts shown in the models have a corresponding counterpart relation running in the opposite direction, but they are not depicted.

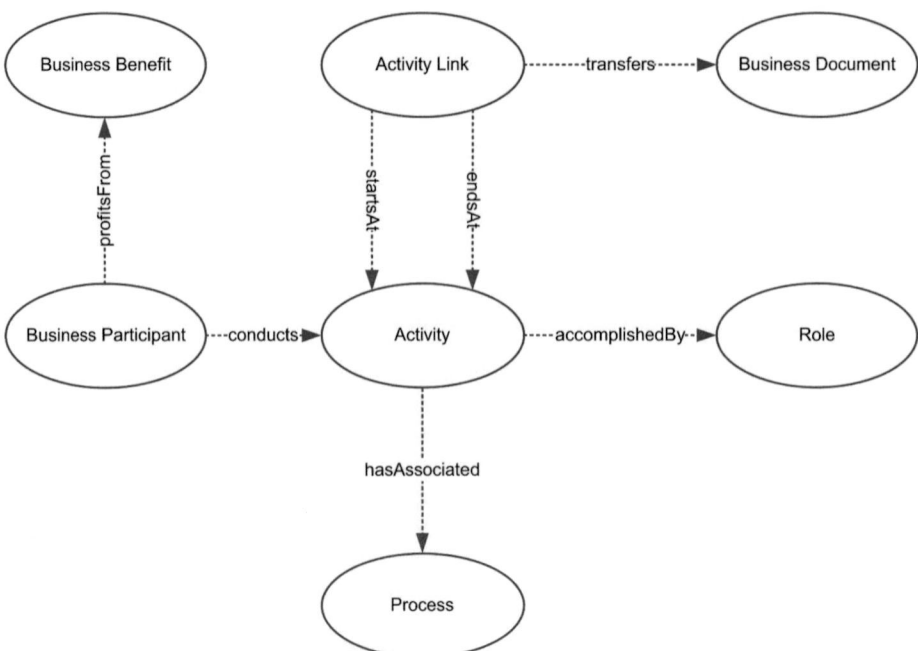

Figure 7.4: Business Map Conceptualization – Business Scenario Map

---

[6]http://www.w3.org/TR/xslt
[7]http://www.w3.org/TR/xpath

Business scenario maps constitute containers for detailed end-to-end business processes (see Fig. 7.4). The process flow between the process activities mostly transcends a mere sequential ordering and thus has to be represented by so called *activity links*. Furthermore, *business documents* are transferred in the course of a business *process* and *roles* accomplishing the activities are specified within the maps. Every *activity* is assigned to exactly one *business participant*. The implementation of the processes specified in the business scenario maps comes along with some *business benefits* (see Fig. 7.4). These are either specific for an individual business participant or hold for the entire business scenario map. As business scenario maps are not the only representation of business processes within the Business Maps in some occasions a link to a process specified in a solution map indicates a semantic equivalence between two map elements.

The main purpose of the Solution Maps is the provision of a framework structuring the business processes supported by SAP or partner products to foster the scoping of customers' IT requirements. The first subtype of solution maps is the application map clustering processes to form *main processes* and *process categories* (see Fig. 7.5). These groupings are not specific to an industry, but refer to generic cross-industry functions like customer relationship management, supplier relationship management, supply chain management, or product lifecycle management. In addition to a *business area* and a responsible *organizational unit* annotated to a *process*, the application maps may also list so called *configuration variants* (see Fig. 7.5). These concepts represent technical implementation variants of a process as they are offered by the SAP *products*. *Process steps* further detail such technical implementations by naming a set of activities conducted for a specific configuration variant. In contrast to the processes defined in business scenario maps, process steps may not be linked differently from a sequential list.

Industry solution maps constitute the second subtype of solution maps (in the following see Fig. 7.6). Similar to application maps they provide a – mostly – two level grouping of processes called *business scenario groups* and *business scenarios*. In some occasions there may be a nested sequence of business scenario groups. In contrast to the application maps, here the different process classes are structured along an industry-specific *value chain*. These value chains comprise a set of *value chain elements* and run from a *supplier* to a *customer*. Every business scenario group spans one or more of these value chain elements and so do its subordinated business scenario groups and business scenarios. The *processes* specified within the industry solution maps have the same structure as explicated for the application maps. The processes are measured by associated *KPIs* and are supposed to achieve a certain *business objective*.

7.2.2 Representational Completeness of the SBP Modeling Framework

Based on the presented conceptualization of Business Maps, we provide a comparison to the modeling concepts available in the SBP modeling framework presented in Part II of this thesis. Table 7.2 contains the Business Maps conceptualizations as depicted in Figs. 7.4, 7.5, 7.6 in the first column[8]. The following three columns stand

---

[8]The concept *process* which appears in all three types of maps is considered once

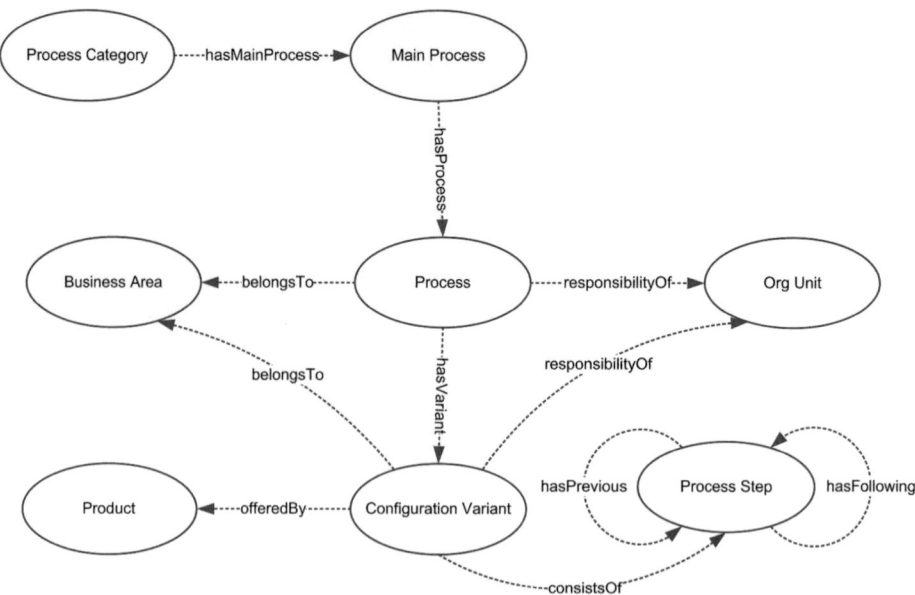

Figure 7.5: Business Map Conceptualization – Application Map

for the concepts defined in the BMO, BPO and BPRO ontology, respectively. The next column represents the concepts defined in the remaining ontologies defined within the process-oriented enterprise ontology framework, and finally in the last column are COBRA modeling concepts.

We can see from the table that out of 23 modeling concepts only the *business benefit*[9] concept is not supported by our modeling framework. Furthermore, 13 modeling concepts are mapped to the BMO, BPO and BPRO ontologies which are discussed in detail in this thesis. *Business document* and *product* map to the concepts defined in the Business Resources Ontology, whereas *process category* and *business area* concepts map to the *business function* concept defined in the Business Functions Ontology (see Section 3.3). The mapping helped to notice this redundancy in the Business Maps conceptualization, resulting in keeping only the *business area* concept. *Collaboration partner*, *supplier* and *consumer* are subcategories of the *business role* concept defined in the Business Roles Ontology. Another redundancy was discovered by mapping the *business participant* and *role* concepts to the COBRA *role* concept, resulting in keeping the latter.

7.2.3   Creating a Semantic Business Process Repository

The modeling content of the Solution Composer comprises a business process repository (BPR)[10] provided by SAP. This repository contains over 1500 real life business process models which capture customer best practices as a result of more than 35

---

[9]This concept stems from the notion of value which is not considered in the modeling framework
[10]https://implementationcontent.sap.com/bpr

Table 7.2: Representational completeness

Business Map Concept	BMO	BPO	BPRO	Other Framework Ontologies	COBRA
Business Benefit	–	–	–	–	–
Business Participant	–	–	–	–	x
Activity	x	–	–	–	–
Activity Link	–	x	–	–	–
Process	–	x	–	–	–
Business Document	–	–	–	x	–
Role	–	–	–	–	x
Process Category	–	–	–	x	–
Main Process	x	–	–	–	–
Business Area	–	–	–	x	–
Org Unit	x	–	–	–	–
Product	–	–	–	x	–
Configuration Variant	–	x	–	–	–
Process Step	–	x	–	–	–
Business Scenario Group	x	–	–	–	–
Business Scenario	–	x	–	–	–
KPI	x	–	–	–	–
Business Objective	x	–	–	–	–
Value Chain	x	–	–	–	–
Value Chain Element	x	–	–	–	–
Collaboration Partner	–	–	–	x	–
Supplier	–	–	–	x	–
Consumer	–	–	–	x	–

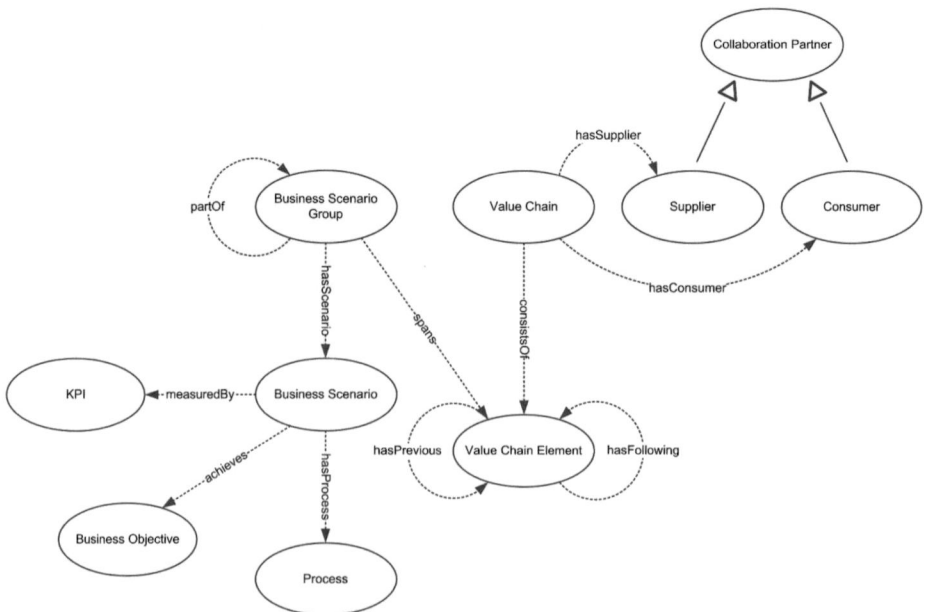

Figure 7.6: Business Map Conceptualization – Industry Solution Map

years of experience in the design and customization of processes within 25 different industries.

In Fig. 7.7, an example business scenario *Customs Management for Export* from BPR is depicted. The scenario comprises three business processes, namely *product classification, transit procedure outbound* and *customs processing export*. By selecting any of the processes we can see its corresponding process steps. Fig. 7.7 also shows the business goals and objectives (upper left) as well as KPIs (upper right) assigned for the scenario. All information about the business scenario is stored as an XML file in the BPR repository.

In order to extract this content and make it available in the representation which is required for the use in the SBP modeling framework, we have written several XSLT transformations. The transformations take the original Solution Composer (SC) XML representation and translate it into the format understandable as input for the Semantic Maestro4BPMN modeling tool (see Section 6.5), which then stores the input in the WSML-Flight representation language. Using XSLT transformations, we were able to convert the entire modeling content (more than 1500 processes) together with their metadata to the representation format used within the SBP modeling framework. By doing so we were also able to extract 278 business goals and objectives and 652 predefined KPIs which can be reused in business motivation modeling. The business goals and KPIs collected from the SC content are modeled as concepts rather than instances in the application ontologies. The rationale for this modeling decision is that a goal from SC does not have values assigned to each of its parameters and thus can be parameterized. Furthermore, this allows

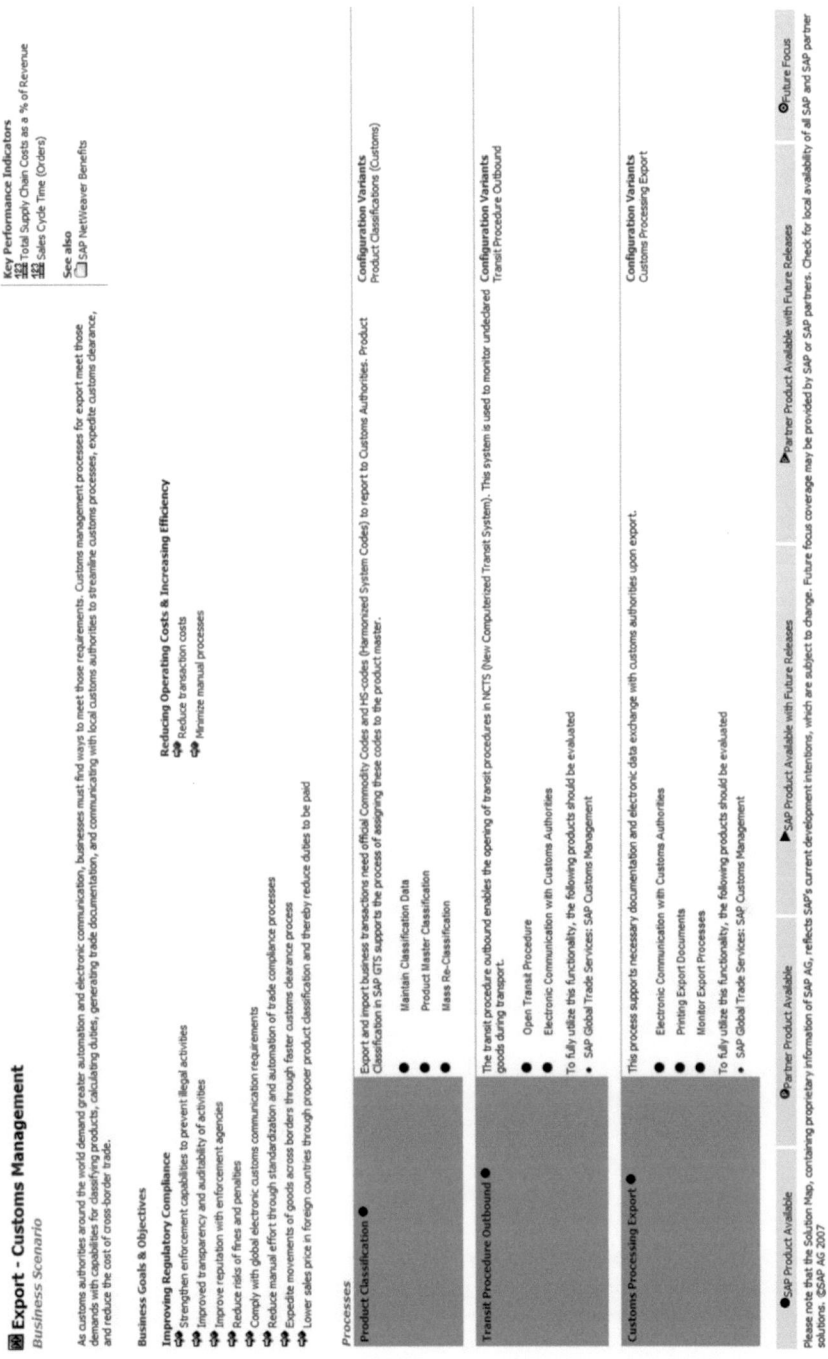

Figure 7.7: Example Business Scenario – Customs Management for Export

for reuse of their definitions when defining similar, but distinct, company-specific goals.

7.2.4   Performance Experiments

The automated extraction of the SC content created a large set of data for testing the applicability, but also the performance and scalability of the proposed modeling methods. In the following, we provide results of the performance experiments for querying business processes using the Semantic Maestro4BPMN modeling tool. The experiments were performed on a Fujitsu Siemens laptop with a Genuine Intel CPU T2400 @ 1.83GHz and 2GB RAM (OS: MS Windows XP). They intend to demonstrate how well the querying method performs when querying large sets of data and how well it scales.

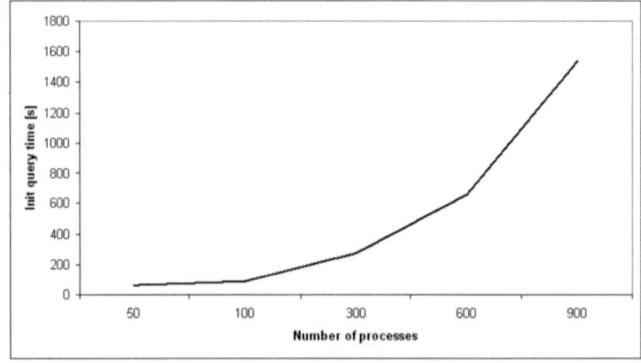

Figure 7.8: Performance of registering processes to the reasoner

Fig. 7.8 shows the performance experiments for registering different number of process descriptions into the reasoner (knowledge base). This procedure has very low performance and thus it must not be initialized often. On the other hand, the performance of performing the queries scales well even for bigger data sets, i.e. over 1000 processes (see Fig. 7.9). We have done two series of experiments here, first without ranking and after with ranking of query results. However, as it can be seen from Fig. 7.9, this has only minor influence on the response time. Similar results are obtained for varying the number of query arguments and their type – required or optional in queries, i.e. this parameter also has no significant influence on query performance.

Under the assumption that the modeling repository will not be updated very frequently, the whole process repository can be loaded at the startup of the model-ing tool. This makes the tool startup time considerably longer, but in turn enables that all querying tasks are evaluated very fast, regardless of the number of query arguments and ranking, as the results in Fig. 7.9 show. The process repository can be re-registered to the reasoner after a certain time in order to consider the newly added models when evaluating the queries.

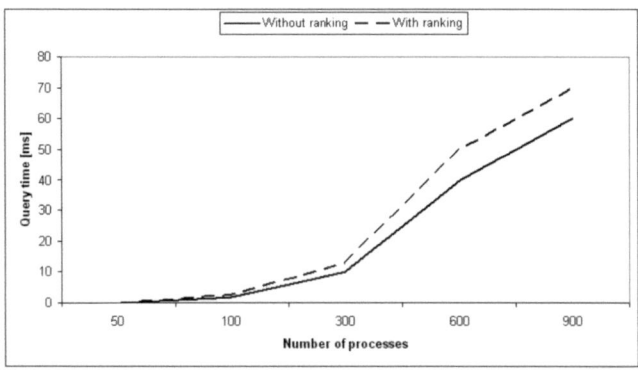

Figure 7.9: Performance of querying processes w/ and w/o ranking

7.3 Maestro4BPR Evaluation Scenarios

In this section, we demonstrate the applicability of the business policy modeling and verification approach presented in Chapter 5. The Maestro4BPR prototypes discussed in Section 5.4 are evaluated using two different business scenarios. Both evaluation scenarios are real-world scenarios provided by the use case partners of the SUPER project and existing SAP products, respectively.

The remainder of this section is structured as follows. For both scenarios, first the scenario context is given along with its business process model. Then, we show how the scenario-relevant business policies and rules are modeled using our approach. Finally, we illustrate how the formalized business rules are used for policy-based process verification in a given scenario.

7.3.1 Access Control

Our first evaluation scenario is part of a broader telecom convergent offer - the Quad-Play offering [FKRS08] - developed by Telekomunikacja Polska S.A. (TP)[11], one of the use case partners of the SUPER project. Quad-Play is defined as a bundled offering that provides customers with four different service lines: voice over IP (VoIP), IP-based television (IPTV), video on-demand (VoD), and mobile voice and data services [FKRS08].

Here, we focus on the VoIP part of the Quad-Play bundle and in particular on the business process concerning VoIP order fulfillment [FKK+08]. We present the business process using the BPMN modeling notation in Fig. 7.10, and provide a short process description in the following.

The process starts with customer identification using the PIN code. After a successful customer authentication, the customer account information is collected and both formal and technical verification of customer account data is performed (see Fig. 7.10). The technical verification checks the infrastructure required for the VoIP service and the already subscribed services. If the customer is not already subscribed to a digital line or DSL services, she is not able to get the VoIP service.

---

[11]http://www.tp.pl/

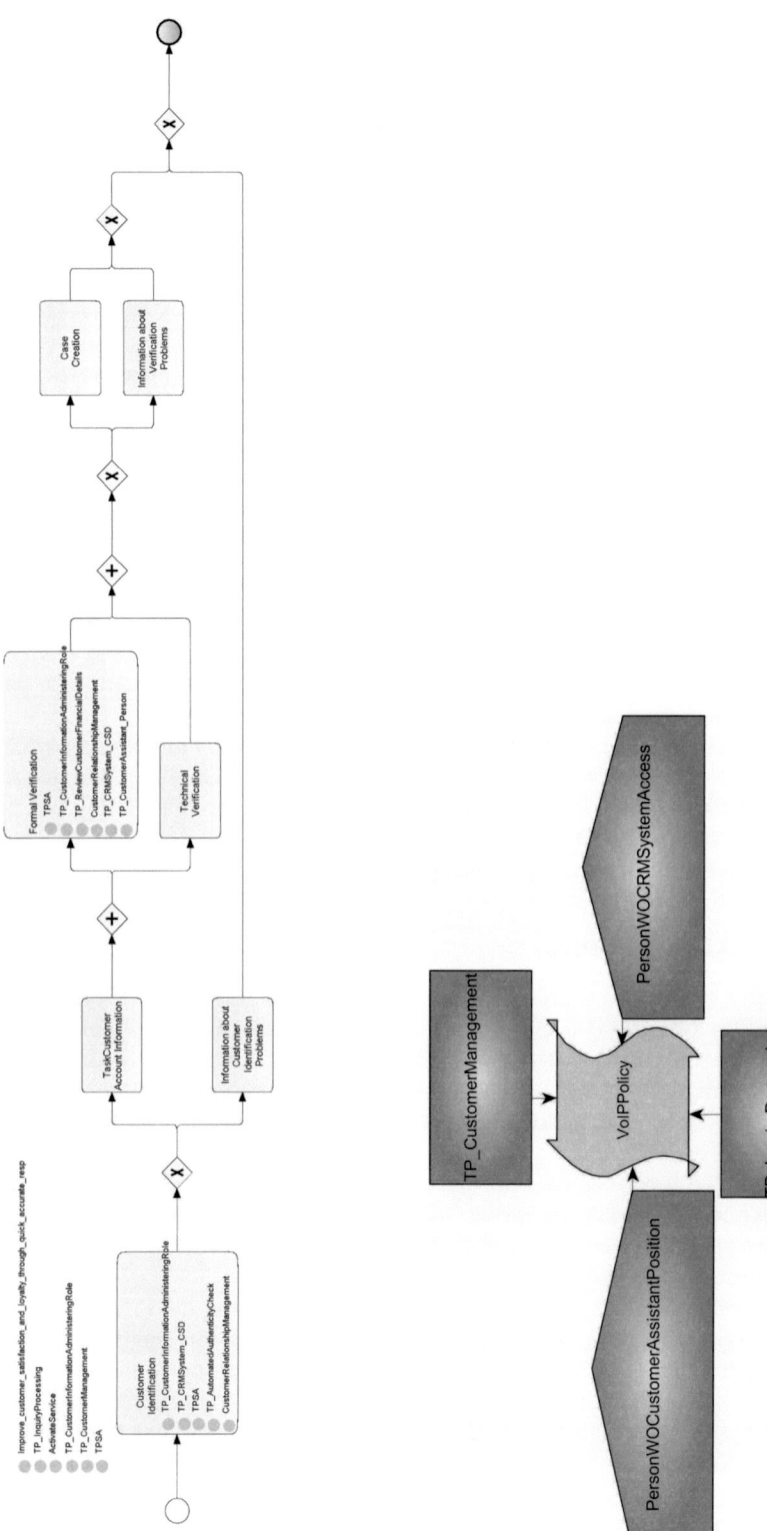

Figure 7.10: VoIP Order Fulfillment Business Process

Figure 7.11: VoIP Business Policy

The formal verification checks whether a customer has paid all previously issued invoices, which requires access to the customer financial data. The successful technical and formal verification follows with the case creation in the CRM system and lets the Back Office Agent to proceed with the sale and establishing a service agreement with the customer. If customer authentication or verification process fails, the information on related problems is generated and passed to the customer.

The semantic annotations of process elements using the domain- and scenario-specific application ontologies are indicated with small circles in Fig. 7.10. The application and domain ontologies extend our process-oriented enterprise ontology framework (see Section 3.3). The instances of the scenario-specific TP ontology are marked with the prefix "TP_", e.g. TP_TPSA, where *TPSA* instance denotes the name of the organizational unit within the company responsible for the process. An example of a domain-specific annotation is the *ActivateService* instance (see Fig. 7.10), defined in the telco domain-specific YATOSP [YAT07] ontology, which denotes that the process belongs to the service activation business domain. These two annotations characterize the whole process, meaning they are automatically transferred for each activity in the overall process. Single process steps can be additionally annotated with more specific metadata, as shown in Fig. 7.10.

We now focus on the formal verification process step, for which we define a business policy and its implementing business rules. As this activity requires access to the customers' financial information, it is annotated with the CRM system of the customer service department (*TP_CRMSystem_CSD*) which stores the financial details of the customers. For security and privacy issues, only an agent assigned to the customer assistant position (annotation *TP_CustomerAssistant_Person*) in the organization and with access to the specific CRM system is allowed to view the financial details of the customers. Fig. 7.11 shows the business policy used to ensure that the VoIP order fulfillment process meets the regulatory requirements. The VoIP policy is implemented by two business rules, namely *PersonWOCRMSystemAccess* and *PersonWOCustomerAssistantPosition*. Apart from these two business rules, in Fig. 7.11 we see contextual annotations *TP_CustomerManagement* and *TP_InquiryProcessing* which indicate that the policy is applicable for the customer management business function, in particular for the inquiry processing activity. This information is used by the *Policy Matchmaker* component (see Section 5.3.3) for finding applicable business policies.

The *PersonWOCRMSystemAccess* business rule ensures that the assigned person has access to the required CRM System. Fig. 7.12 shows the visual as well as the formal representation of the business rule. The rule captures the violating scenario which occurs when the person reviewing the financial details of a customer does not have access to the CRM system used in the reviewing process. In other words, by reading the visual model in Fig. 7.12, the violation happens when: any instance of a *Process*, which belongs to *ReviewCustomerFinancialDetails* set of activities and uses any *CRMSystem* as resource, has a performing *Person* assigned which does not have access to the resource[12].

Fig. 7.13 shows the visual and the formal representation of the *PersonWOCustomerAssistantPosition* business rule. It ensures that the person assigned to the task

---

[12]Note that the instance of the concept *Process* can represent either a complete process model or an individual activity of the complete process (see BPO in Section 6.4.2). In this case, it would match any process or activity which is annotated by the instance of the *ReviewCustomerFinancialDetails* concept.

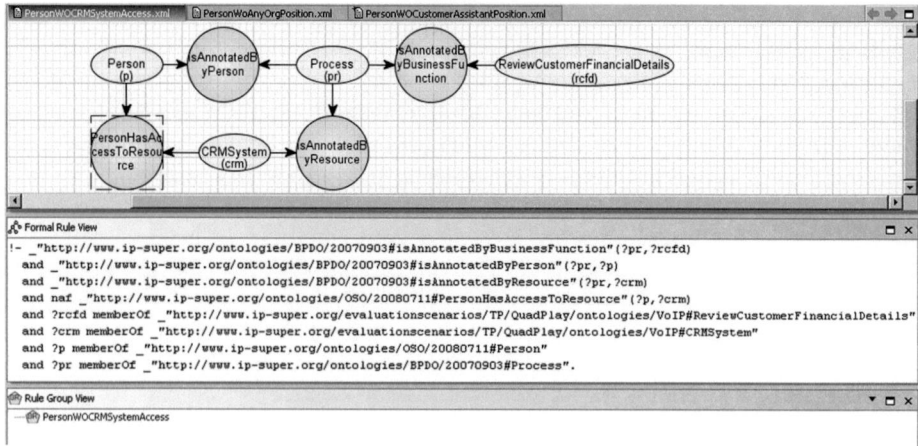

Figure 7.12: *PersonWOCRMSystemAccess* rule depicting the violation scenario

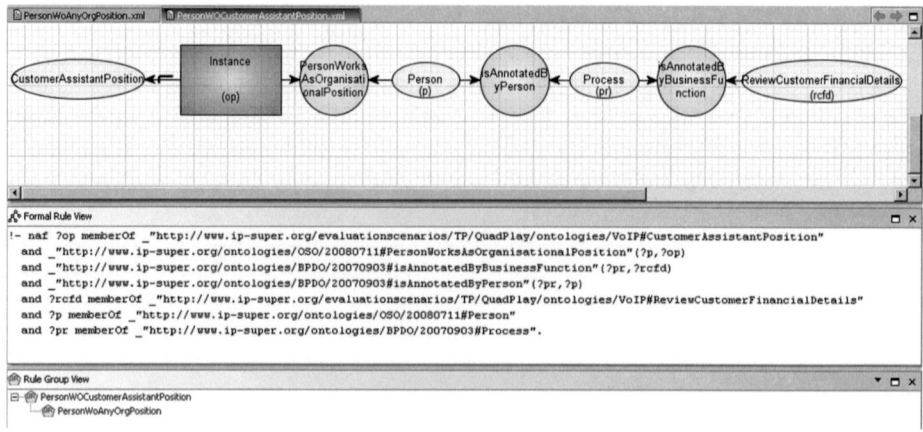

Figure 7.13: *PersonWoCustomerAssistantPosition* rule depicting the violation scenario

occupies a customer assistant position in the organizational structure. This business rule has a related rule which checks if the assigned person is associated with an organizational position within the organizational structure (see Fig. 7.14).

During policy-based process verification, both business rules are loaded into the knowledge base and a consistency check is performed. As both rules model the violation scenario as a constraint, their evaluation to true indicates the presence of a violation scenario in the business process model. The modeler is informed about the verification result through the feedback view and is able to take corresponding action.

In the next section, we present the application of our approach within a separation of duty business scenario in the banking sector.

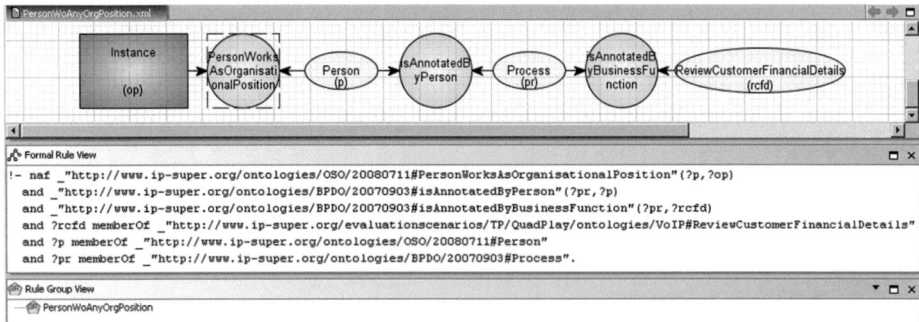

Figure 7.14: *PersonWoOrgPosition* rule depicting the violation scenario

7.3.2 Separation of Duty (SoD)

This scenario is based on the SAP Banking solution obtained from the Banking Business Maps in SAP Solution Composer (see Section 7.2). In particular, we consider a typical loan origination business process which we describe in the following.

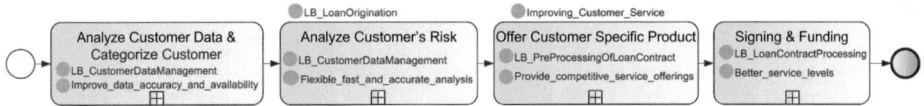

Figure 7.15: Loan Origination Business Process

The loan origination process consists of four main subprocesses, namely: customer data analysis, customer risk analysis, customer product offering, and loan contract signing and funding (see Fig. 7.15). The process is annotated with a *LB_LoanOrigination* business function, where "LB" denotes the instances defined in the scenario-specific application ontology. In addition, the process is annotated with a business goal *Improving_Customer_Service* from the generic Business Motivation Ontology (see Section 3.3). Each of the subprocesses are further annotated with their corresponding business activity types and goals, respectively (see Fig. 7.15).

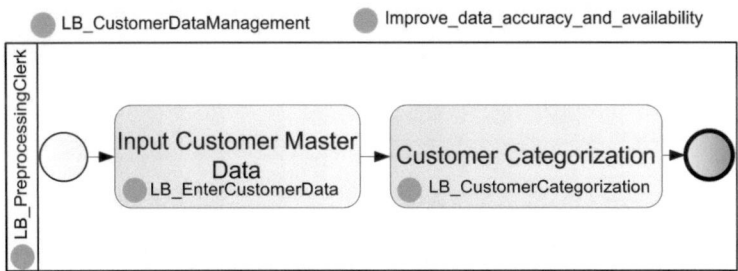

Figure 7.16: Analyze Customer Data & Categorize Customer Subprocess

All subprocesses in Fig. 7.15 have a more detailed process definition attached. For example, the *Analyze Customer Data & Customer Categorization* subprocess involves maintaining customer's master data and categorizing it into various customer segments (see Fig. 7.16). A bank usually maintains this data for the purpose of internal customer rating. Maintaining and categorizing customer data is performed by the employee role *pre-processing clerk* (see Fig. 7.16).

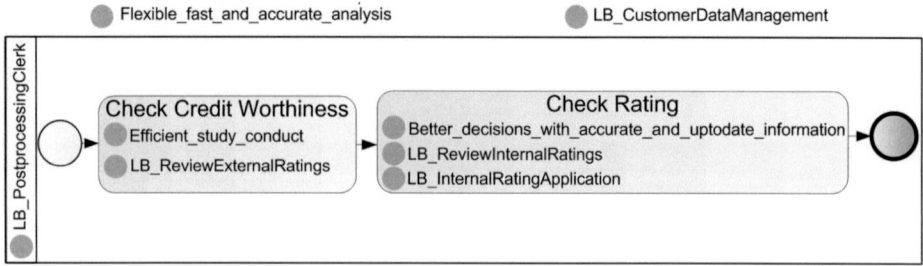

Figure 7.17: Analyze Customer's Risk Subprocess

The *Analyze Customer's Risk* subprocess (see Fig. 7.17) involves obtaining several external and internal ratings in order to check the credit worthiness of a customer (e.g. assets and liabilities of a customer). The analysis of a customer's risk is performed by a *post-processing clerk* (see Fig. 7.17).

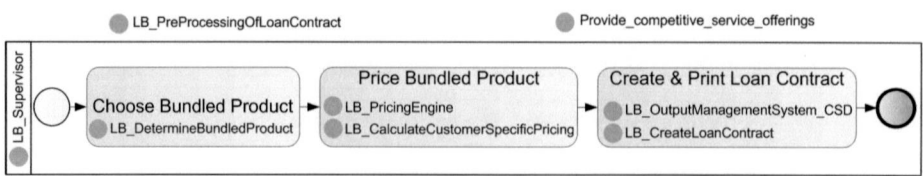

Figure 7.18: Offer Customer Specific Product Subprocess

In the *Offer Customer Specific Product* subprocess (see Fig. 7.18), the *supervisor* role decides which product should be offered to the customer based on the risk involved, and also determines the product price/interest rate and other conditions. Finally, a loan contract to be signed by the customer is created and printed.

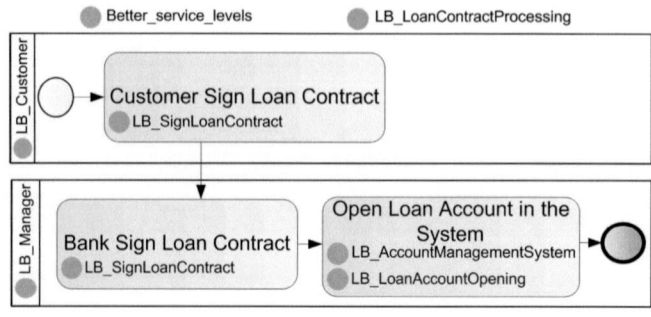

Figure 7.19: Signing & Funding Subprocess

The last step in the overall process, the *Signing & Funding* subprocess (see Fig. 7.19), involves signing of the contract by the customer and the bank management representative. Finally, the account management system is updated with the new customer account.

The loan origination business process involves three sets of mutually exclusive roles where separation of duty (SoD) needs to be ensured in order to prevent fraud. The first set of mutually exclusive roles involves the pre- and post-processing clerk roles. If a single employee is assigned to both of these roles, one could potentially introduce a known person as a customer seeking loan from the bank and provide a good rating, thereby increasing her chances of getting a loan. The second set of mutually exclusive roles is between the post-processing clerk and supervisor roles. This is to ensure that the activities *Check Rating* and *Choose Bundled Product* are performed by a different person, in order to avoid that a product is provided to a customer by manipulation of its ratings even though the customer has high associated risks. The third set of mutually exclusive roles is between the supervisor and manager roles. This is to avoid any inappropriate pricing of loans being approved.

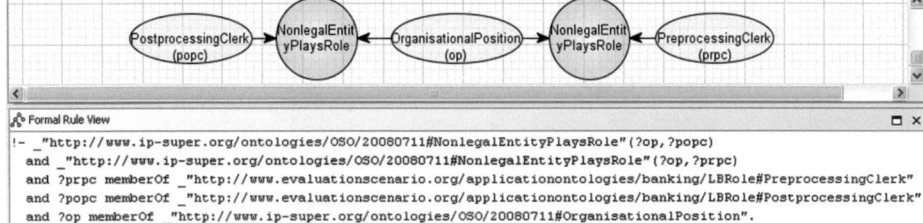

Figure 7.20: Business rule depicting the SoD violation scenario

Fig. 7.20 shows the visual and formal representation of a business rule for the first set of mutually exclusive roles. The rule models the violation scenario where an organizational position is assigned to both, pre- and post-processing clerk roles. Rules for other two sets of mutually exclusive roles can be formulated in a similar manner.

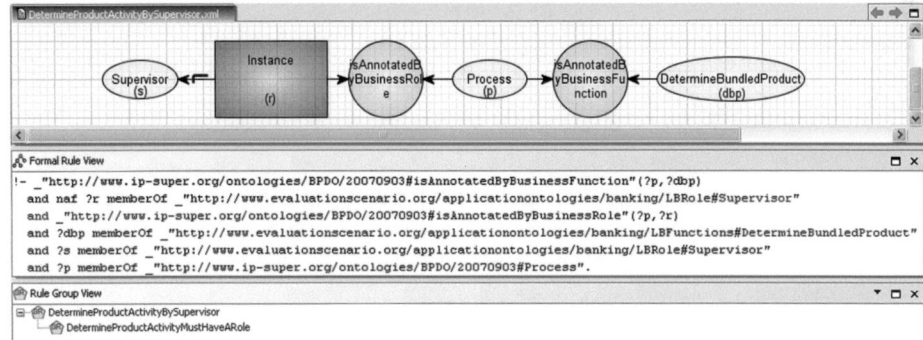

Figure 7.21: Business rule for checking if supervisor role is assigned to *Choose Bundled Product* activity

Business rules can also be formulated for checking if the right employee role is assigned to a particular activity. Fig. 7.21 shows the visual and formal representation of a business rule modeling the violation scenario when the *Choose Bundled*

Product activity is not assigned to the supervisor role. This business rule has a related rule which is executed for checking if any role is assigned to the *Choose Bundled Product* activity (see Fig. 7.22). Similarly, business rules can be formulated for checking other combinations of process activities and roles.

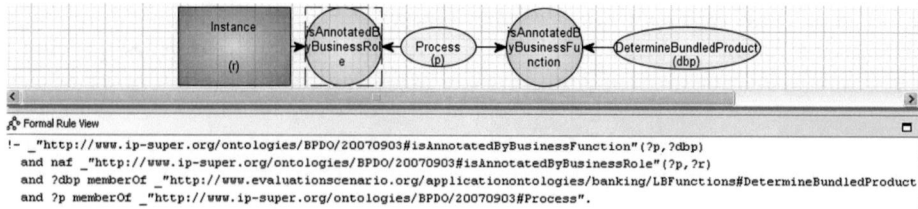

Figure 7.22: Business rule for checking if any role is assigned to *Choose Bundled Product* activity

    The aforementioned business rules can be combined to form one or more business policies and their application context can be defined similar to the previous scenario for use by the *Policy Matchmaker*. During the verification process, the constraints expressed in these business rules are verified by the inferencing engine and the outcome of the verification process is presented to the users through the feedback view.

    Another important aspect that this scenario illustrates is the support for different process perspectives and abstraction levels. If the verification is performed on the detailed subprocess level (e.g. Fig. 7.17), the rules corresponding to this level only are verified. However, the verification can also be performed on a process at a higher abstraction level (see Fig. 7.15). In this case, the system gets the attached detailed subprocess level via the formal definition of the `contains` relation in the BPO (see Section 6.4.2) together with all annotations, and performs the full verification. Hence, the verification can also be performed on a business process model involving multiple modeling abstraction levels. In addition, this scenario illustrates that business rules can be modeled for other perspectives of the enterprise model, in this case the organizational perspective (see Fig. 7.20).

7.3.3 Summary

In this section, we have demonstrated the applicability of our approach in two real-world scenarios used by the use case partners of the SUPER project and in SAP solutions. The focus of interest is the representational expressiveness of the business policy and rule modeling languages as well as support for process verification. In the VoIP order fulfillment scenario, we demonstrate how business rules can be formulated for access control policies to check whether an agent performing a task has access to the resource required by the task. This scenario also shows that business rules can be formulated not only for business process models but also for other parts of the enterprise model such as the organizational structure. The loan origination scenario illustrates the fact that our approach is applicable for scenarios which involve multiple process models and models on different abstraction levels. It also presents how business process models can be verified against SoD policies, which are widely used in the security domain.

The chosen evaluation scenarios focus on security-related business policies as they are most widely prevalent and cover most of the requirements from other areas. It is important to note that our approach and its implemented solution are not restricted to the security domain only.

7.4   Impact

The results of the work presented in this thesis have been used in several projects carried out within SAP aiming at creating impact on different products. In the following, we briefly introduce the projects and discuss our contribution therein.

- *Modeling@SAP* is a long term program aiming at consolidation of the modeling languages, methods and tools used for business process modeling at different levels of abstraction (cf. Fig. 2.2). Examples of modeling languages used at different modeling levels at SAP include: SAP Solution Maps and Collaborative Business Scenarios [SAP07], EPC [KNS92], BPMN [Obj09], BPEL [BPE], UML [Obj07]. Examples of modeling tools used at different levels include: SAP Solution Composer [SAP05a], SAP Solution Manager [SAP09a], SAP Process Composer [SAP], ARIS enterprise modeling applications [DB07]. The key goals of this program are the provision of i) a comprehensive common metamodel which integrates the concepts used at different modeling levels and ii) a modeling methodology which unifies existing modeling methods.

  The results of this thesis contributed to several workstreams within this program. First, we have delivered a report documenting the findings regarding refinement of modeling abstraction levels, process knowledge in models and process perspectives presented in Chapter 3. Second, the results regarding the analysis of the SAP Solution Composer content presented in Section 7.2 have been provided in order to consolidate and improve quality of the existing modeling content. Finally, the features of modeling tools discussed in Sections 4.5, 5.4, 6.5 were used to specify functional and non-functional requirements for the extensions of the productized SAP modeling tools.

- *SAP Strategy Management* [SAP09b] is a new offering in SAP product portfolio which aims at improving the alignment and communication of corporate strategy at both departmental and corporate level. Following the acquisition of the Business Objects company, new opportunities arose for extending the solution to a complete enterprise performance management suite by integrating it to the business intelligence product portfolio of Business Objects.

  As part of the effort in this project, our business motivation modeling language and method (cf. Section 4.4) were delivered in order to bring innovations into the core SAP Strategy Management product functionality. Currently the product features follow closely the Balanced Scorecard approach to strategy implementation [KN96]. In addition, the Business Motivation Ontology (see Fig. 4.3) is intended to be used for facilitating the metamodel integration efforts within the project.

- Implementation of all concepts in the SAP Research Maestro modeling framework was done to prove the feasibility of the approach. In addition, the entire modeling content of SAP Solution Composer has been seamlessly integrated into the SBP modeling framework knowledge base as shown in Section 7.2.3. The last point indicates an issue that has been seen as crucial for the adoption of semantic technologies in business process modeling – compatibility and reuse of existing modeling content.

7.5   Chapter Conclusions

In this chapter, we have evaluated the SBP modeling framework presented in Part II of this thesis from different aspects. Based on the framework foundations presented in Chapter 3, we define a set of criteria and perform a comparative analysis of several influential modeling approaches. The ARIS method comes as the closest to our approach with the core advantages provided through semantic specification and analysis of models in our framework. In Section 7.2, we analyze and conceptualize the rich modeling content provided by SAP Solution Composer in order to validate the representational completeness of the framework. It is shown that over 95% of the Business Maps concepts can be modeled using our framework. We use this fact to automatically extract the existing SC modeling content and make it a part of the framework knowledge base. Profiting from the large repository of semantically described models, we evaluate the performance and scalability of the process querying method on over 1000 process models. The registration of the big amount of ontologies to the reasoner is identified as a bottleneck in querying, however a solution is proposed which provides balance between the desired fast query evaluation and frequent updates from the repository. The third aspect of our evaluation is concerned with the policy and rule modeling approach, where we demonstrate its applicability within two real-life business scenarios. Finally, we show how we created impact by using the results presented in this thesis in several projects carried out at SAP.

Chapter 8

Conclusions and Outlook

This chapter summarizes the contributions and main results of this thesis in Section 8.1. Section 8.2 identifies topics for further research.

8.1 Summary of Contributions

This thesis presents a business process modeling framework based on semantic technologies. The framework consists of modeling languages, methods and tools which aim at facilitating the creation and the improvement of the quality of business process models. We summarize the main contributions of the modeling framework in the following.

In order to provide the framework foundations, we start with a quest on understanding the notion of a conceptual business process model in Chapter 3. Here we analyze a large repository of process models provided by SAP Solution Composer in order to categorize the business knowledge usually captured in models. Further, we approach the knowledge categorization from two viewpoints and identify six process modeling perspectives and three abstraction levels in conceptual process modeling. Based on this categorization, we contribute a *process-oriented enterprise ontology framework* which provides means for formal representation of all identified process perspectives while supporting all modeling abstraction levels. The ontology framework specifies the structure of eight core ontologies which allow for modeling all relevant aspects of business processes in a domain- and application-independent way. It was applied in guiding the design of domain-dependent and application ontologies used for describing several real-world business scenarios in the telco domain.

The introduction of semantic technologies in business process modeling requires certain methodological extensions to the existing process modeling methodologies. For the purpose of providing guidance and directing how SBP modeling framework should be used in process modeling, we contribute the *semantic business process modeling methodology* in Section 3.4. The SBPM methodology is presented in the form of a lifecycle, defining the activities, artifacts and tools involved in semantic business process modeling. Two main points are illustrated in all lifecycle activities: i) how ontologies allow for a unified formal modeling method on different levels of processes and ii) what further advantages does the formal representation of different aspects of processes bring when contrasted to already existing process descriptions.

To this end, we discuss the ontologies used within and the methods supporting each of the activities.

In Chapter 4 we contribute the first part of the SBP modeling framework – a modeling language, method and tool for business motivation modeling. Syntax and semantics for the business motivation modeling language are provided through the Business Motivation Ontology. The motivation modeling method allows for strategic analysis, querying, conflict checks on business motivation models as well as ontology-driven design support in motivation modeling. The COBRA ontology was used as an ontological foundation in designing the BMO, providing the basis for main ontological distinctions. We instantiate the business motivation modeling technique through a prototypical implementation of the Maestro4BM modeling tool, based on the SAP Research Maestro modeling framework.

Chapter 5 contributes the second part of the SBP modeling framework – a modeling language, method and tool for business policies and rules modeling. The Business Policies and Rules Ontology provides the syntax and semantics for the business policy modeling language, while the formal business rule modeling language is based on the metamodel of WSML-Flight. The business policy and rule modeling method allows for visual (yet formal) specification of policies and rules, context-based policy matchmaking and verification of policies and rules against business processes. Prototypical implementations of the Maestro4BP and Maestro4BR modeling tools instantiate the business policy and rule modeling techniques.

The third part of the SBP modeling framework – a modeling language, method and tool for business process modeling is presented in Chapter 6. The Business Process Ontology as a metamodel of the π-calculus provides syntax and semantics for the business process modeling language. The modeling notation in this case is not specifically designed, rather a popular BPMN notation has been reused. Business process modeling method comprises formal specification of business processes, their semantic annotation, formal process query specification and querying mechanism. We instantiate the semantic business process modeling technique through a prototypical implementation of the Maestro4BPMN modeling tool.

Finally, we evaluated the SBP modeling framework from different aspects. First, we define a set of criteria and perform a comparative analysis against several influential modeling approaches. The ARIS method comes as the closest to our approach with the core advantages provided through semantic specification and analysis of models in our framework. Second, we use the conceptualization of SAP Business Maps in order to perform validation of the representational completeness of our framework. It is shown that over 95% of the Business Maps concepts can be modeled using our framework. In addition, we evaluate the performance and scalability of the process querying method on over 1000 extracted process models from practice. The third aspect of the evaluation is concerned with the business policy and rule modeling technique, where we demonstrate its applicability within two different real-world business scenarios. Finally, we discuss the impact created by using the results presented in this thesis in several projects carried out at SAP.

8.2   Outlook

In this section, we outline three streams of research that may be addressed based on the results presented in this thesis.

8.2.1   Extending the SBP Modeling Framework

In Section 3.3 we have described the ontologies constituting the process-oriented enterprise ontology framework. Within the scope of this thesis, we have presented the usage of BMO, BPRO and BPO ontologies in formal modeling of motivational, compliance and behavioral perspective of processes (see Fig. 3.2). Further investigation needs to be done to learn how the formal modeling of organizational, resource and functional perspective[1] can contribute to easier design and higher quality of business process models. In particular, more effort needs to be invested in creating appropriate modeling notations, methods and tools for supporting these process perspectives, based on the respective ontologies. For example, our work in [BFKM08] describes initial results regarding the application of the Business Functions Ontology in business process modeling. The BFO provides means for modeling the functional perspective of processes (see Fig. 3.2) and [BFKM08] presents how BFO concepts may be used for consistent naming of process activities and suggesting appropriate resources in process modeling, which leads to more readable, consistent and higher quality process models.

The provisioning of such additional modeling languages, methods and tools would complete the vision of the SBP modeling framework described in Chapter 3.

8.2.2   Ontology-based Evaluation of OMG Business Modeling Standards

The Object Management Group (OMG) has been working towards a set of specifications for business modeling. At the time of writing this thesis, several of these specifications have become standards, namely: SBVR [Obj08], BMM [OMG08a], BPMM [OMG08b], and BPMN [Obj09][2]. Other specifications such as Organization Structure Metamodel (OSM) and Production Rule Representation (PRR) are still under development.

In Chapter 4, we have demonstrated how an ontological analysis of standards (in this case BMM) can sharpen the intended meaning of modeling concepts and thus improve the quality of the conceptual model by mapping the concepts to the basic ontological distinctions. Such ontologically-backed analysis gives insight into the strengths and limitations of a particular standard, and therefore can provide valuable feedback to the authors, implementers, and users of the given standard.

8.2.3   From Conceptual Models to Running Systems

Service Oriented Architecture (SOA) has received significant popularity in the development of BPM systems [SH06]. It is defined as an architectural principle where

---

[1]Using OSO, BRO, BFO ontologies from Fig. 3.5, respectively

[2]Currently version 2.0 of the standard is under discussion at OMG. It includes extensions regarding the choreography modeling, BPMN formal semantics and metamodel schema

discrete functionalities are packaged into a modular and reusable service that can be consumed in a loosely coupled manner. In an SOA-based BPM, business processes are decoupled from a concrete application using explicit, executable business process models. Based on such models, the available services are orchestrated in order to implement the process activities. This orchestration usually occurs manually which requires significant time and effort on the developers side [GF07]. Using semantic technologies, the operations of discovery, composition and mediation [SGA07, FKZ08] of Web services can be automated and hence the overall process implementation effort may be reduced [Kar07]. In order to enable the automation of these operations, our process-oriented enterprise ontology framework needs to be complemented[3] with ontologies that provide means for the formal modeling of execution-level process knowledge. In addition, appropriate modeling methods and tools need to be provided for modeling of execution-level processes.

---

[3]We have reported our initial investigations in this direction in [MK07, WMD08].

Part IV

Appendix

Appendix A

List of Publications

Journal papers:

- Ivan Markovic, Sukesh Jain, Mahmoud El-Gayyar and Armin B. Cremers. Modeling and Enforcement of Business Policies and Rules in Semantic Business Process Modeling. Communications of Systemics and Informatics World Network (CoSIWN) Journal, 2009.

- Ingo Weber, Ivan Markovic, Christian Drumm. A Conceptual Framework for Semantic Business Process Configuration. Journal of Information Science and Technology, Vol. 5, pages 3–20, 2008.

Conference papers:

- Ivan Markovic, Florian Hasibether. Towards Integrating Perspectives and Abstraction Levels in Business Process Modeling. Proceedings of the 11th International Conference on Enterprise Information Systems (ICEIS), Vol. 3, pages 286–291, 2009.

- Carlos Pedrinaci, Ivan Markovic, Florian Hasibether, John Domingue. Strategy-driven Business Process Analysis. Proceedings of the 12th International Conference on Business Information Systems (BIS), pages 169–180, 2009.

- Agata Filipowska, Monika Kaczmarek, Martin Hepp, Ivan Markovic. Organisational Ontology Framework for Semantic Business Process Management. Proceedings of the 12th International Conference on Business Information Systems (BIS), pages 1–12, 2009.

- Ivan Markovic, Sukesh Jain, Mahmoud El-Gayyar and Armin B. Cremers. Modeling and Enforcement of Business Policies and Rules in Semantic Business Process Modeling. Proceedings of 3rd International Conference on Adaptive Business Information Systems (ABIS), 2009.

- Ivan Markovic, Florian Hasibether, Sukesh Jain, Nenad Stojanovic. Process-oriented Semantic Business Modeling. Proceedings of the 9th International Conference on Business Informatics (Wirtschaftsinformatik), Vol. 1, pages 683–694, 2009.

- Matthias Born, Agata Filipowska, Monika Kaczmarek, Ivan Markovic. Business Functions Ontology and its Application in Semantic Business Process

Modeling. Proceedings of the 19th Australasian Conference on Information Systems, 2008.

- Ivan Markovic, Marek Kowalkiewicz. Linking Business Goals to Process Models in Semantic Business Process Modeling. Proceedings of the 12th IEEE International Conference on Enterprise Computing (EDOC), pages 332–338, 2008.

- David de Francisco, Ivan Markovic, Javier Martinez, Henar Munoz, Noelia Perez. Methodological Extensions for Semantic Business Process Modeling. Proceedings of the 10th International Conference on Enterprise Information Systems (ICEIS), Vol. 2, pages 410–415, 2008.

- Patrik Spiess, Dinh Khoa Nguyen, Ingo Weber, Ivan Markovic, and Michael Beigl. Modelling, Simulation, and Performance Analysis of Business Processes Involving Ubiquitous Systems. Proceedings of the 20th International Conference on Advanced Information Systems Engineering (CAiSE), pages 579–582, 2008.

- Ivan Markovic. Advanced Querying and Reasoning on Business Process Models. Proceedings of the 11th International Conference on Business Information Systems (BIS), pages 189–200, 2008.

- Ivan Markovic, Alessandro Costa Pereira, Nenad Stojanovic. A Framework for Querying in Business Process Modeling. In Proceedings of the Multikonferenz Wirtschaftsinformatik (MKWI), 2008.

- Ingo Weber, Ivan Markovic, Christian Drumm. A Conceptual Framework for Composition in Business Process Management. Proceedings of the 10th International Conference on Business Information Systems (BIS), pages 54–66, 2007.

Workshop papers:

- Agata Filipowska, Monika Kaczmarek, Marek Kowalkiewicz, Ivan Markovic, Xuan Zhou. Organizational Ontologies to Support Semantic Business Process Management. Proceedings of the 4th International Workshop on Semantic Business Process Management (SBPM), 2009.

- Matthias Born, Christian Brelage, Ivan Markovic, Daniel Pfeiffer, Ingo Weber. Auto-completion for Executable Business Process Models. Proceedings of the Business Process Management Workshops, pages 510–515, 2008.

- Marwane El Kharbili, Ivan Markovic, Sebastian Stein, Elke Pulvermueller. Towards Policy-Powered Semantic Enterprise Compliance Management. 3rd International Workshop on Semantic Business Process Management (SBPM), 2008.

- Marwane El Kharbili, Sebastian Stein, Ivan Markovic, Elke Pulvermueller. Towards a Framework for Semantic Business Process Compliance Management. Proceedings of the 1st International Workshop on Governance, Risk and Compliance - Applications in Information Systems (GRCIS), 2008.

- Ivan Markovic, Mario Karrenbrock. Semantic Web Service Discovery for Business Process Models. Proceedings of the Web Information Systems Engineering Workshops, pages 272-283, 2007.

- Ivan Markovic, Alessandro Costa Pereira, David de Francisco, Henar Munoz. Querying in Business Process Modeling. Proceedings of the International Conference on Service Oriented Computing Workshops, pages 234–245, 2007.

- Ivan Markovic, Alessandro Costa Pereira. Towards a Formal Framework for Reuse in Business Process Modeling. Proceedings of the Business Process Management Workshops, pages 484–495, 2007.

Demo papers:

- Ivan Markovic, Sukesh Jain, Mahmoud El-Gayyar, Armin B. Cremers, and Nenad Stojanovic. Modeling and Enforcement of Business Policies on Process Models with Maestro. Proceedings of the Demo Session at the 6th European Semantic Web Conference (ESWC), pages 873–877, 2009.

- Matthias Born, Joerg Hofmann, Tomasz Kaczmarek, Marek Kowalkiewicz, Ivan Markovic, James Scicluna, Ingo Weber, and Xuan Zhou. Semantic Annotation and Composition of Business Processes with Maestro for BPMN. Proceedings of the Demo Session at the 5th European Semantic Web Conference (ESWC), pages 772–776, 2008.

- Matthias Born, Joerg Hofmann, Tomasz Kaczmarek, Marek Kowalkiewicz, Ivan Markovic, James Scicluna, Ingo Weber, and Xuan Zhou. Supporting Execution-Level Business Process Modeling with Semantic Technologies. Proceedings of the Demo Session at the 14th International Conference on Database Systems for Advanced Applications (DASFAA), pages 759–763, 2009.

Popular publications:

- Matthias Born, Christian Drumm, Ivan Markovic, Ingo Weber SUPER - Raising Business Process Management Back to the Business Level, ERCIM News Vol. 70 Special Theme on Service-Oriented Computing, 2007.

Appendix B

Business Motivation Ontology

ontology BMO

    importsOntology _"http://www.ip−super.org/ontologies/COBRA/20080921#COBRA"

/* Acting entities */

concept OrganizationalUnit **subConceptOf** cobra#Agent
    nonFunctionalProperties
        dc#description **hasValue** "An Organizational Unit is in charge of defining ends,
            determining strategies and is responsible for business Activities ."
    endNonFunctionalProperties
    hasName **ofType** (0 1) _string
    hasDescription **ofType** (0 1) _string

relation definesEnd(**ofType** OrganizationUnit, **ofType** End)

relation EndDefinedBy(**ofType** End, **ofType** OrganizationUnit)

axiom OrganizationUnitEndAxiom
    definedBy
    definesEnd(?x,?y) :− EndDefinedBy(?y,?x) **and** ?x **memberOf** OrganizationUnit **and** ?y
        memberOf End.
    EndDefinedBy(?y,?x) :− definesEnd(?x,?y) **and** ?x **memberOf** End **and** ?y **memberOf**
        OrganizationUnit.

relation establishes(**ofType** OrganizationUnit, **ofType** Means)

relation establishedBy(**ofType** Means, **ofType** OrganizationUnit)

axiom OrganizationUnitMeansAxiom
    definedBy
    establishes(?x,?y) :− EndDefinedBy(?y,?x) **and** ?x **memberOf** OrganizationUnit **and** ?y
        memberOf Means.
    EndDefinedBy(?y,?x) :− establishes(?x,?y) **and** ?x **memberOf** Means **and** ?y **memberOf**
        OrganizationUnit.

relation determines(**ofType** OrganizationUnit, **ofType** Strategy)

relation determinedBy(**ofType** Strategy, **ofType** OrganizationUnit)

axiom OrganizationUnitStrategyAxiom

definedBy
determines(?x,?y) :− determinedBy(?y,?x) **and** ?x **memberOf** OrganizationUnit **and** ?y **memberOf** Strategy.
determinedBy(?y,?x) :− determines(?x,?y) **and** ?x **memberOf** Strategy **and** ?y **memberOf** OrganizationUnit.

relation responsibleFor(**ofType** OrganizationUnit, **ofType** Activity)

relation responsibilityOf (**ofType** Activity , **ofType** OrganizationUnit)

axiom OrganizationUnitActivityAxiom
definedBy
responsibleFor(?x,?y) :− responsibilityOf (?y,?x) **and** ?x **memberOf** OrganizationUnit **and** ?y **memberOf** Activity.
responsibilityOf (?y,?x) :− responsibleFor(?x,?y) **and** ?x **memberOf** Activity **and** ?y **memberOf** OrganizationUnit.

relation makes(**ofType** OrganizationUnit, **ofType** Assessment)

relation madeBy(**ofType** Assessment, **ofType** OrganizationUnit)

axiom OrganizationUnitAssessmentAxiom
definedBy
makes(?x,?y) :− madeBy(?y,?x) **and** ?x **memberOf** OrganizationUnit **and** ?y **memberOf** Assessment.
madeBy(?y,?x) :− makes(?x,?y) **and** ?x **memberOf** Assessment **and** ?y **memberOf** OrganizationUnit.

/* Ends */

concept End **subConceptOf** cobra#NonAgentiveNonPhysicalEntity
nonFunctionalProperties
dc#description **hasValue** "Ends are about what an enterprise wants to be. The definitionb of an end does not say how it will be achieved."
endNonFunctionalProperties
hasName **ofType** (0 1) _string
hasDescription **ofType** (0 1) _string

relation judgedIn(**ofType** End, **ofType** Assessment)

relation onAchievementOf (**ofType** Assessment, **ofType** End)

axiom EndAssessmentAxiom
definedBy
judgedIn(?x,?y) :− onAchievementOf(?y,?x) **and** ?x **memberOf** End **and** ?y **memberOf** Assessment.
onAchievementOf(?y,?x) :− judgedIn(?x,?y) **and** ?x **memberOf** Assessment **and** ?y **memberOf** End.

concept DesiredResult **subConceptOf** End
nonFunctionalProperties
dc#description **hasValue** "A desired result is either a less specific goal or a more specific objective . "
endNonFunctionalProperties
hasStatus **ofType** (0 1) DesiredResultAssessmentStatus

concept Vision **subConceptOf** End
nonFunctionalProperties

dc#description **hasValue** "A vision is an overall image of what the organization wants to be or become."
endNonFunctionalProperties

relation madeOperativeBy(**ofType** Vision, **ofType** Mission)

relation makesOperative(**ofType** Mission, **ofType** Vision)

axiom VisionMissionAxiom
    definedBy
    madeOperativeBy(?x,?y) :— makesOperative(?y,?x) **and** ?x **memberOf** Vision **and** ?y **memberOf** Mission.
    makesOperative(?y,?x) :— madeOperativeBy(?x,?y) **and** ?x **memberOf** Vision **and** ?y **memberOf** Mission.

concept Goal **subConceptOf** DesiredResult
    nonFunctionalProperties
        dc#description **hasValue** "A goal is something a business wants to achieve."
    endNonFunctionalProperties
    isSatisfied **ofType** (0 1) _boolean
    hasPriority **ofType** _integer
    hasEvidence **ofType** _integer
    hasDeadline **ofType** _date
    satisfaction **ofType** (0 1) Label
    denial **ofType** (0 1) Label

relation hasMetric (**ofType** Goal, **ofType** Metric)

relation measures (**ofType** Metric, **ofType** Goal)

axiom GoalMetricAxiom
    definedBy
    hasMetric(?x,?y) :— measuredBy(?y,?x) **and** ?x **memberOf** Goal **and** ?y **memberOf** Metric
    .
    measuredBy(?y,?x) :— hasMetric(?x,?y) **and** ?x **memberOf** Metric **and** ?y **memberOf** Goal
    .

relation amplifies (**ofType** Goal, **ofType** Vision)

relation amplifiedBy (**ofType** Vision, **ofType** Goal)

axiom GoalVisionAxiom
    definedBy
    amplifies(?x,?y) :— amplifiedBy(?y,?x) **and** ?x **memberOf** Goal **and** ?y **memberOf** Vision.
    amplifiedBy(?y,?x) :— amplifies(?x,?y) **and** ?x **memberOf** Vision **and** ?y **memberOf** Goal.

concept DesiredOutcomeAssessmentResult **subConceptOf** cobra#QualitativeAnalysisResult
instance Achievement **memberOf** DesiredOutcomeAssessmentResult
instance Failure **memberOf** DesiredOutcomeAssessmentResult

concept DesiredOutcomeAssessment **subConceptOf** cobra#QualitativeAnalysis

relation DesiredOutcomeAssessmentHasResult (**ofType** DesiredOutcomeAssessment, **ofType** DesiredOutcomeAssessmentResult, **ofType** DesiredOutcome)

concept Objective **subConceptOf** Goal
    nonFunctionalProperties

           dc#description **hasValue** "An objective is a measurable goal. It is a step along the way towards a goal."
    endNonFunctionalProperties
relation quantifies (**ofType** Objective, **ofType** Goal)

relation isQuantifiedBy(**ofType** Goal, **ofType** Objective)

axiom ObjectiveGoalAxiom
     definedBy
     quantifies (?x,?y) :− isQuantifiedBy(?y,?x) **and** ?x **memberOf** Objective **and** ?y
        memberOf Goal.
     isQuantifiedBy(?y,?x) :− quantifies (?x,?y) **and** ?x **memberOf** Goal **and** ?y **memberOf**
        Objective.

/* Means */

concept Means **subConceptOf** cobra#NonAgentiveNonPhysicalEntity
     nonFunctionalProperties
           dc#description **hasValue** "Means are about what an enterprise has decided to do in
             order to become what it wants to be. A means is something that may be called
             upon, activated, or enforced to achieve Ends. It does include neither tasks nor
             responsibility for tasks."
     endNonFunctionalProperties
     hasName **ofType** _string
     hasDescription **ofType** _string

relation affectedBy (**ofType** Means, **ofType** Assessment)

relation affectsEmploymentOf (**ofType** Assessment, **ofType** Means)

axiom MeansAssessmentAxiom
     definedBy
     affectedBy(?x,?y) :− affectsEmploymentOf(?y,?x) **and** ?x **memberOf** Means **and** ?y
        memberOf Assessment.
     affectsEmploymentOf(?y,?x) :− affectedBy(?x,?y) **and** ?x **memberOf** Assessment **and** ?y
        memberOf Means.

concept Mission **subConceptOf** Means
     nonFunctionalProperties
           dc#description **hasValue** "A mission indicates ongoing operational activity of the
             enterprise. Its definition should be broad enough to cover all strategies and
             the complete area of operations."
     endNonFunctionalProperties

concept CourseOfAction **subConceptOf** Means
     nonFunctionalProperties
           dc#description **hasValue** "A Course of Action defines what has to be done, not how
             well it has to be done. Metrics of performance are defined in objectives that
             are supported by the course of action. Courses of action do not necessarily
             have to support desired results directly , they can enable other courses of
             action."
     endNonFunctionalProperties

relation channelsEffortsTowards (**ofType** CourseOfAction, **ofType** DesiredOutcome)

relation supportedBy (**ofType** DesiredOutcome, **ofType** CourseOfAction)

axiom CourseOfActionDesiredOutcomeAxiom

definedBy
channelsEffortsTowards(?x,?y) :− supportedBy(?y,?x) **and** ?x **memberOf** CourseOfAction
   and ?y **memberOf** DesiredOutcome.
supportedBy(?y,?x) :− channelsEffortsTowards(?x,?y) **and** ?x **memberOf** DesiredOutcome
   and ?y **memberOf** CourseOfAction.

concept Strategy **subConceptOf** CourseOfAction
   nonFunctionalProperties
      dc#description **hasValue** "Strategies are Courses of Action that are long term and
         broad in scope."
   endNonFunctionalProperties
relation isComponentOfPlanFor (**ofType** Strategy, **ofType** Mission)

relation plannedByMeansOf (**ofType** Mission, **ofType** Strategy)

axiom StrategyMissionAxiom
   definedBy
   isComponentOfPlanFor(?x,?y) :− plannedByMeansOf(?y,?x) **and** ?x **memberOf** Strategy
      and ?y **memberOf** Mission.
   plannedByMeansOf(?y,?x) :− isComponentOfPlanFor(?x,?y) **and** ?x **memberOf** Mission
      and ?y **memberOf** Strategy.

concept Tactic **subConceptOf** CourseOfAction
   nonFunctionalProperties
      dc#description **hasValue** "Each strategy is implemented by tactics, which tend to be
         shorter term and narrower in scope. A tactic may contribute to the
         implementation of more than one strategy."
   endNonFunctionalProperties

relation implements (**ofType** Tactic, **ofType** Strategy)

relation implementedBy (**ofType** Strategy, **ofType** Tactic)

axiom TacticStrategyAxiom
   definedBy
   implements(?x,?y) :− implementedBy(?y,?x) **and** ?x **memberOf** Tactic **and** ?y **memberOf**
      Strategy.
   implementedBy(?y,?x) :− implements(?x,?y) **and** ?x **memberOf** Strategy **and** ?y
      memberOf Tactic.

concept Directive **subConceptOf** Means
   nonFunctionalProperties
      dc#description **hasValue** "Directives are set up to govern the course of action."
   endNonFunctionalProperties
   hasEnforcementLevel **ofType** EnforcementLevel

relation supportsAchievementOf (**ofType** Directive, **ofType** DesiredOutcome)

relation hasAchievementSupportedBy (**ofType** DesiredOutcome, **ofType** Directive)

axiom DirectiveDesiredOutcomeAxiom
   definedBy
   supportsAchievementOf(?x,?y) :− hasAchievementSupportedBy(?y,?x) **and** ?x **memberOf**
      Directive **and** ?y **memberOf** DesiredOutcome.
   hasAchievementSupportedBy(?y,?x) :− supportsAchievementOf(?x,?y) **and** ?x **memberOf**
      DesiredOutcome **and** ?y **memberOf** Directive.

axiom supportsAchievementOfTransitivityAxiom

        definedBy
        supportsAchievementOf(?x,?z) :− ?x **memberOf** Directive **and** ?y **memberOf**
            DesiredOutcome **and** ?z **memberOf** DesiredOutcome **and** supportsAchievementOf(?x,
            ?y) **and** isSubGoalOf(?y,?z).

relation governs (**ofType** Directive, **ofType** CourseOfAction)

relation governedBy (**ofType** CourseOfAction, **ofType** Directive)

axiom DirectiveCourseOfActionAxiom
        definedBy
        governs(?x,?y) :− governedBy(?y,?x) **and** ?x **memberOf** Directive **and** ?y **memberOf**
            CourseOfAction.
        governedBy(?y,?x) :− governs(?x,?y) **and** ?x **memberOf** CourseOfAction **and** ?y
            memberOf Directive.

relation sourceOf (**ofType** Directive, **ofType** CourseOfAction)

relation formulatedBasedOn (**ofType** CourseOfAction, **ofType** Directive)

axiom DirectiveCourseOfActionAxiom
        definedBy
        sourceOf(?x,?y) :− formulatedBasedOn(?y,?x) **and** ?x **memberOf** Directive **and** ?y
            memberOf CourseOfAction.
        formulatedBasedOn(?y,?x) :− sourceOf(?x,?y) **and** ?x **memberOf** CourseOfAction **and** ?y
            memberOf Directive.

relation guides (**ofType** Directive, **ofType** Activity)

relation guidedBy (**ofType** Activity, **ofType** Directive)

axiom DirectiveActivityAxiom
        definedBy
        guides(?x,?y) :− guidedBy(?y,?x) **and** ?x **memberOf** Directive **and** ?y **memberOf** Activity.
        guidedBy(?y,?x) :− guides(?x,?y) **and** ?x **memberOf** Activity **and** ?y **memberOf** Directive.

relation hasEnforcementLevelEffectedBy (**ofType** Directive, **ofType** Tactic)

relation effectsEnforcementLevelOf (**ofType** Tactic, **ofType** Directive)

axiom DirectiveTacticAxiom
        definedBy
        hasEnforcementLevelEffectedBy(?x,?y) :− effectsEnforcementLevelOf(?y,?x) **and** ?x
            memberOf Directive **and** ?y **memberOf** Tactic.
        effectsEnforcementLevelOf(?y,?x) :− hasEnforcementLevelEffectedBy(?x,?y) **and** ?x
            memberOf Tactic **and** ?y **memberOf** Directive.

concept EnforcementLevel
        nonFunctionalProperties
            dc#description **hasValue** "An Enforcement Level represent alternatives, which
                indicates the severity of action imposed to put or keep a directive in force."
        endNonFunctionalProperties
        hasName **ofType** _string
        hasDescription **ofType** _string

instance StrictlyEnforced **memberOf** EnforcementLevel
        hasName **hasValue** "Strictly enforced"

hasDescription **hasValue** "If rule is violated a penalty is applied."

instance DeferredEnforcement **memberOf** EnforcementLevel
       hasName **hasValue** "Deferred enforcement"
       hasDescription **hasValue** "Strictly enforced, but enforcement may be delayed with required
          skills"

instance PreAuthorizedOverride **memberOf** EnforcementLevel
       hasName **hasValue** "Pre−authorized override"
       hasDescription **hasValue** "Enforced, but exceptions allowed, with prior approval for actors
          with before−the−fact override authorization."

instance PostJustifiedOverride **memberOf** EnforcementLevel
       hasName **hasValue** "Post−justified override"
       hasDescription **hasValue** "If not approved after the fact , you may be subject to sanction or
          other consequences."

instance OverrideWithExplanation **memberOf** EnforcementLevel
       hasName **hasValue** "Override with explanation"
       hasDescription **hasValue** "Comment must be provided when the violation occurs."

instance Guideline **memberOf** EnforcementLevel
       hasName **hasValue** "Guideline"
       hasDescription **hasValue** "Suggested, but not enforced."

/* Activity */

concept Activity **subConceptOf** cobra#Activity
       nonFunctionalProperties
              dc#description **hasValue** "An activity is the ultimate means of realizing a course
                  of action. This concept allows for specification of any business activity (
                  process or task) at a high−level."
       endNonFunctionalProperties
       hasDescription **ofType** (1) _string

relation responsibilityOf (**ofType** Activity , **ofType** OrganizationUnit)

relation responsibleFor (**ofType** OrganizationUnit, **ofType** Activity)

axiom ActivityOrganizationUnitAxiom
       definedBy
       responsibilityOf (?x,?y) :− responsibleFor(?y,?x) **and** ?x **memberOf** Activity **and** ?y
          memberOf OrganizationUnit.
       responsibleFor(?y,?x) :− responsibilityOf (?x,?y) **and** ?x **memberOf** OrganizationUnit **and**
          ?y **memberOf** Activity.

relation realizes (**ofType** Activity , **ofType** CourseOfAction)

relation isRealizedBy (**ofType** CourseOfAction, **ofType** Activity)

axiom ActivityAxiom
       definedBy
       realizes (?x,?y) :− isRealizedBy(?y,?x) **and** ?x **memberOf** Activity **and** ?y **memberOf**
          CourseOfAction.
       isRealizedBy(?y,?x) :− realizes(?x,?y) **and** ?x **memberOf** CourseOfAction **and** ?y
          memberOf Activity.

/* Influencers */

concept Influencer **subConceptOf** cobra#AgentiveRole
    nonFunctionalProperties
        dc#description **hasValue** "An Influencer can be anything that has the capability to
          produce an effect on the business."
    endNonFunctionalProperties
    hasName **ofType** (1) _string
    hasDescription **ofType** (1) _string
    assessedAs **ofType** Assessment

relation recognizedBy (**ofType** Influencer, **ofType** OrganizationUnit)

relation recognizes (**ofType** OrganizationUnit, **ofType** Influencer)

axiom InfluencerOrganizationUnitAxiom
    definedBy
    recognizedBy(?x,?y) :− recognizes(?y,?x) **and** ?x **memberOf** Influencer **and** ?y **memberOf**
        OrganizationUnit.
    recognizes(?y,?x) :− recognizedBy(?x,?y) **and** ?x **memberOf** OrganizationUnit **and** ?y
        memberOf Influencer.

relation judgedIn (**ofType** Influencer, **ofType** Assessment)

relation judges (**ofType** Assessment, **ofType** Influencer)

axiom InfluencerAssessmentAxiom
    definedBy
    judgedIn(?x,?y) :− judges(?y,?x) **and** ?x **memberOf** Influencer **and** ?y **memberOf**
        Assessment.
    judges(?y,?x) :− judgedIn(?x,?y) **and** ?x **memberOf** Assessment **and** ?y **memberOf**
        Influencer.

concept InternalInfluencer **subConceptOf** Influencer

concept ExternalInfluencer **subConceptOf** Influencer

concept DesiredOutcomeAssessmentResult **subConceptOf** cobra#QualitativeAnalysisResult
instance Achievement **memberOf** DesiredOutcomeAssessmentResult
instance Failure **memberOf** DesiredOutcomeAssessmentResult

concept DesiredOutcomeAssessment **subConceptOf** cobra#QualitativeAnalysis

relation DesiredOutcomeAssessmentHasResult (**ofType** DesiredOutcomeAssessment, **ofType**
    DesiredOutcomeAssessmentResult, **ofType** DesiredOutcome)

/* Metrics */

concept Metric **subConceptOf** cobra#QuantitativeAnalysis
    nonFunctionalProperties
        dc#description **hasValue** "Any kind of Metric."
    endNonFunctionalProperties
    hasName **ofType** _string
    hasDescription **ofType** _string
    hasCalculation **ofType** _string
    hasPerspective **ofType** MeasurementPerspective
    hasTarget **ofType** _string
    hasType **ofType** _string

concept KPI **subConceptOf** cobra#NonAgentiveRole
    nonFunctionalProperties
        dc#description **hasValue** "A key performance indicator is a role of Metric."
    endNonFunctionalProperties

relation playsKPIRole (**ofType** Metric, **ofType** KPI, **ofType** Objective) **subRelationOf**
    cobra#playsRoleIn

concept MeasurementPerspective
    nonFunctionalProperties
        dc#description **hasValue** "A Metric can be relevant on several perspectives.
            Following Kaplan and Norton (1992) one can distinguish a (1) Financial, (2)
            Customer, (3) Internal Business Processes and (4) Learning & Growth
            perspective."
    endNonFunctionalProperties

instance Financial_Perspective **memberOf** MeasurementPerspective
instance Customer_Perspective **memberOf** MeasurementPerspective
instance Process_Perspective **memberOf** MeasurementPerspective
instance Intangible_Perspective **memberOf** MeasurementPerspective

concept Assessment **subConceptOf** cobra#QualitativeAnalysis
    nonFunctionalProperties
        dc#description **hasValue** "An assessment is the procedure of the judgement of
            some influencer."
    endNonFunctionalProperties
    hasName **ofType** (1) _string
    hasDescription **ofType** (1) _string

instance SWOT **memberOf** Assessment

relation playsInfluencerRole (**ofType** cobra#Agent, **ofType** Influencer, **ofType** Assessment)

relation providesImpetusFor (**ofType** Assessment, **ofType** Directive)

relation motivatedByAssessment (**ofType** Directive, **ofType** Assessment)

axiom AssessmentDirectiveAxiom
    definedBy
    providesImpetusFor(?x,?y) :− motivatedByAssessment(?y,?x) **and** ?x **memberOf**
        Assessment **and** ?y **memberOf** Directive.
    motivatedByAssessment(?y,?x) :− providesImpetusFor(?x,?y) **and** ?x **memberOf** Directive
        and ?y **memberOf** Assessment.

concept Strength **subConceptOf** InternalInfluencer
concept Weakness **subConceptOf** InternalInfluencer
concept Opportunity **subConceptOf** ExternalInfluencer
concept Threat **subConceptOf** ExternalInfluencer

/* Relations */

relation isSubGoalOf(**ofType** Goal, **ofType** Goal)
    nonFunctionalProperties
        dc#description **hasValue** "A goal can have one or more subgoals."
    endNonFunctionalProperties

relation isRootGoal(**ofType** Goal)
    nonFunctionalProperties

          dc#description **hasValue** "A goal tree has a root goal. "
    endNonFunctionalProperties

relation isAncGoalOf(**ofType** Goal, **ofType** Goal)
    nonFunctionalProperties
          dc#description **hasValue** "All goals connected to a goal by the subgoal relation are
                it 's ancestor goals."
    endNonFunctionalProperties

relation isLeafGoal (**ofType** Goal)
    nonFunctionalProperties
          dc#description **hasValue** "A goal which has no subgoals."
          dc#relation **hasValue** "concept Goal"
    endNonFunctionalProperties

relation isNotRootGoal(**ofType** Goal)
    nonFunctionalProperties
          dc#description **hasValue** "All goals which are not a root goal. "
          dc#relation **hasValue** "concept Goal"
    endNonFunctionalProperties

relation isIntermediateGoal (**ofType** Goal)
    nonFunctionalProperties
          dc#description **hasValue** "A goal that is neither a root goal nor a leaf goal."
          dc#relation **hasValue** "concept Goal"
    endNonFunctionalProperties

relation UnsatisfiedGoals(**ofType** Goal)
    nonFunctionalProperties
          dc#description **hasValue** "All goals which are not known to be satisfied . "
          dc#relation **hasValue** "concept Goal"
    endNonFunctionalProperties

relation higherPriority (**ofType** Goal, **ofType** Goal)
    nonFunctionalProperties
          dc#description **hasValue** "Goal 1 is of higher priority than goal 2. "
    endNonFunctionalProperties

relation lowerPriority (**ofType** Goal, **ofType** Goal)
    nonFunctionalProperties
          dc#description **hasValue** "Goal 1 is of lower priority than goal 2."
    endNonFunctionalProperties

relation conflicts (**ofType** Goal, **ofType** Goal)
    nonFunctionalProperties
          dc#description **hasValue** "A goal is in conflict with another if it hinders the
                other and has lower priority . "
    endNonFunctionalProperties

/* Axioms */

axiom GoalObjective
    nonFunctionalProperties
          dc#description **hasValue** "A goal is said to be an objective, if it is SMART."
    endNonFunctionalProperties
    definedBy
    ?x **memberOf** Objective :− ?x **memberOf** Goal **and** ?y **memberOf** Metric **and** hasMetric(
        ?x,?y).

axiom QuantifiedGoals
    nonFunctionalProperties
        dc#description **hasValue** "A goal quantifies another, if it is an objective and is
            its direct subgoal."
    endNonFunctionalProperties
    definedBy
        ?x[quantifies **hasValue** ?y] :− ?x **memberOf** Objective **and** ?y **memberOf** Goal
            and ?x[hasParentGoal **hasValue** ?y].

axiom GoalPartition
    nonFunctionalProperties
        dc#description **hasValue** "A goal is part of another, if it is subgoal of another."
    endNonFunctionalProperties
    definedBy
        ?x[partOf **hasValue** ?y] :− ?x **memberOf** Goal **and** ?y **memberOf** Goal **and** ?x[
            hasParentGoal **hasValue** ?y].

axiom PriorityDef
    nonFunctionalProperties
        dc#description **hasValue** "Goals are prioritized according to their   attribute ."
        dc#relation **hasValue** "relation higherPriority (?x,?y), relation   lowerPriority (?x,?y
)"
    endNonFunctionalProperties
    definedBy
    higherPriority (?x,?y) :− ?x[hasPriority **hasValue** ?a] **and** ?y[hasPriority **hasValue** ?b]
    and ?x **memberOf** Goal **and** ?y **memberOf** Goal **and** wsml#greaterThan(?a,?b).
    lowerPriority (?x,?y) :− higherPriority (?y,?x).

axiom PriorityConflictAxiom
    nonFunctionalProperties
        dc#description **hasValue** "A goal is in conflict with another if it hinders the
            other and has lower priority ."
        dc#description **hasValue** "relation conflicts (?x,?y)"
    endNonFunctionalProperties
    definedBy
    conflicts (?x,?y) :− lowerPriority (?x,?y) **and** (WeakNegativeContribution(?x,?y) **or**
        StrongNegativeContribution(?x,?y)).

axiom swotDef
    nonFunctionalProperties
        dc#description **hasValue** "External influencers are either opportunities or threats
            and internal influencers are either strength or weaknesses."
        dc#relation **hasValue** "concept Influencer"
    endNonFunctionalProperties
    definedBy
    !− (?x **memberOf** InternalInfluencer **and** (?x **memberOf** Threat **or** ?x **memberOf**
        Opportunity)).
    !− (?x **memberOf** ExternalInfluencer **and** (?x **memberOf** Weakness **or** ?x **memberOf**
        Strenght)).

axiom InfluencerRoleEitherInternalOrExternal
    nonFunctionalProperties
        dc#description **hasValue** "An Influencer can not be both, internal and external at
            the same time"
        dc#relation **hasValue** "concept Influencer"
    endNonFunctionalProperties
    definedBy

!— ?x **memberOf** Influencer **and** ?y **memberOf** Influencer **and**
   ?x **memberOf** InternalInfluencer **and** ?y **memberOf** ExternalInfluencer **and** ?x != ?y.

axiom isSubGoalDef
    nonFunctionalProperties
        dc#description **hasValue** "Refinement is a special type of subgoal relation."
        dc#relation **hasValue** "concept Goal"
    endNonFunctionalProperties
    definedBy
    isSubGoalOf(?x,?z) :— ?x **memberOf** Goal **and** ?y **memberOf** Goal **and** ?z **memberOf**
        Goal **and** Refinement(?x,?y,?z).
    isSubGoalOf(?y,?z) :— ?x **memberOf** Goal **and** ?y **memberOf** Goal **and** ?z **memberOf**
        Goal **and** Refinement(?x,?y,?z).

axiom isNotRootGoalDef
    nonFunctionalProperties
        dc#description **hasValue** "Definition of all goals which are not a root goal."
        dc#relation **hasValue** "concept Goal"
    endNonFunctionalProperties
    definedBy
    isNotRootGoal(?y) :— ?y **memberOf** Goal **and** ?x **memberOf** Goal **and** isSubGoalOf(?y,?x
)
    and naf isSubGoalOf(?x,?y).

axiom isRootGoalDef
    nonFunctionalProperties
        dc#description **hasValue** "A root goal is a goal, which is not known to be inside
            the goal tree. Thus, it has no parent goals."
        dc#relation **hasValue** "concept Goal"
    endNonFunctionalProperties
    definedBy
    isRootGoal(?y) :— ?y **memberOf** Goal **and naf** isNotRootGoal(?y).

axiom isIntermediateGoalDef
    nonFunctionalProperties
        dc#description **hasValue** "An intermediate goal is subgoal of another and has
            subgoals itself."
        dc#relation **hasValue** "concept Goal"
    endNonFunctionalProperties
    definedBy
    isIntermediateGoal(?y) :— ?x **memberOf** Goal **and** ?y **memberOf** Goal **and** ?z **memberOf**
        Goal
    and isSubGoalOf(?x,?y) **and** isSubGoalOf(?y,?z).

axiom isLeafGoalDef
    nonFunctionalProperties
        dc#description **hasValue** "A leaf goal is a goal, which is not known to be a root
            goal nor is it known to be an intermediate goal."
        dc#relation **hasValue** "concept Goal"
    endNonFunctionalProperties
    definedBy
    isLeafGoal(?x) :— ?x **memberOf** Goal **and naf** isRootGoal(?x) **and naf** isIntermediateGoal(
        ?x).

axiom UnsatisfiedGoalsDef
    nonFunctionalProperties
        dc#description **hasValue** "All goals that are not explicity known or infered to be
            satisfied "

dc#relation **hasValue** "concept Goal"
endNonFunctionalProperties
definedBy
UnsatisfiedGoals(?x) :− ?x **memberOf** Goal **and naf** partySatisfaction(?x).

axiom ParentGoalfromSubGoal
    nonFunctionalProperties
        dc#description **hasValue** "A goal which is known to be a subgoal of another has the
            one as its parent goal."
        dc#relation **hasValue** "concept Goal"
    endNonFunctionalProperties
    definedBy
        ?x[hasParentGoal **hasValue** ?y] :− ?x **memberOf** Goal **and** ?y **memberOf** Goal
           and isSubGoalOf(?x,?y).

axiom SubGoalfromParentGoal
    nonFunctionalProperties
        dc#description **hasValue** "Two goals which are known to be in the subgoal relation
           are infered to be parent and subgoal respectively."
        dc#relation **hasValue** "concept Goal"
    endNonFunctionalProperties
    definedBy
        isSubGoalOf(?x,?y) :− ?x **memberOf** Goal **and** ?y **memberOf** Goal **and** ?x[
           hasParentGoal **hasValue** ?y].

axiom SubGoalNonTransitive
    nonFunctionalProperties
        dc#description **hasValue** "The subgoal relation is non−transitive."
        dc#relation **hasValue** "concept Goal"
    endNonFunctionalProperties
    definedBy
        !− isSubGoalOf(?x,?x) **and** ?x **memberOf** Goal.

axiom GoalTreeNonCyclic
    nonFunctionalProperties
        dc#description **hasValue** "There are no cycles in a goal tree."
        dc#relation **hasValue** "relation isAncGoalOf"
    endNonFunctionalProperties
    definedBy
        !− isAncGoalOf(?x,?x).

axiom isAncGoalOf
    nonFunctionalProperties
        dc#description **hasValue** "A goal is another goal's ancestor, if there is link via
           the subgoal relation."
        dc#relation **hasValue** "isAncGoalOf(ofType Goal, ofType Goal)"
    endNonFunctionalProperties
    definedBy
        isAncGoalOf(?x,?y) :− isSubGoalOf(?x,?y).
        isAncGoalOf(?x,?z) :− isSubGoalOf(?x,?y) **and** isSubGoalOf(?y,?z).

axiom StrategyDirectiveActivityAxiom
    definedBy
        realizes (?x, ?z) :−   ?x **memberOf** Activity **and** ?y **memberOf** Directive
        and ?z **memberOf** Strategy **and** governs(?y, ?x) **and** formulatedBasedOn(?z, ?y).

/* Goal contribution semantics */

concept Label
instance full **memberOf** Label
instance partial **memberOf** Label
instance none **memberOf** Label

concept Helper **subConceptOf** Goal

// Satifaction & denial relations

relation fullSatisfaction (**ofType** Goal)
relation partlySatisfaction (**ofType** Goal)
relation fullDenial (**ofType** Goal)
relation partlyDenial (**ofType** Goal)

// Invariant Axioms

axiom InvariantAxioms
 definedBy
   partlySatisfaction (?x) :− fullSatisfaction (?x).
   partlyDenial(?x) :− fullDenial (?x).

relation Refinement(**ofType** Goal, **ofType** Goal, **ofType** Goal)

relation necessaryGoals(**ofType** Goal, **ofType** Goal, **ofType** Goal) **subRelationOf** Refinement
axiom necessaryGoalsAxiom
 definedBy
  fullSatisfaction (?z) :− necessaryGoals(?x,?y,?z) **and** fullSatisfaction(?x) **and** fullSatisfaction (?y
).
  partlySatisfaction (?z) :− necessaryGoals(?x,?y,?z) **and** partlySatisfaction(?x) **and**
       partlySatisfaction(?y).
  fullDenial (?z) :− necessaryGoals(?x,?y,?z) **and** (fullDenial(?x) **or** fullDenial (?y)).
  partlyDenial(?z) :− necessaryGoals(?x,?y,?z) **and** (partlyDenial(?x) **or** partlyDenial(?y)).

relation sufficientGoals (**ofType** Goal, **ofType** Goal, **ofType** Goal) **subRelationOf** Refinement
axiom sufficientGoalsAxiom
 definedBy
  fullSatisfaction (?z) :− sufficientGoals(?x,?y,?z) **and** (fullSatisfaction (?x) **or** fullSatisfaction (
       ?y)).
  partlySatisfaction (?z) :− sufficientGoals(?x,?y,?z) **and** (partlySatisfaction (?x) **or**
       partlySatisfaction (?y)).
  fullDenial (?z) :− sufficientGoals(?x,?y,?z) **and** (fullDenial (?x) **and** fullDenial(?y)).
  partlyDenial(?z) :− sufficientGoals(?x,?y,?z) **and** (partlyDenial(?x) **and** partlyDenial(?y)).

// Contribution links

relation Contribution (**ofType** Goal, **ofType** Goal)
        nonFunctionalProperties
            dc#description **hasValue** "A goal can influence another goal in a positive or
               negative way."
        endNonFunctionalProperties

relation WeakPositiveSatisfactionContribution (**ofType** Goal, **ofType** Goal) **subRelationOf**
     Contribution
axiom WeakPositiveSatisfactionContributionAxiom
 definedBy
  partlySatisfaction (?y) :− WeakPositiveSatisfactionContribution(?x,?y) **and** partlySatisfaction (?x).

relation WeakNegativeSatisfactionContribution (**ofType** Goal, **ofType** Goal) **subRelationOf**
    Contribution
axiom WeakNegativeSatisfactionContributionAxiom
  definedBy
  partlyDenial(?y) :− WeakNegativeSatisfactionContribution(?x,?y) **and** partlySatisfaction(?x).

relation StrongPositiveSatisfactionContribution (**ofType** Goal, **ofType** Goal) **subRelationOf**
    Contribution
axiom StrongPositiveSatisfactionContributionAxiom
  definedBy
  fullSatisfaction (?y) :− StrongPositiveSatisfactionContribution(?x,?y) **and** fullSatisfaction (?x).
  partlySatisfaction (?y) :− StrongPositiveSatisfactionContribution(?x,?y) **and** partlySatisfaction (?x
).

relation StrongNegativeSatisfactionContribution (**ofType** Goal, **ofType** Goal) **subRelationOf**
    Contribution
axiom StrongNegativeSatisfactionContributionAxiom
  definedBy
  fullDenial (?y) :− StrongNegativeSatisfactionContribution(?x,?y) **and** fullSatisfaction (?x).
  partlyDenial(?y) :− StrongNegativeSatisfactionContribution(?x,?y) **and** partlySatisfaction(?x).

relation WeakPositiveDenialContribution (**ofType** Goal, **ofType** Goal) **subRelationOf** Contribution
axiom WeakPositiveDenialContributionAxiom
  definedBy
  partlyDenial(?y) :− WeakPositiveDenialContribution(?x,?y) **and** partlyDenial(?x).

relation WeakNegativeDenialContribution (**ofType** Goal, **ofType** Goal) **subRelationOf**
    Contribution
axiom WeakNegativeDenialContributionAxiom
  definedBy
  partlyDenial(?y) :− WeakNegativeDenialContribution(?x,?y) **and** partlySatisfaction(?x).

relation StrongPositiveDenialContribution (**ofType** Goal, **ofType** Goal) **subRelationOf**
    Contribution
axiom StrongPositiveDenialContributionAxiom
  definedBy
  fullDenial (?y) :− StrongPositiveDenialContribution(?x,?y) **and** fullDenial (?x).
  partlyDenial(?y) :− StrongPositiveDenialContribution(?x,?y) **and** partlyDenial(?x).

relation StrongNegativeDenialContribution (**ofType** Goal, **ofType** Goal) **subRelationOf**
    Contribution
axiom StrongNegativeDenialContributionAxiom
  definedBy
  fullSatisfaction (?y) :− StrongNegativeDenialContribution(?x,?y) **and** fullDenial(?x).
  partlySatisfaction (?y) :− StrongNegativeDenialContribution(?x,?y) **and** partlyDenial(?x).

// *Aggregated contributions*

relation WeakPositiveContribution (**ofType** Goal, **ofType** Goal) **subRelationOf** Contribution
axiom WeakPositiveContributionAxiom
  definedBy
  WeakPositiveSatisfactionContribution(?x,?y) :− WeakPositiveContribution(?x,?y).
  WeakPositiveDenialContribution(?x,?y) :− WeakPositiveContribution(?x,?y).

relation WeakNegativeContribution (**ofType** Goal, **ofType** Goal) **subRelationOf** Contribution
axiom WeakNegativeContributionAxiom
  definedBy
  WeakNegativeSatisfactionContribution(?x,?y) :− WeakNegativeContribution(?x,?y).

WeakNegativeDenialContribution(?x,?y) :— WeakNegativeContribution(?x,?y).

relation StrongPositiveContribution (**ofType** Goal, **ofType** Goal) **subRelationOf** Contribution
axiom StrongPositiveContributionAxiom
  definedBy
  StrongPositiveSatisfactionContribution (?x,?y) :— StrongPositiveContribution(?x,?y).
  StrongPositiveDenialContribution(?x,?y) :— StrongPositiveContribution(?x,?y).

relation StrongNegativeContribution (**ofType** Goal, **ofType** Goal) **subRelationOf** Contribution
axiom StrongNegativeContributionAxiom
  definedBy
  StrongNegativeSatisfactionContribution(?x,?y) :— StrongNegativeContribution(?x,?y).
  StrongNegativeDenialContribution(?x,?y) :— StrongNegativeContribution(?x,?y).

// Conflicts

relation GoalConflict (**ofType** Goal)
relation WeakConflict(**ofType** Goal) **subRelationOf** GoalConflict
relation StrongConflict(**ofType** Goal) **subRelationOf** GoalConflict

axiom ConflictAxiom
  definedBy
  WeakConflict(?x) :— partlySatisfaction (?x) **and** partlyDenial(?x).
  StrongConflict(?x) :— fullSatisfaction (?x) **and** fullDenial(?x).

// Inferrence rules for satifaction & denial attributes

axiom GoalEvidenceAxiom
  definedBy
  ?x[denial **hasValue** full] :— fullDenial (?x) **and naf** WeakConflict(?x).
  ?x[denial **hasValue** partial] :— partlyDenial(?x) **and naf** fullDenial (?x) **and naf** WeakConflict(?x)

  ?x[satisfaction **hasValue** full] :— fullSatisfaction (?x) **and naf** WeakConflict(?x).
  ?x[satisfaction **hasValue** partial] :— partlySatisfaction (?x) **and naf** fullSatisfaction (?x) **and**
    naf WeakConflict(?x).
  ?x[denial **hasValue** none] :— ?x **memberOf** Goal **and naf** partlyDenial(?x) **and naf** WeakConflict
    (?x).
  ?x[satisfaction **hasValue** none] :— ?x **memberOf** Goal **and naf** partlySatisfaction(?x) **and naf**
    WeakConflict(?x).

Listing B.1: Business Motivation Ontology

Appendix C

Business Motivation Visual Modeling Constructs

Table C.1: Visual Constructs

Modeling Construct	Visual Notation
Ends	
Vision {*VisionName*}	Vision Name
Goal {*GoalName*}	Goal Name
Objective {*ObjectiveName*}	Objective Name
Strong positive contribution relation	++
Weak positive contribution relation	+
Strong negative contribution relation	--
Weak negative contribution relation	-
AND-decomposition relation	AND
OR-decomposition relation	OR
Association relation	

Continued on next page

Table C.1 – continued from previous page

Modeling Construct	Visual Notation
Means	
Mission {*MissionName*}	Mission Name
Strategy {*StrategyName*}	Strategy
Tactic {*TacticName*}	Tactic Name
Metrics	
Metric {*MetricName*}	Metric Name
Influencers	
External Influencer {*ExtInflName*}	External Influencer Name
Internal Influencer {*IntInflName*}	Internal Influencer Name
Assessment {*AssessmentName*}	Assessment Name
External Constructs	
Activity {*ActivityName*}	Activity Name
Organizational Unit {*OrgUnitName*}	Organizational Unit Name

Table C.1: Visual Constructs

Appendix D

Business Process Ontology

ontology BPO

    importsOntology
        { _"http :// www.ip−super.org/ontologies/RO/20080624#BRO",
                 _"http :// www.ip−super.org/ontologies/BFO/20080317#BFO",
                 _"http :// www.ip−super.org/ontologies/BPRO/20080829#BPRO",
           _"http :// www.ip−super.org/ontologies/OUO/20080711#OUO",
           _"http :// www.ip−super.org/ontologies/BResO/20070907#BResO",
           _"http :// www.ip−super.org/ontologies/organisation/BMO/v1.1.3#BMO"
        }

concept Process **subConceptOf** bmo#Activity
           hasID **ofType** _string
      hasDefinition **ofType** (0 1) Process
      hasSubprocessDefinition **ofType** (0 1) Process
      hasNames **ofType** PassingName
          hasLabel **ofType** _string
          hasType **ofType** _string

concept Name
           hasID **ofType** _string

// Abstract Concept for pi−process sub definitions

concept Summation **subConceptOf** Process
      hasNext **ofType** (1 1) Process

// Names which should be scoped inside this process definition

concept Restriction **subConceptOf** Summation
      onNames **ofType** (1 *) Name

// Process replicates its instances

concept Replication **subConceptOf** Summation

// Abstract Concept

concept MultiplePath **subConceptOf** Process
      subdivide **ofType** (2 *) Process

// Choose just one of multiple paths

concept ExclusiveChoice **subConceptOf** MultiplePath

// Execute all paths in parallel

concept Concurrent **subConceptOf** MultiplePath

// pi−prefix: super concept for Communication and InternalProcessing (Local)

concept Prefix **subConceptOf** Summation

// Super Concepts for Input and Output Communication

concept Communication **subConceptOf** Prefix
    hasName **ofType** (0 1) Name

// Sending a name through a communication channel

concept Output **subConceptOf** Communication

// Receiving a name through a communication channel

concept Input **subConceptOf** Communication

// Internal Processing of any activity

concept Local **subConceptOf** Prefix

// Perform Processing of activity if the Condition holds

concept Match **subConceptOf** Prefix
    hasCondition **ofType** (0 1) _string

relation isAnnotatedBy/2

// A functional categorization of a process

relation isAnnotatedByBusinessFunction(**ofType** Process, **ofType** bfo#ActivityOrStep)
    subRelationOf isAnnotatedBy

axiom hasBusinessFunctionRelDefn
definedBy
isAnnotatedByBusinessFunction(?x,?y) :− isAnnotatedBy(?x,?y) **and** ?y **memberOf**
    bfo#ActivityOrStep.

// An Objective supported by a process

relation isAnnotatedByBusinessObjective(**ofType** Process, **ofType** bmo#Objective)
    subRelationOf isAnnotatedBy

axiom hasBusinessObjectiveRelDefn
definedBy
isAnnotatedByBusinessObjective(?x,?y) :− isAnnotatedBy(?x,?y) **and** ?y **memberOf**
    bmo#Objective.

// A Role performing a process

relation isAnnotatedByBusinessRole(**ofType** Process, **ofType** bro#Role) **subRelationOf**
  isAnnotatedBy

axiom hasBusinessRoleRelDefn
definedBy
isAnnotatedByBusinessRole(?x,?y) :− isAnnotatedBy(?x,?y) **and** ?y **memberOf** bro#Role.

// An Organizational unit responsible for a process

relation isAnnotatedByOrganizationalUnit(**ofType** Process, **ofType** ouo#OrganizationalUnit)
    subRelationOf isAnnotatedBy

axiom hasOrganizationalUnitRelDefn
definedBy
isAnnotatedByOrganizationalUnit(?x, ?y) :− isAnnotatedBy(?x,?y) **and** ?y **memberOf**
  ouo#OrganizationalUnit.

// A Resource required by a process

relation isAnnotatedByBusinessResource(**ofType** Process, **ofType** breso#Object) **subRelationOf**
    bpo#isAnnotatedBy

axiom hasBusinessResourceRelDefn
definedBy
isAnnotatedByBusinessResource(?x, ?y) :− isAnnotatedBy(?x,?y) **and** ?y **memberOf** breso#Object
  .

// A Policy associated with a process

relation isAnnotatedByBusinessPolicy(**ofType** Process, **ofType** bpro#Policy) **subRelationOf**
  isAnnotatedBy

axiom isAnnotatedByBusinessPolicyRelDefn
definedBy
isAnnotatedByBusinessPolicy(?x,?y) :− isAnnotatedBy(?x,?y) **and** ?y **memberOf** bpro#Policy.

// A Rule associated with a process

relation isAnnotatedByBusinessRule(**ofType** Process, **ofType** bpro#Rule) **subRelationOf**
  isAnnotatedBy

axiom isAnnotatedByBusinessRuleRelDefn
definedBy
isAnnotatedByBusinessRule(?x,?y) :− isAnnotatedBy(?x,?y) **and** ?y **memberOf** bpro#Rule.

// Represents a Process that does not continue execution

instance Null **memberOf** Process
    hasName **hasValue** "Null"

relation contains(**ofType** Process, **ofType** Process)

axiom processContainment
definedBy
contains(?x, ?r) :− ?x[hasDefinition **hasValue** ?y] **memberOf** Process **and** ?y[hasNext **hasValue**
    ?z] **memberOf** Restriction **and**

?z[subdivide **hasValue** ?r] **memberOf** Concurrent.

axiom subProcessContainment
definedBy
contains(?x, ?y) :− ?x[hasSubprocessDefinition **hasValue** ?y] **memberOf** Process **and** ?y
    memberOf Process.

axiom processContainmentTransitivity
definedBy
contains(?x,?z) :− contains(?x,?y) **and** contains(?y,?z).

Listing D.1: Business Process Ontology

Appendix E

BPO representation of the Simple Merge pattern in Fig. 6.3

instance a8ab71071210c101301210c1202cd0015SubProcess_1 **memberOf** bpo#Process
bpo#hasID **hasValue** "XorGatewaya8ab71071210c101301210c1202cd0015_1"
bpo#hasType **hasValue** "Gateway"
bpo#hasNames **hasValue** {a8ab71071210c101301210c1203130017,
a8ab71071210c101301210c120d170019, a8ab71071210c101301210c1228e8001d }
bpo#hasDefinition **hasValue** a8ab71071210c101301210c1202cd0015Tau

instance a8ab71071210c101301210c1202cd0015Tau **memberOf** bpo#Local
bpo#hasID **hasValue** "tau"
bpo#hasNext **hasValue** a8ab71071210c101301210c1202cd00150Send

instance a8ab71071210c101301210c1202cd00150Send **memberOf** bpo#Output
bpo#hasID **hasValue** "a8ab71071210c101301210c1228e8001d"
bpo#hasNext **hasValue** bpo#Null

instance a8ab71071210c101301210c1202cd0015Process **memberOf** bpo#Process
bpo#hasID **hasValue** "XorGatewaya8ab71071210c101301210c1202cd0015"
bpo#hasType **hasValue** "Gateway"
bpo#hasNames **hasValue** {a8ab71071210c101301210c1203130017,
a8ab71071210c101301210c120d170019, a8ab71071210c101301210c1228e8001d }
bpo#hasDefinition **hasValue** a8ab71071210c101301210c1202cd0015XOR

instance a8ab71071210c101301210c1202cd0015XOR **memberOf** bpo#ExclusiveChoice
bpo#hasID **hasValue** "ExclusiveChoice"
bpo#subdivide **hasValue** {a8ab71071210c101301210c1202cd00150Receive,
a8ab71071210c101301210c1202cd00151Receive }

instance a8ab71071210c101301210c1202cd00150Receive **memberOf** bpo#Input
bpo#hasID **hasValue** "a8ab71071210c101301210c1203130017"
bpo#hasNext **hasValue** a8ab71071210c101301210c1202cd0015Process

instance a8ab71071210c101301210c1202cd0015Process **memberOf** bpo#Process
bpo#hasID **hasValue** {"XorGatewaya8ab71071210c101301210c1202cd0015_1", "
XorGatewaya8ab71071210c101301210c1202cd0015" }
bpo#hasNames **hasValue** {a8ab71071210c101301210c1203130017,
a8ab71071210c101301210c120d170019, a8ab71071210c101301210c1228e8001d }

instance a8ab71071210c101301210c1202cd00151Receive **memberOf** bpo#Input
bpo#hasID **hasValue** "a8ab71071210c101301210c120d170019"

bpo#hasNext **hasValue** a8ab71071210c101301210c1202cd0015Process

Listing E.1: Simple Merge Pattern from Fig. 6.3

Appendix F

Business Policies and Rules Ontology

ontology BPRO

> **importsOntology**
> { _"http :// www.ip−super.org/ontologies/BFO/20080317#BFO_20080317",
>   _"http :// www.ip−super.org/ontologies/RO/20080624#BRO",
>   _"http :// www.heppnetz.de/ontologies/pro#BRE",
>   _"http :// www.ip−super.org/ontologies/BPO/20070903#BPO",
>   _"http :// www.ip−super.org/ontologies/organisation/BMO/v1.1.3#BMO" }

concept Policy **subConceptOf** bmo#Directive
hasPolicyName **ofType** _string
hasNaturalLangDescription **ofType** _string

concept Rule **subConceptOf** bmo#Directive
hasRuleName **ofType** _string
hasNaturalLangDescription **ofType** _string

relation annotation/2

relation implements(**ofType** Policy, **ofType** Rule) **subRelationOf** annotation

relation hasContext/2 **subRelationOf** annotation

relation hasBusinessFunction(**ofType** Policy, **ofType** bfo#Function) **subRelationOf** hasContext

relation hasBusinessRole(**ofType** Policy, **ofType** bro#Role) **subRelationOf** hasContext

relation hasBusinessResource(**ofType** Policy, **ofType** bre#Object) **subRelationOf** hasContext

relation appliesToBusinessProcess(**ofType** Policy, **ofType** bpdo#Process) **subRelationOf**
    annotation

relation isEnforcedOnBusinessProcess(**ofType** Rule, **ofType** bpdo#Process) **subRelationOf**
    annotation

relation callsBusinessRule(**ofType** Rule, **ofType** Rule) **subRelationOf** annotation

relation containsPolicy(**ofType** Policy, **ofType** Policy) **subRelationOf** annotation

relation usesTerm/2

axiom usesTermDefn
definedBy
!– usesTerm(?x,?y) **and naf** ?x **memberOf** Rule.

axiom appliesToBusinessProcessRelDefn
definedBy
appliesToBusinessProcess(?x,?y) :– annotation(?x,?y) **and** ?x **memberOf** Policy **and** ?y
    memberOf bpdo#Process.

axiom processAnnotationPolicyDefn
definedBy
annotation(?po, ?pr) :– bpdo#isAnnotatedBy(?pr, ?po) **and** ?pr **memberOf** bpdo#Process **and** ?po
    memberOf Policy.

axiom isEnforcedOnBusinessProcessRelDefn
definedBy
isEnforcedOnBusinessProcess(?x, ?y) :– annotation(?x,?y) **and** ?x **memberOf** Rule **and** ?y
    memberOf bpdo#Process.

axiom processAnnotationDefn
definedBy
annotation(?r, ?p) :– bpdo#isAnnotatedBy(?p, ?r) **and** ?p **memberOf** bpdo#Process **and** ?r
    memberOf Rule.

axiom implementsDefn
definedBy
implements(?x, ?y) :– annotation(?x, ?y) **and** ?x **memberOf** Policy **and** ?y **memberOf** Rule.

axiom callsBusinessRuleDefn
definedBy
callsBusinessRule(?x, ?y) :– annotation(?x, ?y) **and** ?x **memberOf** Rule **and** ?y **memberOf** Rule
    and ?x != ?y.

axiom containsPolicyDefn
definedBy
containsPolicy(?x, ?y) :– annotation(?x, ?y) **and** ?x **memberOf** Policy **and** ?y **memberOf** Policy
    and ?x != ?y.

axiom hasContextDefn
definedBy
hasContext(?x, ?y) :– annotation(?x, ?y) **and** ?x **memberOf** Policy **and naf** ?y **memberOf** Policy
    and naf ?y **memberOf** Rule **and naf** ?y **memberOf** bpdo#Process.

axiom callsBusinessRuleReflexivityDefn
definedBy
!– callsBusinessRule(?x,?x) **and** ?x **memberOf** Rule.

axiom containsPolicyReflexivityDefn
definedBy
!– containsPolicy(?x,?x) **and** ?x **memberOf** Policy.

Listing F.1: Business Policies and Rules Ontology

Appendix G

Policy Recommendation Ontology

ontology BPRecO

    importsOntology
        { _"http :// www.ip−super.org/ontologies/BPDO/20070903#BPDO",
              _"http :// www.ip−super.org/ontologies/BPRO/20080829#BPRO" }

relation memberOfSubConcept/3

axiom memberOfSubConceptDefn
definedBy
memberOfSubConcept(?m, ?c, ?sc) :− ?m **memberOf** ?c **and** ?sc **subConceptOf** ?c **and** ?sc !=
    ?c **and** ?m **memberOf** ?sc.

relation directConceptOnly/2

axiom directConceptOnlyDefn
definedBy
directConceptOnly(?x, ?c) :− ?x **memberOf** ?c **and naf** memberOfSubConcept(?x, ?c, ?y).

relation match/3
relation noMatch/3

relation generalizedMatch/4
relation specializedMatch/4
relation ancestralMatch/4

axiom generalizedMatchDef
definedBy
generalizedMatch(?pr, ?po, ?pa, ?poa) :− bpdo#isAnnotatedBy(?pr, ?pa) **and naf** match(?pr, ?po,
    ?pa) **and** bpro#policyHasContext(?po, ?poa) **and naf** bpdo#isAnnotatedBy(?pr, ?po) **and**
    directConceptOnly(?pa, ?padc) **and** directConceptOnly(?poa, ?poadc) **and** ?padc
    subConceptOf ?poadc.

axiom specializedMatchDef
definedBy
specializedMatch(?pr, ?po, ?pa, ?poa) :− bpdo#isAnnotatedBy(?pr, ?pa) **and naf** match(?pr, ?po,
    ?pa) **and naf** generalizedMatch(?pr, ?po, ?pa, ?poa) **and naf** bpdo#isAnnotatedBy(?pr, ?po)
    and bpro#policyHasContext(?po, ?poa) **and** directConceptOnly(?pa, ?padc) **and**
    directConceptOnly(?poa, ?poadc) **and** ?poadc **subConceptOf** ?padc.

axiom ancestralMatchDef

definedBy
ancestralMatch(?pr, ?po, ?pa, ?poa) :− bpdo#isAnnotatedBy(?pr, ?pa) **and naf** match(?pr, ?po,
    ?pa) **and naf** generalizedMatch(?pr, ?po, ?pa, ?poa) **and naf** specializedMatch(?pr, ?po, ?pa,
    ?poa) **and naf** bpdo#isAnnotatedBy(?pr, ?po) **and** bpro#policyHasContext(?po, ?poa) **and** ?pa
    memberOf ?c **and** ?poa **memberOf** ?c.

axiom matchRel
definedBy
match(?Pr, ?Po, ?x) :− bpdo#isAnnotatedBy(?Pr, ?x) **and** bpro#policyHasContext(?Po, ?x) **and naf**
    bpdo#isAnnotatedBy(?Pr, ?Po).

axiom noMatchRel
definedBy
noMatch(?Pr, ?Po, ?x) :− bpdo#isAnnotatedBy(?Pr, ?x) **and naf** bpro#policyHasContext(?Po, ?x)
    and ?Po **memberOf** bpro#Policy **and naf** relaxedMatch(?Pr, ?Po, ?x, ?y).

axiom matchRelConstraint
definedBy
!− match(?x, ?y, ?z) **and** (**naf** ?x **memberOf** bpdo#Process **or naf** ?y **memberOf** bpro#Policy).

axiom noMatchRelConstraint
definedBy
!− noMatch(?x, ?y, ?z) **and** (**naf** ?x **memberOf** bpdo#Process **or naf** ?y **memberOf** bpro#Policy).

axiom generalizedMatchRelConstraint
definedBy
!− generalizedMatch(?pr, ?po, ?pa, ?poa) **and** (**naf** ?pr **memberOf** bpdo#Process **or naf** ?po
    memberOf bpro#Policy).

axiom specializedMatchRelConstraint
definedBy
!− specializedMatch(?pr, ?po, ?pa, ?poa) **and** (**naf** ?pr **memberOf** bpdo#Process **or naf** ?po
    memberOf bpro#Policy).

axiom ancestralMatchRelConstraint
definedBy
!− ancestralMatch(?pr, ?po, ?pa, ?poa) **and** (**naf** ?pr **memberOf** bpdo#Process **or naf** ?po
    memberOf bpro#Policy).

Listing G.1: Policy Recommendation Ontology

Appendix H

Business Policies and Rules Visual Modeling Constructs

This appendix describes the visual constructs (notation) used for the modeling of business policies and business rules.

Since the ontology language of choice for the formalization of business policies and rules is WSML-Flight, our first step in creating a notation for visual modeling of business policies and rules was to create a metamodel of the WSML-Flight language constructs, shown in Fig. H.1. Based on this metamodel, a visual notation for WSML-Flight language was designed, as depicted in Table H.1 (right column).

It is important to note that a WSML-Flight logical expression can be *atomic* or *compound*. We provide the visual representation of atomic expressions in Table H.2, whereas compound expressions combine the atomic expressions using the unary and binary *operators* (see Fig. H.1). For the purpose of visual representation, connectors are used to connect and combine different atomic expressions. In the process of translation to formal representation, these connectors are translated to the conjunction operator.

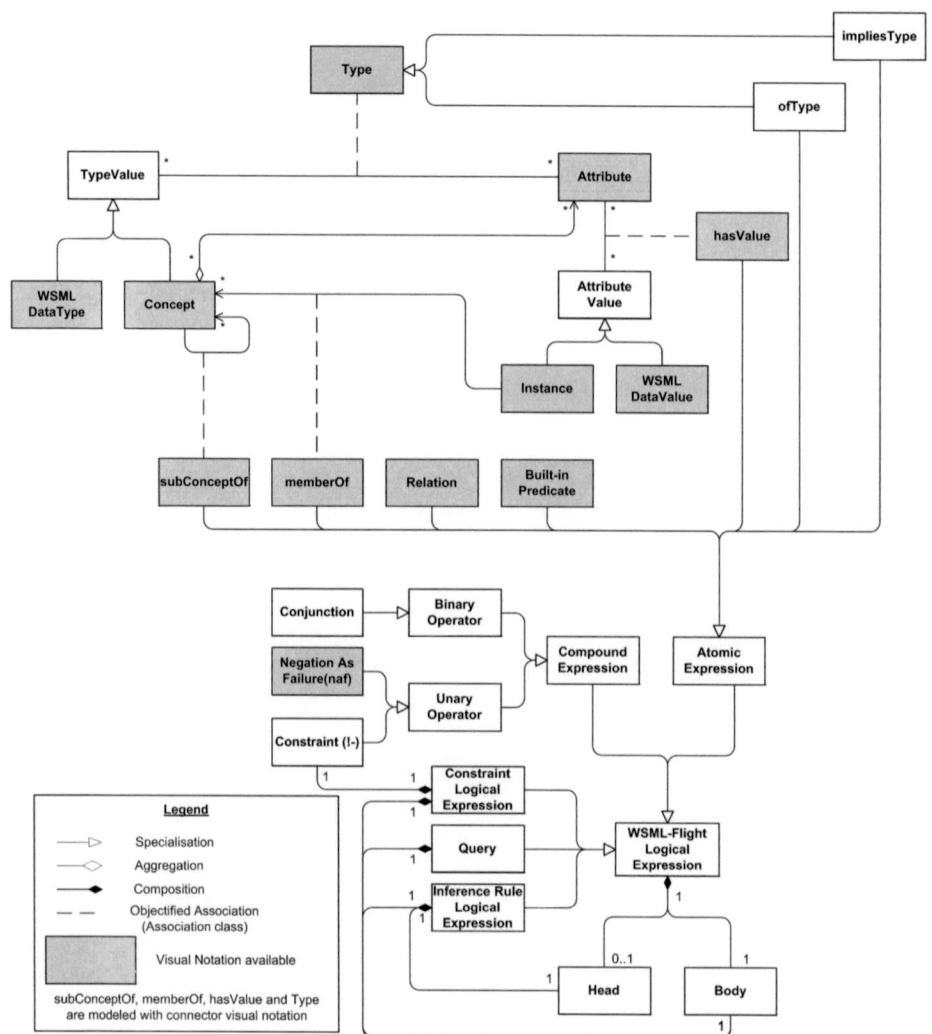

Figure H.1: Metamodel of the WSML-Flight language based on [dBFK+08]

Table H.1: Visual Notation for the Business Policy and Rule Modeling Language

Ontological Construct	Visual Representation
concept {*ConceptName*}	ConceptName
attribute[1] {*AttributeName*}	AttributeName
instance {*InstanceName*}	InstanceName
relation {*RelationName*}	RelationName
WSML-Flight Built-ins	
Data types[2] Ex. {*_string*}	_string
Predicates[2] Ex. {*inequal*}	inequal
Data value[3] {*WSML Data Value*}	AttributeValue
WSML-Flight Logical Expressions (see Section 2.3.4)	
Head or *conclusion* (connector)	
Body or *condition* (connector)	
naf for *relation* and *built-in predicates*	Ex. RelationName
naf for *body* or condition part of WSML-Flight other than *relation*	Ex.
Business Policy and Business Rule visual representations	
Business Policy	Policy Name
Business Rule	Rule Name

[1] *Attribute* is not a keyword in WSML-Flight. Attributes are defined directly after concept definition.

[2] For a list of built-in data types and predicates supported by WSML-Flight we refer the reader to [dBFK+08, dBLPF06].

[3] Defines values for attributes with WSML built-in data types such as *string*. *Data value* is not a keyword in WSML-Flight. Data values are assigned to attributes of an instance directly after instance definition.

Table H.2: Visual Modeling of WSML-Flight Atomic Expressions

Atomic Expression	Visual Representation
subConceptOf Ex. C_1 *subConceptOf* C_2	
memberOf Ex. I_1 *memberOf* C_1	
ofType/impliesType[1] Ex. $C_1[A_1$ *ofType* _string] $C_1[A_1$ *impliesType* _string] $C_1[A_1$ *ofType* $C_2]$ $C_1[A_1$ *impliesType* $C_2]$	
hasValue Ex. $I_1[A_1$ *hasValue* $l_1]$ $I_1[A_1$ *hasValue* $I_2]$	
relation[2] Ex. $R_1(I_1,I_2)$	
Built-in predicates {*inequal*}[2] Ex. *inequal*(I_1,I_2) $I_1 \mathrel{!=} I_2$	

[1] In visual representation, *ofType/impliesType* is inferred from the attribute definition.

[2] The order of parameters in visual representation is captured through the attribute view of the developed prototype (see Section 5.4.1).

References

[AAA+07] A Alves, A. Arkin, S. Askary, C. Barreto, B. Bloch, F. Curbera, M. Ford, Y. Goland, A. Guízar, N. Kartha, C. K. Liu, R. Khalaf, D. König, M. Marin, V. Mehta, S. Thatte, D. van der Rijn, P. Yendluri, and A. Yiu. Web Services Business Process Execution Language version 2.0. Committee specification, OASIS, January 2007.

[ADR07] Gustavo Alonso, Peter Dadam, and Michael Rosemann, editors. *Business Process Management, 5th International Conference, BPM 2007, Brisbane, Australia, September 24-28, 2007, Proceedings*, volume 4714 of *Lecture Notes in Computer Science*. Springer, 2007.

[ADW08] Ahmed Awad, Gero Decker, and Mathias Weske. Efficient compliance checking using BPMN-Q and temporal logic. In Marlon Dumas, Manfred Reichert, and Ming-Chien Shan, editors, *BPM*, volume 5240 of *Lecture Notes in Computer Science*, pages 326–341. Springer, 2008.

[AH05] W.M.P. van der Aalst and A.H.M. ter Hofstede. YAWL: Yet another workflow language. *Information Systems*, 30(4):245–275, 2005.

[AHKB03] W. M. P. Van Der Aalst, A. H. M. Ter Hofstede, B. Kiepuszewski, and A. P. Barros. Workflow patterns. *Distrib. Parallel Databases*, 14(1):5–51, 2003.

[And00] Diagrams '00: Proceedings of the first international conference on theory and application of diagrams. London, UK, 2000. Springer-Verlag.

[Ans65] Igor Ansoff. *Corporate Strategy*. McGraw-Hill, New York, 1965.

[AS06] Sudhir Agarwal and Rudi Studer. Automatic matchmaking of web services. In *ICWS '06: Proceedings of the IEEE International Conference on Web Services (ICWS'06)*, pages 45–54, Washington, DC, USA, 2006. IEEE Computer Society.

[BBM+08] Matthias Born, Christian Brelage, Ivan Markovic, Daniel Pfeiffer, and Ingo Weber. Auto-completion for executable business process models. In *Business Process Management Workshops*, pages 510–515, 2008.

[BCM+03] Franz Baader, Diego Calvanese, Deborah L. McGuinness, Daniele Nardi, and Peter F. Patel-Schneider, editors. *The Description Logic Handbook: Theory, Implementation, and Applications*. Cambridge University Press, 2003.

[BEKM06] Catriel Beeri, Anat Eyal, Simon Kamenkovich, and Tova Milo. Querying business processes. In Umeshwar Dayal, Kyu-Young Whang, David B. Lomet, Gustavo Alonso, Guy M. Lohman, Martin L. Kersten, Sang Kyun Cha, and Young-Kuk Kim, editors, *VLDB*, pages 343–354. ACM, 2006.

[BF08]   Barry Bishop and Florian Fischer. IRIS - integrated rule inference system. In *Proceedings of the 1st Workshop on Advancing Reasoning on the Web: Scalability and Commonsense (ARea2008), in conjunction with the 5th European Semantic Web Conference*, June 2008.

[BFKM08] Matthias Born, Agata Filipowska, Monika Kaczmarek, and Ivan Markovic. Business functions ontology and its application in semantic business process modelling. In *Proceedings of the 19th Australasian Conference on Information Systems, Christchurch, New Zealand*, 2008.

[BHK⁺08] Martin Bichler, Thomas Hess, Helmut Krcmar, Ulrike Lechner, Florian Matthes, Arnold Picot, Benjamin Speitkamp, and Petra Wolf, editors. *Multikonferenz Wirtschaftsinformatik, MKWI 2008, München, 26.2.2008 - 28.2.2008, Proceedings*. GITO-Verlag, Berlin, 2008.

[BIS⁺07] Wasana Bandara, Marta Indulska, Shazia Sadiq, Sandy Chong, Michael Rosemann, and Peter Green. Major issues in business process management: An expert perspective. Technical report, School of ITEE, University of Queensland, Australia, 2007.

[BLHL01] Tim Berners-Lee, James Hendler, and Ora Lassila. The semantic web. *Scientific American*, May 2001.

[BN05]   Travis Breaux and James Niehaus. Requirements for a policy-enforceable agent architecture. Technical Report TR-2005-17, Department of Computer Science, North Carolina State University, Raleigh, NC, USA, March 2005.

[Boe81]   Barry W. Boehm. *Software Engineering Economics*. Prentice-Hall, Englewood Cliffs, USA, 1981.

[Boe88]   Barry W. Boehm. A spiral model of software development and enhancement. *Computer*, 21(5):61–72, 1988.

[Bon06]   Pierro A. Bonatti. Flexible and usable policies. In *Proc. of W3C Workshop on Languages for Privacy Policy Negotiation and Semantics-Driven Enforcement*, Ispra, Italy, October 2006.

[Bör07]   Egon Börger. Modeling workflow patterns from first principles. In Christine Parent, Klaus-Dieter Schewe, Veda C. Storey, and Bernhard Thalheim, editors, *ER*, volume 4801 of *Lecture Notes in Computer Science*, pages 1–20. Springer, 2007.

[BP06]   Anja Bog and Frank Puhlmann. A tool for the simulation of pi-calculus systems. In *Open.BPM 2006: Geschäftsprozessmanagement mit Open Source-Technologien, Hamburg, Germany*, 2006.

[BPE]   Business Process Execution Language for Web Services. http://www.ibm.com/developerworks/library/specification/ws-bpel

[BPM]   BPMI. Business Process Query Language. http://www.service-architecture.com/web-services/articles/business_process_query_language_bpql.html.

[BR02]   G.J. Browne and V. Ramesh. Improving information requirements determination: a cognitive perspective. *Information & Management*, 39:625–645, 2002.

[Bri03] S. Briais. Abc bisimulation checker. Available at: http://lamp.epfl.ch/sbri-ais/abc/abc.html, 2003.

[BRvU00] Jörg Becker, Michael Rosemann, and Christoph von Uthmann. Guide-lines of business process modeling. In *Business Process Management, Models, Techniques, and Empirical Studies*, pages 30–49, London, UK, 2000. Springer-Verlag.

[CH08] M. Cantara and J. Hill. Bpm primer: Getting the basics right first. Technical report, Gartner, Inc., 2008.

[Cha05] James Chang. *Business Process Management Systems: Strategy and Implementa-tion*. Auerbach Publications, 2005.

[CK99] A. Chandra and R. Krovi. Representational congruence and information re-trieval: towards an extended model of cognitive fit. *Decision Support Systems*, 25:271–288, 1999.

[CKO92] Bill Curtis, Marc I. Kellner, and Jim Over. Process modeling. *Commun. ACM*, 35(9):75–90, 1992.

[CR05] Martin J. Creaner and John P. Reilly. *NGOSS Distilled: The Essential Guide to Next Generation Telecoms Management*. The Lean Corporation, 2005.

[CRF03] William W. Cohen, Pradeep Ravikumar, and Stephen E. Fienberg. A com-parison of string distance metrics for name-matching tasks. In Subbarao Kambhampati and Craig A. Knoblock, editors, *IIWeb*, pages 73–78, 2003.

[Dah97] Michael Dahr. *Deductive Databases: Theory and Applications*. Thomson, 1997.

[Dav93] Thomas H. Davenport. *Process innovation: reengineering work through infor-mation technology*. Harvard Business School Press, Boston, MA, USA, 1993.

[Dav98] Thomas H. Davenport. Putting the enterprise into the enterprise system. *Harvard Business Review*, 76(4):121–131, July-August 1998.

[DB07] Rob Davis and Eric Brabänder. *ARIS Design Platform*. Springer, 2007.

[dBFK+08] Jos de Bruijn, Dieter Fensel, Mick Kerrigan, Uwe Keller, Holger Lausen, and James Scicluna. *Modeling Semantic Web Services: The Web Service Modeling Language*. Springer, 1 edition, July 2008.

[dBLPF06] Jos de Bruijn, Holger Lausen, Axel Polleres, and Dieter Fensel. The Web Service Modeling Language WSML: An Overview. In *The Semantic Web: Research and Applications, 3rd ESCW Proceedings*, volume 4011, pages 590–604, June 2006.

[DeM82] T. DeMarco. *Controlling Software Projects: Management, Measurement & Esti-mation*. Yourdon Press, New York, 1982.

[Des05] Jörg Desel. *Process Aware Information Systems: Bridging People and Software Through Process Technology*, chapter Process modeling using petri nets. Wiley Interscience, 2005.

[DFS06] Schahram Dustdar, José Luiz Fiadeiro, and Amit P. Sheth, editors. *Business Process Management, 4th International Conference, BPM 2006, Vienna, Austria, September 5-7, 2006, Proceedings*, volume 4102 of *Lecture Notes in Computer Science*. Springer, 2006.

[DHL90] U. Dayal, M. Hsu, and R. Ladin. Organizing long-running activities with triggers and transactions. In *Proceedings of the 1990 ACM SIGMOD international conference on Management of data*, pages 204–214. ACM Press, New York, 1990.

[DKZD06] G. Decker, M. Kirov, J. M. Zaha, and M. Dumas. Maestro for let's dance: An environment for modeling service interactions. In *BPM Demo Session 2006*, Vienna, Austria, September 2006.

[Dör07] F. Dörr. Semantic extensions of business process modeling tools. Master thesis, Department of Computer Science, Technische Universität Darmstadt, April 2007.

[DPW04] Jörg Desel, Barbara Pernici, and Mathias Weske, editors. *Business Process Management: Second International Conference, BPM 2004, Potsdam, Germany, June 17-18, 2004. Proceedings*, volume 3080 of *Lecture Notes in Computer Science*. Springer, 2004.

[DR01] J. Dehnert and P. Rittgen. Relaxed soundness of business processes. In K.R. Dittrich, A. Geppert, and M.C. Norrie, editors, *Proceedings of the 13th International Conference on Advanced Information Systems Engineering (CAiSE'01)*, volume 2068 of *Lecture Notes in Computer Science*, pages 157–170. Springer-Verlag, Berlin, 2001.

[DRS08] Marlon Dumas, Manfred Reichert, and Ming-Chien Shan, editors. *Business Process Management, 6th International Conference, BPM 2008, Milan, Italy, September 2-4, 2008. Proceedings*, volume 5240 of *Lecture Notes in Computer Science*. Springer, 2008.

[DtH01] Marlon Dumas and Arthur H. M. ter Hofstede. UML activity diagrams as a workflow specification language. In Martin Gogolla and Cris Kobryn, editors, *UML 2001 - The Unified Modeling Language. Modeling Languages, Concepts, and Tools. 4th International Conference, Toronto, Canada, October 2001, Proceedings*, volume 2185 of *LNCS*, pages 76–90. Springer, 2001.

[DvdAtH05] Marlon Dumas, Wil M. van der Aalst, and Arthur H. ter Hofstede. *Process-Aware Information Systems: Bridging People and Software Through Process Technology*. Wiley-Interscience, 2005.

[EKSMP08] Marwane El Kharbili, Sebastian Stein, Ivan Markovic, and Elke Pulvermüller. Towards policy-powered semantic enterprise compliance management – discussion paper. In *3rd International Workshop on Semantic Business Process Management (SBPM)*, CEUR Workshop Proceedings, Tenerife, Spain, June 2008.

[ER03] A. Enders and H.D. Rombach. *A Handbook of Software and Systems Engineering: Empirical Observations, Laws and Theories*. Addison-Wesley, Reading, MA, USA, 2003.

[EW03]   Steffen Exeler and Sven Wilms. Change management with ARIS. In *Bus. Proc. Change Management*. Springer, 2003.

[FESS07] Alexander Förster, Gregor Engels, Tim Schattkowsky, and Ragnhild Van Der Straeten. Verification of business process quality constraints based on visual process patterns. In *TASE '07: Proceedings of the First Joint IEEE/IFIP Symposium on Theoretical Aspects of Software Engineering*, pages 197–208, Los Alamitos, CA, USA, 2007. IEEE Computer Society.

[FG94]   Mark S. Fox and Michael Grüninger. Ontologies for enterprise integration. In *Proceedings of the International Conference on Cooperative Information Systems (CoopIS)*, pages 82–89, 1994.

[FG98]   Mark S. Fox and Michael Gruninger. Enterprise modelling. *AI Magazine*, 19:109–121, Fall 1998.

[FHKM09] Agata Filipowska, Martin Hepp, Monika Kaczmarek, and Ivan Markovic. Organisational ontology framework for semantic business process management. In Witold Abramowicz, editor, *BIS*, volume 21 of *Lecture Notes in Business Information Processing*, pages 1–12. Springer, 2009.

[FKK+08] Agata Filipowska, Monika Kaczmarek, Marwane El Kharbili, Ivan Markovic, and Pierre Grenon. Ontology stack for high-level business process knowledge. Technical report, SUPER Project, Deliverable D1.6, 2008.

[FKRS08] J. Frankowski, H. Kupidura, P. Rubach, and E. Szczekocka. Business process management for convergent services provisioning using the super platform. In *Proceedings of the International Conference on Intelligence in Service Delivery Networks (ICIN)*, 2008.

[FKZ08] Dieter Fensel, Mick Kerrigan, and Michal Zaremba, editors. *Implementing Semantic Web Services, The SESA Framework*. Springer-Verlag, Berlin, Heidelberg, 2008.

[FLM+04] Ariel Fuxman, Lin Liu, John Mylopoulos, Marco Roveri, and Paolo Traverso. Specifying and analyzing early requirements in Tropos. *Req. Eng.*, 9(2):132–150, 2004.

[FLP+06] D. Fensel, H. Lausen, A. Polleres, J. Bruijn, M. Stollberg, D. Roman, and J. Domingue. *Enabling Semantic Web Services: The Web Service Modeling Ontology*. Springer, 1 edition, November 2006.

[Fox92] Mark S. Fox. The TOVE project towards a Common-Sense model of the enterprise. In *Proc. of the 5th int. conf. on Industrial and engineering applications of artificial intelligence and expert systems*, volume 604, pages 25–34, Paderborn, Germany, June 1992. Springer.

[FSK+09] Paola Fantini, Alberto Savoldelli, Marwane El Kharbili, Jana Koehler, Christian Brelage, and Matthias Born. Super deliverable d2.4: Semantic business process modelling & quality assurance. Technical report, 2009.

[FSM+06] Paola Fantini, Alberto Savoldelli, Micaela Milanesi, Giulio Carizzoni, Jana Koehler, Martin Hepp Sebastian Stein and, Ralf Angeli and, Dumitru Roman, Christian Brelage, and Matthias Born. Semantic business process life cycle. Technical report, SUPER Deliverable, June 2006.

[GBCL04] Aldo Gangemi, Stefano Borgo, Carola Catenacci, and Jos Lehmann. Task taxonomies for knowledge content d07. Technical report, Metokis Project, 2004.

[GD08] Kirk Gould and Christine Dicken. Process as an asset. *BPTrends*, 2008.

[GDDS06] Dragan Gasevic, Dragan Djuric, Vladan Devedzic, and Bran Selic. *Model Driven Architecture and Ontology Development*. Springer-Verlag New York, Inc., Secaucus, NJ, USA, 2006.

[GF07] Laurence Goasduff and Carina Forsling. Business Process Management Suites (BPMS) Will Be Among the Fastest Growing Software Markets through 2011, Says Gartner. Technical report, Gartner Press Release, http://www.gartner.com/it/page.jsp?id=502645, 2007.

[GHA07] S. Grimm, P. Hitzler, and A. Abecker. Knowledge representation and ontologies. In R. Studer, S. Grimm, and A. Abecker, editors, *Semantic Web Services : Concepts, Technologies, and Applications*, chapter 3, pages 51–105. Springer, Berlin, 1 edition, June 2007.

[GHJV95] E. Gamma, R. Helm, R. Johnson, and J. Vlissides. *Design patterns: elements of reusable object-oriented software*. Addison-Wesley Longman Publishing Co., Inc. Boston, MA, USA, 1995.

[GHSW08] Guido Governatori, Jörg Hoffmann, Shazia Sadiq, and Ingo Weber. Detecting regulatory compliance for business process models through semantic annotations. In *BPD-08: 4th International Workshop on Business Process Design*, September 2008.

[GL07] Volker Gruhn and Ralf Laue. *Technologies for Business Information Systems*, chapter Approaches for Business Process Model Complexity Metrics, pages 13–24. Springer, 2007.

[GMNS03] Paolo Giorgini, John Mylopoulos, Eleonora Nicchiarelli, and Roberto Sebastiani. Formal reasoning techniques for goal models. *J. Data Semantics*, 2800:1–20, 2003.

[GMP+08] Paolo Giorgini, John Mylopoulos, Loris Penserini, Anna Perini, and Angelo Susi. Tropos at the age of eight: On-going research at fbk, unitn and ut. In Jaelson Brelaz de Castro, Xavier Franch, Anna Perini, and Eric Yu, editors, *iStar*, volume 322 of *CEUR Workshop Proceedings*, pages 83–89. CEUR-WS.org, 2008.

[GMS06] Guido Governatori, Zoran Milosevic, and Shazia Sadiq. Compliance checking between business processes and business contracts. In *EDOC '06: Proceedings of the 10th IEEE International Enterprise Distributed Object Computing Conference*, pages 221–232, Washington, DC, USA, 2006. IEEE Computer Society.

[GN87] Michael R. Genesereth and Nils Nilsson. *The Logical Foundations of Artificial Intelligence*. Morgan Kaufmann, 1987.

[GOS09] N. Guarino, D. Oberle, and S. Staab. What is an ontology? *Handbook on Ontologies, Second Edition*, International handbooks on information systems. Springer Verlag:1–17, 2009.

[Gro94] Standish Group. The chaos report. Available on-line at `http://www.standishgroup.com/sample_research/chaos_1994_1.php`, 1994.

[Gro95] Standish Group. Unfinished voyages. Available on-line at `http://www.standishgroup.com/sample_research/unfinished_voyages_1.php`, 1995.

[Gru93] T. R. Gruber. Towards principles for the design of ontologies used for knowledge sharing. In N. Guarino and R. Poli, editors, *Formal Ontology in Conceptual Analysis and Knowledge Representation*, Deventer, The Netherlands, 1993. Kluwer Academic Publishers.

[GS95] J. Galler and A.-W. Scheer. Workflow-projekte: Vom geschäftsprozessmodell zur unternehmensspezifischen workflow-anwendung. *Information Management*, 10(1):20–27, 1995.

[Gua97] Nicola Guarino. Semantic matching: Formal ontological distinctions for information organization, extraction, and integration. In Maria Teresa Pazienza, editor, *SCIE*, volume 1299 of *Lecture Notes in Computer Science*, pages 139–170. Springer, 1997.

[Gua98] N. Guarino. Formal ontology and information systems. In N. Guarino, editor, *Formal Ontology in Information Systems*, pages 3–18. IOS Press, Amsterdam, 1998.

[GV06] Stijn Goedertier and Jan Vanthienen. Compliant and flexible business processes with business rules. In *BPMDS*, 2006.

[Ham90] Michael Hammer. Reengineering work: Don't automate, obliterate. *Harvard Business Review*, pages 105–112, July-August 1990.

[HC93] Michael Hammer and Charles Champy. *Reengineering the Corporation*. Harper Business, 1993.

[HCDK07] Janelle B. Hill, Michele Cantara, Eric Deitert, and Marc Kerremans. Gartner magic quadrant for business process management suites. Technical report, Gartner Report, G00152906, 2007.

[HCKP09] Janelle B. Hill, Michele Cantara, Marc Kerremans, and Daryl C. Plummer. Gartner magic quadrant for business process management suites. Technical report, Gartner Report, G00164485, 2009.

[HHK⁺07] Martin Hepp, Knut Hinkelmann, Dimitris Karagiannis, Rüdiger Klein, and Nenad Stojanovic, editors. *Proceedings of the Workshop on Semantic Business Process and Product Lifecycle Management held in conjunction with the 3rd European Semantic Web Conference (ESWC 2007), Innsbruck, Austria, June 7, 2007*, volume 251 of *CEUR Workshop Proceedings*. CEUR-WS.org, 2007.

[HLD⁺05] Martin Hepp, Frank Leymann, John Domingue, Alexander Wahler, and Dieter Fensel. Semantic business process management: A vision towards using semantic web services for business process management. In *ICEBE '05: Proceedings of the IEEE International Conference on e-Business Engineering*, pages 535–540, Washington, DC, USA, 2005. IEEE Computer Society.

[HMPR04] A. R. Hevner, S. T. March, J. Park, and S. Ram. Design science in information systems research. *MIS Quarterly*, 28(1):75–105, 2004.

[HPSB⁺04] I. Horrocks, P. F. Patel-Schneider, H. Boley, S. Tabet, B. Grosof, and M. Dean. SWRL: A Semantic Web Rule Language Combining OWL and RuleML. W3C Member Submission http://www.w3.org/Submission/SWRL/, May 2004.

[HR07] Martin Hepp and Dimitru Roman. An ontology framework for semantic business process management. In *Proceedings of the 8th international Conference Wirtschaftsinformatik*, Karlsruhe, Germany, February 28 – March 2 2007.

[HS06] H.-J. Happel and L. Stojanovic. Ontoprocess - a prototype for semantic business process verification using SWRL rules. In *Demosession of the 3rd European Semantic Web Conference (ESWC' 06)*, Budva, Montenegro, June 2006.

[IBM06] IBM. *Best Practices for Using WebSphere Business Modeler and Monitor*. IBM Redbooks, 2006.

[IBM09] IBM. Websphere business modeler. http://www-01.ibm.com/software/integration/wbimodeler/, 2009.

[ICO07] ICOM/CIDOC CRM Special Interest Group. CIDOC Conceptual Reference Model. http://cidoc.ics.forth.gr/docs/cidoc_crm_version_4.2.2.pdf, August 2007.

[ISR02] ISR. Editorial statement and policy. Information Systems Research (13:4), December 2002.

[JB96] S. Jablonski and C. Bussler. *Workflow Management: Modeling Concepts, Architecture, and Implementation*. International Thomson Computer Press, London, UK, 1996.

[Kar95] Dimitris Karagiannis. Bpms: business process management systems. *SIGOIS Bull.*, 16(1):10–13, 1995.

[Kar07] Dimitris Karagiannis. What can web services learn from business process modeling? In *ACT4SOC*, page 3, 2007.

[Kar08] Dimitris Karagiannis. A business process-based modelling extension for regulatory compliance. In *Multikonferenz Wirtschaftsinformatik*, 2008.

[KF94] H. Kim and M.S Fox. Formal models of quality and iso 9000 compliance: An information systems approach. In *American Quality Congress (AQC) Conference*, 1994.

[KG] George Koliadis and Aditya Ghose. Relating business process models to goal-oriented requirements models in kaos. In *PKAW 2006*, pages 25–39.

[KK02] D. Karagiannis and H. Kühn. Metamodelling platforms. In *EC-WEB '02: Proceedings of the Third International Conference on E-Commerce and Web Technologies*, London, UK, 2002. Springer-Verlag.

[KLW95] Michael Kifer, Georg Lausen, and James Wu. Logical foundations of object-oriented and frame-based languages. *J. ACM*, 42(4):741–843, July 1995.

[KMS07] Dimitris Karagiannis, John Mylopoulos, and Margit Schwab. Business process-based regulation compliance: The case of the sarbanes-oxley act. In *Proceedings of the 15th IEEE International Conference on Requirements Engineering*, pages 315–321, 2007.

[KN92]   Robert S. Kaplan and David P. Norton. The Balanced Scorecard - Measures that Drive Performance. *Harvard Business Review*, January/February 1992.

[KN96]   Robert S. Kaplan and David P. Norton. *The Balanced Scorecard : Translating Strategy Into Action*. Harvard Business School Press, Boston, Mass., 1996.

[KNS92]   G. Keller, M. Nüttgens, and A.-W Scheer. Semantische Prozessmodellierung auf der Grundlage Ereignisgesteuerter Prozessketten. *Tech.R., Uni. d. Saarlandes*, 1992.

[KSMP08] Marwane El Kharbili, Sebastian Stein, Ivan Markovic, and Elke Pulvermueller. Towards a framework for semantic business process compliance management. In *Proc. 1st Int'l Workshop on Governance, Risk and Compliance - Applications in Information Systems (GRCIS'08)*, 2008.

[KV07]   J. Koehler and J. Vanhatalo. Process anti-patterns: How to avoid the common traps of business process modeling. *IBM WebSphere Developer Technical Journal*, 10(2):4, 2007.

[Lam07]   Steffen Lamparter. *Policy-based Contracting in Semantic Web Service Markets*. PhD thesis, University of Karlsruhe (TH), 2007.

[LGRMD08] L. Thao Ly, K. Göser, S. Rinderle-Ma, and P. Dadam. Compliance of semantic constraints - a requirements analysis for process management systems. In *Proc. 1st Int'l Workshop on Governance, Risk and Compliance - Applications in Information Systems (GRCIS'08)*, Montpellier, France, June 2008.

[LH03]   L. Li and I. Horrocks. A software framework for matchmaking based on semantic web technology. In *Proc. of the 12th int. conf. on World Wide Web*, pages 331–339. ACM, 2003.

[Lin78]   William James Linton. *Poetry of America: Selections from one hundred American poets from 1776 to 1876*. 1878.

[Lin08]   Yun Lin. *Semantic Annotation for Process Models: Facilitating Process Knowledge Management via Semantic Interoperability*. PhD thesis, Norwegian University of Science and Technology, Trondheim, Norway, 2008.

[Llo87]   J. Wylie Lloyd. *Foundations of Logic Programming*. Springer, 2 sub edition, November 1987.

[LMX07]   Y. Liu, S. Müller, and K. Xu. A static compliance-checking framework for business process models. *IBM Systems Journal*, 46(2):335–361, April 2007.

[LNO+89] G. Lausen, T. Németh, A. Oberweis, F. Schönthaler, and W. Stucky. The income approach for conceptual modelling and prototyping of information systems. In *CASE89: The First Nordic Conference on Advanced Systems Engineering*, 1989.

[LSS94]   O.I. Lindland, G. Sindre, and A. Solvberg. Understanding quality in conceptual modeling. *Software, IEEE*, 11(2):42—49, March 1994.

[Mai03]   A. Maier. Integration with ontologies. In U. Reimer, A. Abecker, S. Staab, and G. Stumme, editors, *WM2003: Professionelles Wissensmanagement - Erfahrungen und Visionen*, Luzern, Switzerland, April 2003.

[Mar03]   A. Martens. On compatibility of web services. volume 65, pages 12–20, 2003.

[MBG⁺03]   Claudio Masolo, Stefano Borgo, Aldo Gangemi, Nicola Guarino, Alessandro Oltramari, and Luc Schneider. WonderWeb Deliverable D17. The WonderWeb Library of Foundational Ontologies and the DOLCE ontology. http://www.loa-cnr.it/Papers/DOLCE2.1-FOL.pdf, May 2003.

[Mcg03]   Deborah L. Mcguinness. *Ontologies Come of Age*. MIT Press, 2003.

[MCZ04]   Yujie Mou, Jian Cao, and Shen-Sheng Zhang. A process component model for enterprise business knowledge reuse. In *IEEE International Conference on Services Computing (SCC)*, pages 409–412. IEEE Computer Society, 2004.

[Men07]   Jan Mendling. *Detection and Prediction of Errors in EPC Business Process Models*. PhD thesis, Vienna University of Economics and Business Administration, May 2007.

[Men08]   Jan Mendling. *Metrics for Process Models: Empirical Foundations of Verification, Error Prediction, and Guidelines for Correctness*. Springer, 2008.

[MESW01]   B. Moore, E. Ellesson, J. Strassner, and A. Westerinen. Policy core information model – version 1 specification. http://portal.acm.org/citation.cfm?id=RFC3060, 2001.

[MH09]   Ivan Markovic and Florian Hasibether. Towards integrating perspectives and abstraction levels in business process modeling. In *ICEIS (3)*, pages 286–291, 2009.

[MHJS09]   Ivan Markovic, Florian Hasibether, Sukesh Jain, and Nenad Stojanovic. Process-oriented semantic business modeling. In *Wirtschaftsinformatik (1)*, pages 683–694, 2009.

[MK07]   Ivan Markovic and Mario Karrenbrock. Semantic web service discovery for business process models. In *WISE Workshops*, pages 272–283, 2007.

[MK08]   Ivan Markovic and Marek Kowalkiewicz. Linking business goals to process models in semantic business process modeling. In *EDOC*, pages 332–338, 2008.

[MLA05]   Henry Mintzberg, Joseph Lampel, and Bruce Ahlstrand. *Strategy Safari: A Guided Tour Through The Wilds of Strategic Management*. Free Press, May 2005.

[MMG02]   M. L. Markus, A. Majchrzak, and L. Gasser. A design theory for systems that support emergent knowledge processes. *MIS Quarterly*, 26(3):179–212, 2002.

[Moo05]   Daniel L. Moody. Theoretical and practical issues in evaluating the quality of conceptual models: current state and future directions. *Data Knowl. Eng*, 55(3):243–276, 2005.

[Mor98]   G. Morgan. *Images of Organization*. Sage Pubns, 1998.

[MP07]   Ivan Markovic and Alessandro Costa Pereira. Towards a formal framework for reuse in business process modeling. In Arthur H. M. ter Hofstede, Boualem Benatallah, and Hye-Young Paik, editors, *Business Process Management Workshops*, volume 4928 of *Lecture Notes in Computer Science*, pages 484–495. Springer, 2007.

[MPW89] R. Milner, J. Parrow, and D. Walker. A calculus of mobile processes, parts I and II. Technical Report 86, University of Edinburgh, June 1989.

[MR08] Michael Zur Muehlen and Jan Recker. How much language is enough? theoretical and practical use of the business process modeling notation. In *CAiSE '08: Proceedings of the 20th international conference on Advanced Information Systems Engineering*, pages 465–479, Berlin, Heidelberg, 2008. Springer-Verlag.

[MS95] Salvatore T. March and Gerald F. Smith. Design and natural science research on information technology. *Decis. Support Syst.*, 15(4):251–266, 1995.

[Nil71] Nils J. Nilsson. *Problem-Solving Methods in Artificial Intelligence*. McGraw-Hill Pub. Co., 1971.

[NM07] G. J. Nalepa and M. A. Mach. Conceptual modeling of business rules and processes with the xtt method. In *Proc. of CMS'07: Computer Methods and Systems*, Kraków, Poland, November 2007.

[NPC03] S. Neumann, C. Probst, and C.Wernsmann. *Process Management: A Guide for the Design of Business Processes*, chapter Continuous Process Management, pages 233–250. Springer, Berlin, 2003.

[NS06] K. Namiri and N. Stojanovic. Towards business level verification of cross organizational business processes. In *Workshop on Semantics for Business Process Management* `http://km.aifb.uni-karlsruhe.de/ws/sbpm2006/papers/sbpm06_Namiri.pdf`, pages 101–112, Budva, Montenegro, June 11–14 2006.

[Obj07] Object Management Group. Unified modeling language (uml), November 2007.

[Obj08] Object Management Group. Semantics of Business Vocabulary and Business Rules (SBVR), ver1.0. `http://www.omg.org/spec/SBVR/index.htm`, January 2008.

[Obj09] Object Management Group. Business process modeling notation, v1.2. `http://www.omg.org/spec/BPMN/index.htm`, January 2009. Object Management Group (OMG) Released version of Business Process Modeling Notation (BPMN).

[OMG08a] OMG. Business Motivation Model v1.0. `http://www.omg.org/spec/BMM`, 2008.

[OMG08b] OMG. Business Process Maturity Model v1.0. `http://www.omg.org/spec/BPMM/1.0/`, 2008.

[Ont] Ontoprise GmbH. Ontostudio manual. `http://www.ontoprise.de/help/index.jsp`.

[Ora09] Oracle. Oracle bpel process manager. `http://www.oracle.com/technology/products/ias/bpel/index.html`, 2009.

[OSS94] Andreas Oberweis, Gabriele Scherrer, and Wolffried Stucky. Income/star: Methodology and tools for the development of distributed information systems. *Inf. Syst.*, 19(8):643–682, 1994.

[Pal07]   Nathaniel Palmer. A survey of business process initiatives. Technical report, Business Process Trends, 2007.

[PDdM08]   Carlos Pedrinaci, John Domingue, and Ana Karla Alves de Medeiros. A core ontology for business process analysis. In Sean Bechhofer, Manfred Hauswirth, Jörg Hoffmann, and Manolis Koubarakis, editors, *ESWC*, volume 5021 of *Lecture Notes in Computer Science*, pages 49–64. Springer, 2008.

[Pet62]   C. A. Petri. *Communication with Automata*. PhD Dissertation, Universität Bonn, Germany, 1962.

[PKPS02]   Massimo Paolucci, Takahiro Kawamura, Terry R. Payne, and Katia P. Sycara. Semantic matching of web services capabilities. In Ian Horrocks and James A. Hendler, editors, *International Semantic Web Conference*, volume 2342 of *Lecture Notes in Computer Science*, pages 333–347. Springer, 2002.

[Por85]   Michael Porter. *Competitive Advantage*. The Free Press, 1985.

[Pre05]   Roger S. Pressman. *Software Engineering: A Practitioner's Approach*. McGraw-Hill Professional, 6th edition, 2005.

[Puh06a]   Frank Puhlmann. A tool chain for lazy soundness. In *Proceedings of the Demo Session at the International Conference on Business Process Management*, pages 9–16, 2006.

[Puh06b]   Frank Puhlmann. Why do we actually need the pi-calculus for business process management? In Witold Abramowicz and Heinrich C. Mayr, editors, *Proceedings of the International Conference on Business Information Systems*, volume 85 of *LNI*, pages 77–89. GI, 2006.

[PW05]   F. Puhlmann and M. Weske. Using the pi-Calculus for formalizing workflow patterns. *Business Process Management*, 3649:153–168, 2005.

[PW06]   Frank Puhlmann and Mathias Weske. Investigations on soundness regarding lazy activities. In *Business Process Management*, pages 145–160, 2006.

[RB01]   Erhard Rahm and P Bernstein. A survey of approaches to automatic schema matching. *VLDB Journal*, 10(4):334–350, 2001.

[RK07]   Dumitru Roman and Michael Kifer. Reasoning about the behavior of semantic web services with concurrent transaction logic. In *VLDB '07: Proceedings of the 33rd international conference on Very large data bases*, pages 627–638. VLDB Endowment, 2007.

[Ros03a]   M. Rosemann. *Process Management: A Guide for the Design of Business Processes*, chapter Preparation of Process Modeling, pages 41–78. Springer-Verlag, 2003.

[Ros03b]   R. G. Ross. *Principles of the Business Rule Approach*. Addison-Wesley Professional, February 2003.

[RtHvdAM06]   N. Russel, A. ter Hofstede, W. M. P. van der Aalst, and N. Mulyar. Workflow control-flow patterns. a revised view. Technical report, Draft Manuscript BPMCenter.org, 2006.

[RZ96] D. Riehle and H. Züllighoven. Understanding and using patterns in software development. *Theory and Practice of Object Systems*, 2(1):3–13, 1996.

[San96] Sangiorgi. A theory of bisimulation for the pi-calculus. *ACTAINF: Acta Informatica*, 33, 1996.

[SAP] SAP AG. Sap netweaver bpm process composer. `http://www.sap.com/platform/netweaver/components/sapnetweaverbpm/index.epx`, 2008.

[SAP05a] SAP AG. Sap solution composer - what is it? `http://www.sap.com/solutions/businessmaps/pdf/MISC_SAP_Solution_Composer_8_2005.pdf`, 2005.

[SAP05b] SAP AG. Solution Composer Quick Guide. `http://www.sap.com/solutions/businessmaps/pdf/Misc_Composer_Quick_Guide_12_2005.pdf`, 2005.

[SAP07] SAP AG. Sap business maps. `http://www.sap.com/solutions/businessmaps/index.epx`, 2007.

[SAP09a] SAP AG. Sap solution manager. `http://www.sap.com/platform/netweaver/components/solutionmanager/index.epx`, 2009.

[SAP09b] SAP AG. Sap strategy management. `http://www.sap.com/solutions/sapbusinessobjects/large/enterprise-performance-management/strategy/index.epx`, 2009.

[Sav05] Savvion. Business process lifecycle management with savvion businessmanager. Technical report, Savvion, 2005.

[SBF98] Rudi Studer, Richard V. Benjamins, and Dieter Fensel. Knowledge engineering: Principles and methods. *Data & Knowledge Engineering*, 25(1-2):161–197, March 1998.

[Sch88] August-Wilhelm Scheer. *Wirtschaftsinformatik: Referenzmodelle für industrielle Geschäftsprozesse*. Springer, 1988.

[Sch99] August-Wilhelm Scheer. *ARIS. Business Process Modeling*. Springer, 1999.

[Sch00a] A.-W. Scheer. *ARIS - Business Process Frameworks*. Springer, 3rd edition, March 2000.

[Sch00b] A.-W. Scheer. *ARIS - Business Process Modeling*. Springer, Berlin, Heidelberg, 3rd edition, March 2000.

[SEI09] Carnegy Melon University Software Engineering Institute. Capability maturity model integration. `http://www.sei.cmu.edu/cmmi/general/index.html`, May 2009.

[SF06] H. Smith and P. Fingar. *Business Process Management: The Third Wave*. Meghan Kiffer Press, October 2006.

[SGA07] Rudi Studer, Stephan Grimm, and Andreas Abecker, editors. *Semantic Web Services, Concepts, Technologies, and Applications*. Springer-Verlag, Berlin, Heidelberg, 2007.

[SGM04] Roberto Sebastiani, Paolo Giorgini, and John Mylopoulos. Simple and minimum-cost satisfiability for goal models. In *Proc. CAiSE 2004*, 2004.

[SGN07] Shazia Wasim Sadiq, Guido Governatori, and Kioumars Namiri. Modeling control objectives for business process compliance. In *BPM*, pages 149–164, 2007.

[SH06] Jim Sinur and Janelle B. Hill. Align BPM and SOA Initiatives Now to Increase Chances of Becoming a Leader by 2010. Gartner Predicts 2007, 10 November 2006.

[SHP03] E. Sirin, J. Hendler, and B. Parsia. Semi-automatic composition of web services using semantic descriptions. *In Web Services: Modeling, Architecture and Infrastructure workshop in ICEIS*, pages 17–24, 2003.

[Sim96] Herbert A. Simon. *The Sciences of the Artificial - 3rd Edition*. The MIT Press, October 1996.

[SKN92] A.-W. Scheer, G. Keller, and M. Nuttgens. Semantische prozessmodellierung auf der grundlage "ereignisgesteuerter prozessketten (epk)". *Veroffentlichungen des Instituts fur Wirtschaftsinformatik*, 89, 1992.

[Smi07] Ralph F. Smith. *Business Process Management and the Balanced Scorecard: Using Processes as Strategic Drivers*. John Wiley & Sons, Inc., 2007.

[SPH03] A. Speck, E. Pulvermüller, and D. Heuzeroth. Validation of business process models. In *Proc. of ECOOP 2003 Workshop Correctness of Model-based Software Composition (CMC)*, volume 2003-13, pages 75–83, Darmstadt, Germany, July 2003. Universitaet Karlsruhe, Fakultaet fuer Informatik.

[SSSS01] Steffen Staab, Rudi Studer, Hans-Peter Schnurr, and York Sure. Knowledge processes and ontologies. *IEEE Intelligent Systems*, 16(1):26–34, 2001.

[STA05] August-Wilhelm Scheer, Oliver Thomas, and Otmar Adam. *Process Aware Information Systems: Bridging People and Software Through Process Technology.*, chapter Process modeling using event-driven process chains. Wiley Interscience, 2005.

[Tay11] Frederick W. Taylor. *The Principles of Scientific Management*. 1911.

[TBJ+03] G. Tonti, J. M. Bradshaw, R. Jeffers, R. Montanari, N. Suri, and A. Uszok. Semantic web languages for policy representation and reasoning: A comparison of KAoS, rei, and ponder. *The Semantic Web ISWC 2003*, 2870:419–437, 2003.

[TFG94] D. Tham, M.S. Fox, and M. Gruninger. A cost ontology for enterprise modelling. In *3rd Workshop on Enabling Technologies, West Virginia University*, 1994.

[UG96] Mike Uschold and Michael Gruninger. Ontologies: Principles, methods and applications. *Know. Eng. Rev.*, 11:93–155, 1996.

[UG04] M. Uschold and M. Gruninger. Ontologies and semantics for seamless connectivity. *SIGMOD Rec.*, 33(4):58–64, December 2004.

[UKH+98] Mike Uschold, Martin King, South Bridge Rosanne House, Stuart Moralee, and Yannis Zorgios. The enterprise ontology. *The Knowledge Engineering Review*, 13:31–89, 1998.

[Ult06] Ultimus. What makes human-centric bpm different? Technical report, Ultimus, 2006.

[VCM+07] I. Vanderfeesten, J. Cardoso, J. Mendling, H. Reijers, and W. van der Aalst. Quality metrics for business process models. *BPM & Workflow Handbook, Workflow Management Coalition*, pages 179–190, 2007.

[vdA97] Wil M. P. van der Aalst. Verification of workflow nets. In *ICATPN '97: Proceedings of the 18th International Conference on Application and Theory of Petri Nets*, pages 407–426, London, UK, 1997. Springer-Verlag.

[vdA98] W.M.P. van der Aalst. The application of petri nets to workflow management. *The Journal of Circuits, Systems and Computers*, 8(1):21–66, 1998.

[vdA00] Wil M. P. van der Aalst. Workflow verification: Finding control-flow errors using petri-net-based techniques. In *Business Process Management, Models, Techniques, and Empirical Studies*, pages 161–183, London, UK, 2000. Springer-Verlag.

[vdA04] W. M. P. van der Aalst. Business process management demystified: A tutorial on models, systems and standards for workflow management. In J. Desel, W. Reisig, and G. Rozenberg, editors, *Lectures on Concurrency and Petri Nets*, volume 3098 of *Lecture Notes in Computer Science*, pages 1–65. Springer-Verlag, Berlin, 2004.

[vdABCC05] Wil M. P. van der Aalst, Boualem Benatallah, Fabio Casati, and Francisco Curbera, editors. *Business Process Management, 3rd International Conference, BPM 2005, Nancy, France, September 5-8, 2005, Proceedings*, volume 3649. 2005.

[vdAtHW03] Wil M. P. van der Aalst, Arthur H. M. ter Hofstede, and Mathias Weske, editors. *Business Process Management, International Conference, BPM 2003, Eindhoven, The Netherlands, June 26-27, 2003, Proceedings*, volume 2678 of *Lecture Notes in Computer Science*. Springer, 2003.

[vdAvH02] W. van der Aalst and K. van Hee. *Workflow Management*. MIT Press, 2002.

[VL01] Axel Van Lamsweerde. Goal-oriented requirements engineering: A guided tour. In *RE '01: Proceedings of the Fifth IEEE International Symposium on Requirements Engineering*, page 249, Washington, DC, USA, 2001. IEEE Computer Society.

[VM94] B. Victor and F. Moller. The Mobility Workbench — a tool for the π-calculus. In David Dill, editor, *Proc. of the 6th Int. Conf. on Computer Aided Verification*, volume 818, pages 428–440. Springer, 1994.

[WAM+07] Ueli Wahli, Vedavyas Avula, Hannah Macleod, Mohamed Saeed, and Anders Vinther. *Business Process Management: Modeling through Monitoring Using WebSphere V6.0.2 Products*. IBM Redbooks, 2007.

[Web09] Ingo Weber. *Semantic Methods for Execution-level Business Process Modeling*. PhD thesis, Universität Karlsruhe (TH), November 2009. Springer, Lecture Notes in Business Information Processing (LNBIP) Vol. 40.

[Wes07] M. Weske. *Business Process Management: Concepts, Languages, Architectures*. Springer, 2007.

[WfM99] Workflow Management Coalition WfMC. Terminology & glossary. `http://wfmc.org/View-document-details/WFMC-TC-1011-Ver-3-Terminology-and-Glossary-English.html`, 1999. Retrieved: December 4, 2008.

[Whi04] S. A. White. Process modeling notations and workflow patterns. *BPTrends—Business Process Trends*, March 2004.

[WHMN07] Ingo Weber, Jörg Hoffmann, Jan Mendling, and Jörg Nitzsche. Towards a methodology for semantic business process modeling and configuration. In *SeMSoC-07: Proceedings of the 2nd International Workshop on Business Oriented Aspects concerning Semantics and Methodologies in Service-oriented Computing*, September 2007.

[WMD08] Ingo Weber, Ivan Markovic, and Christian Drumm. A conceptual framework for semantic business process configuration. *Journal of Information Science and Technology (JIST)*, 5(2):3–20, 2008.

[Wor04] World Wide Web Consortium (W3C). Web ontology language (owl). W3C Recommendation `http://www.w3.org/2004/OWL/`, February 2004.

[WW95]   Y. Wand and R. Weber. On the deep structure of information systems. *Information Systems Journal*, 5:203–223, 1995.

[WW02]   Y. Wand and R. Weber. Research commentary: Information systems and conceptual modeling–a research agenda. *Information Systems Research*, 13(4):363–376, December 2002.

[XLY07] Gang Xue, Joan Lu, and Shaowen Yao. Investigating workflow patterns in term of pi-calculus. In Weiming Shen, Yun Yang, Jianming Yong, Igor Hawryszkiewycz, Zongkai Lin, Jean-Paul A. Barthès, Mary Lou Maher, Qi Hao, and Minh Hong Tran, editors, *Proceedings of the 11th International Conference on Computer Supported Cooperative Work in Design, CSCWD*, pages 823–827. IEEE, 2007.

[YAT07] D.8.2. yatosp framework (draft). Technical report, SUPER Deliverable, 2007.

[Yu95]   Eric Yu. *Modelling Strategic Relationships for Process Reengineering*. PhD thesis, Univ. of Toronto, 1995.

[zur04] Michael zur Muehlen. *Workflow-based Process Controlling. Foundation, Design, and Implementation of Workflow-driven Process Information Systems.*, volume 6 of *Advances in Information Systems and Management Science*. Logos, Berlin, 2004.